P9-CFY-358

HEARING
GOD'S VOICE

HEARING
GOD'S VOICE

HENRY AND RICHARD
BLACKABY

BROADMAN
&HOLMAN
PUBLISHERS

NASHVILLE, TENNESSEE

OHIO CHRISTIAN UNIVERSITY

0–8054–2493–8

Published by Broadman & Holman Publishers,
Nashville, Tennessee
The authors are represented by the literary agency of
Wolgemuth & Associates, Inc.

Subject Heading: CHRISTIAN LIVING
Dewey Decimal Classification: 248

2 3 4 5 6 7 8 9 10 07 06 05 04 03 02

DEDICATION

I dedicate this book to my wife Marilynn, who has filled my life and our family with godly wisdom day after day for forty-two years. I honor her for uniquely and faithfully hearing from God and sharing lovingly with us all.

Henry Blackaby

I dedicate this book to my wonderful wife, Lisa. She has often been the first to hear God speaking to our family, and at times she has had to encourage me to be still and to listen so I could hear God speaking too. It has truly been a joy to listen to God together and to respond to God's invitations to do things with him we could never have dreamed God would do through our lives.

Richard Blackaby

CONTENTS

PREFACE

God said, "Why was there no man when I came? When I called, why was there none to answer?" (Isa. 50:2). He could ask that same question today. People everywhere struggle to know clearly what God is saying to them. Christian leaders and ministers candidly admit they have difficulty discerning God's voice. Everywhere we go, we meet Christians who tell us they do not hear God speak to them. Even more alarming are those who conclude they do not hear from God because he does not speak to people.

God *is* speaking. The problem is people have become disoriented to his voice. When the book *Experiencing God* was published, the hunger it exposed among God's people was amazing. Christians all over the world longed to know and to experience the Person they claimed was most important in their lives.

No one anticipated that *Experiencing God* would be so widely received. It was simply a little study designed to reorient people to God. It was based on our experience as we had walked with God through the years and the insights we learned along the way about his character and his ways. Over and over people say, "I knew in my head much of what the course taught. I had just never experienced those truths personally. *Experiencing God* helped me understand how to really know God." No one was more surprised than we were when God, in his grace, used that material to change countless lives and churches. The heart of *Experiencing God* is the simple truth that God is a Person who relates to people by speaking to them and by guiding them into his will.

Of course, every book has its detractors. Some critics maintain that the premise for *Experiencing God* is false. They argue that God does not speak to people. While this explains the heavenly silence that is their experience, it contradicts everything the Bible teaches. *Experiencing God* has been criticized for suggesting that Christians can relate to God in an intimate, personal way.

Some oppose its teachings on the basis that people have no right to claim such a close relationship with God. We would agree. No one has that right. It is a privilege—a gift from God. Other critics express knee-jerk reactions to the excesses of people who claim to follow *Experiencing God* teachings but who actually violate them. In this case both reveal a lack of knowledge of what *Experiencing God* actually teaches.

The last book we did together, *Spiritual Leadership: Moving People on to God's Agenda,* saw pastors and denominational leaders as well as Christian CEOs embrace the definition of a spiritual leader as someone who "moves people on to God's agenda." However, it became increasingly apparent how few leaders understand what God's agenda is. Most Christians agree that God's will is the key to successful leadership. Furthermore, experienced leaders know their role is to move people from where they are to where they need to be. However, the point of vulnerability for many leaders is this: How do I know what God's agenda is? If I don't know when God is speaking to me, how will I know what God's will is for the people I lead?

Spiritual Leadership highlighted the enormous need for people to learn how to hear from God. Effective spiritual leaders must know when God is speaking to them. In fact, every Christian must know how to recognize God's voice; otherwise, how can we obey him? Apart from God's personal involvement in our lives, our life experience will be no different from that of nonbelievers. We may have some extra rules and a stricter moral code to follow; but unless we communicate regularly with our Lord, we'll miss out on much that God desires for us. Moreover, we'll rob others of gifts God wanted to give them through us.

In light of both the ongoing heart cry for people to know when God is speaking to them and in response to those who question whether God communicates with people at all, we have written this book. We want to address this fundamental yet controversial issue: Does God speak to people today? If so, how does he do so? It is impossible to read the Bible without seeing a clear pattern of God speaking to people. Yet because some have not heard God speak to them personally, they conclude that God chooses not to speak today. They are choosing to view Scripture from the vantage point of their experience. Instead, people must learn to view their experience against the backdrop of the Bible. When we do not experience the truths expressed in Scripture, it is our experience that is in question, not the Bible!

Some argue that God revealed in Scripture all we need to know about his nature, his ways, and his purposes. We fully agree! You will not discover a truth about God that he has not expressed through his written Word. So why does God speak to us? He takes the revelation found in his Word and applies it to our lives. When he does, we not only *know about* him from his revelation in Scripture, but we also *know* him by experience. Thus we know from the Scriptures that God is love. But we also experience that love personally, so "God loves *people*" becomes "God loves me."

God does speak to people today, but we don't want you merely to take our word for it. We want *you* to hear his voice. We want *you* to experience his guidance. Throughout this book we refer to numerous Scriptures that address the issue of God speaking. It would benefit you to take time to prayerfully read over each verse. Let the Holy Spirit use the words of Scripture to verify the truth of what we are saying. We also cite the examples of some of the great Christians of history. With remarkable consistency, those God has used in mighty ways have been people who heard from God and obediently responded to what he said. We include examples from our own lives. We have both heard God speak to us many times. That does not qualify us as "super saints." We believe it makes us normal Christians. We simply testify that we *know* God speaks to people because he has spoken to us.

Take time to read this book carefully. It may be that through these pages you will hear God speak to you in ways you never have before. Be careful as you read. Throughout Scripture, when people heard God speak, their lives were never the same again. We pray God will clearly speak to you as you read this material. If you have been living your Christian life at a level below what God desires for you, we pray this book will help you begin to enjoy the richest dimensions of the Christian life.

THE QUESTION:
DOES GOD SPEAK TO
PEOPLE TODAY?

CHAPTER ONE

Does God Really Call People to Be Missionaries in Africa?

Does God *really* have a specific will for everyone?" Doug[1] asked us, "If he does, how does he reveal that will?" Bewilderment was drawn like a curtain across his face. Then he shared his story. As a young man, Doug had been convinced God was calling him to medical missions. He had responded to God's Word by entering medical school. His educational achievements were exceptional, and he soon caught the attention of various medical research centers. As he was deluged with offers from major hospitals, he struggled to reconcile this new career direction with his call to the mission field. Friends and family assured him this was God's blessing. He could serve God at home in America as effectively as he could on the mission field. Maybe more so. Eventually, Doug became the director of immunology for one of the most prestigious medical institutions in the United States.

The years raced by. Doug achieved a life that surpassed most men's dreams. He and his wife enjoyed a loving, solid marriage. Their children were happy and healthy. They lived in a beautiful home. They were loved and supported by a solid church and a wide circle of friends. Still Doug could not deny the persistent uneasiness in his spirit. He was living a good Christian life. He was a faithful church member. Was it possible he was still missing God's will?

What about the call he received as a teenager? Was it real? He was convinced it was. But that was so long ago; did it even apply any more? Now he was a man in a responsible position with a wife and children. Asking them to transplant their lives to a remote, possibly dangerous country to fulfill a calling he received as a teenager seemed reckless and foolhardy. Surely God wouldn't ask him to do that. It didn't make sense. Perhaps he was just going through a midlife crisis. There was a poignant urgency in Doug's manner as he persisted with his questions. He *had* to know. Was God really speaking to him? Too much hung in the balance to make a mistake.

The Issue

Does God speak to people today? Doug is one of many, many people we have encountered who are urgently asking this question. In fact, this issue is at the heart of the Christian life. Christians want to choose the spouse God knows is best for them. They need direction with their careers. Baffled parents are desperate for God's wisdom in rearing their children. Every day numerous events magnify the awareness that Christians need a timely, specific word from God. Most Christians acknowledge their need for God's guidance. Many people regularly seek it. The problem is that they are not sure they recognize God's voice. In moments of honest reflection, they may doubt whether God actually speaks to anyone today, except perhaps to a select few.

Life can be aggravatingly complex. The best choices are not always readily apparent. Christians are regularly reminded by their own deficiencies of their need for divine guidance. The Scriptures assure them that God is all knowing and perfectly loving. Passages such as Jeremiah 29:11 talk about God's specific will for others, but does this apply to all Christians? Does it apply to them?

Even a casual perusal of the Bible reveals a consistent pattern of God speaking to people. However, some argue that biblical history does not necessarily translate into modern experience. Talking donkeys and burning bushes are not common, contemporary occurrences. Nevertheless, a closer examination of the Scriptures reveals that while God did indeed speak on matters of great significance through supernatural means, he also clearly communicated with men and women from all walks of life regarding matters of seemingly lesser importance.

What significance does this hold for Christians today? Does God give specific guidance to people? If so, how does he do it? Does he only use the words of Scripture? Does he still speak through dreams and visions?

Theories abound on how God communicates with people. If we were to list every view that has been advocated in books, seminars, and the media, we would need a book series rather than this one volume. However, we have observed at least four broad categories of thought on the subject.

God's Written Word: His Only Word

Some believe God rarely, if ever, speaks to people today. Proponents of this view contend that God perfectly revealed everything people need to know about himself, salvation, and the Christian life in the Bible. Regarding God's will, they argue that apart from what people can discern in the Bible, they need no further word from God. Since the Bible was divinely inspired by the Holy Spirit, God has no need to supplement it with a fresh word today. For God to speak to someone today would be to "add" to Scripture. Rather than seeking personal communication with God, people should concentrate on following the teachings and commandments already found in Scripture. Advocates of this view tend to act as if the Holy Spirit spoke to *inspire* Scripture but he does not speak today to *apply* Scripture. As long as people are careful not to violate the laws and principles set forth in the Bible, they are capable of making their own choices and are free to do so.

In his 1980 book *Decision Making and the Will of God: A Biblical Alternative to the Traditional View*, Gary Friesen critiques the "traditional" view that God communicates his specific will to each person. Friesen suggests that

Christians should make decisions based on "The Way of Wisdom."[2] That is, where the Bible presents a command or principle, it is to be obeyed. Where the Bible does not give specific instruction, Christians are free to make their own choices. Friesen claims, "Any decision made within the moral will of God is acceptable to God."[3] Friesen's position is that God treats people the way a parent treats a child. God's desire is not to guide his children to make the correct decision every time but to help them learn to make responsible, wise decisions on their own. The key, therefore, is not so much *what* is decided but *how* the decision is made. This approach would say, for example, that God does not directly reveal whom you should marry but he allows you to choose your own spouse as long as you choose wisely and do not violate biblical injunctions.

People who hold this view generally contend that biblical heroes such as Abraham, Moses, Peter, and Paul are not meant to serve as models for modern Christians. God did speak directly to them, but that was then. God needed to speak to them in order to write the Bible. However, now that the Bible is in place, God does not need to speak directly to people as he once did. The example of Jesus is discounted with the disclaimer that he was the Son of God; therefore his example is not normative for mortal Christians. People who are of the opinion that God's written Word is his final word conclude that modern believers can and should make prudent decisions on their own. They do not need God's direct involvement in their decision-making process. If their decisions are biblically sound, they are perfectly pleasing to God.

This decision-making approach has proven appealing to many because it aligns with two widely held assumptions about God: (1) God is too busy managing a vast universe to bother with the personal lives of billions of people and their comparatively minor issues; (2) God made people in his image, so we must be capable of making good decisions. After all, he gave us our brains.

On the positive side, this approach points believers to God's Word. Certainly Christians should always make their decisions in conformity with biblical injunctions and teachings. In that regard Friesen's decision-making approach is preferable to nonbelievers' methods, which run the gamut from strict human logic (drawing up a list of pros and cons) to pure emotion (if it feels good, do it). This view falls short, however, because it fails to consider the full richness of relationship God intends for the Christian life. The Scriptures tell us that God *wants* to be involved in the lives of his people! That is why he created us—for an intimate relationship with him. Moreover, the truth that God made us in his image should not be erroneously extended to imply that he made us his equal. God is all-powerful and all-knowing. We, obviously, are not.

Friesen argues, "Most of the time, our five senses are reliable interpreters of reality, for God designed them to be trustworthy."[4] However, Isaiah 55:8–9 indicates the best human thinking is far below God's wisdom: "'For my thoughts are not your thoughts, neither are your ways my ways,' declares the LORD. 'For as the heavens are higher than the earth, so are my ways higher than your ways, and my thoughts than your thoughts'" (NIV).

People who make decisions based merely on what seems most advisable to them will inevitably choose something inferior to God's best. History's overwhelming testimony is that the most brilliant human reasoning has proven inadequate to save humanity from its own frailty. To claim people can determine the best course of action apart from God's guidance is to ignore Scripture's clear teaching concerning humankind's degenerate condition (Jer. 17:9; Rom. 3:9–18). Numerous warnings throughout the Bible advise against making decisions apart from God's involvement: The writer of Proverbs warned: "There is a way which seems right to a man, but its end is the way of death" (Prov. 14:12). The apostle Paul speaks of God as "able to do above and beyond all that we ask or think—according to the power that works in you" (Eph. 3:20).

It is no secret that God's ways are vastly superior to our ways. It is inconceivable that God would ask his children to make independent choices that robbed them of the good he knew they could experience. While God does allow people the freedom to make their own decisions,

Scripture clearly demonstrates that God also lets people know what his will is.

Jesus, the ultimate model for the Christian life, did not rely on his own best thinking, but depended completely on his heavenly father for wisdom in everything: He acknowledged, "I can do nothing on My own. Only as I hear do I judge, and My judgment is righteous, because I do not seek My own will, but the will of him who sent me" (John 5:30). The sinless Son of God, the only Person who perfectly fulfilled the Father's will, did not make decisions independent of the heavenly Father's personal direction. It seems absurd to think that anyone else should.

Some people are understandably wary of any talk about hearing a direct word from God because of the rampant, exaggerated abuses of this claim, both now and throughout history. People can recoil from talk of God speaking to people because they think this can refer only to God's audible voice. In response, some argue that God's Word in the Bible is sufficient for us today and for every age. Some may see the concept of God speaking today as a threat to the Bible's authority. Is the Bible the *only* means God has at his disposal for speaking to people? Is prayer a one-way conversation where we do all the talking, or does God also speak to us during our communion with him? Does God speak to us through godly friends or through our circumstances? While there certainly have been abuses by some who claimed to hear from God in nonbiblical ways, does that discount the legitimate avenues through which God speaks? While the Bible is God's definitive, authoritative word to us, is God not capable of *applying* that word to our lives in numerous ways?

There always have been and always will be those who justify bizarre actions with the claim they are acting on direct orders from God. Such perversions of God's name demonstrate the inherent dangers in a second approach to decision-making wherein God's fresh word is treated as superseding God's written Word.

Christian Experience: A Preeminent Guide

Montanus was a pagan priest who converted to Christianity in A.D. 155. Soon after, he pronounced that he and two prophetesses, Priscilla and Maximilla, had been possessed by the Holy Spirit. Those who followed them, he said, were the spiritual elite. The trio prophesied that their movement was the beginning of history's final age leading to Christ's Second Coming. Montanus based much of his theology and practice not on the Scriptures but on revelations he claimed he received directly from the Holy Spirit. Not surprisingly, though the movement attracted many followers, the official church condemned it as heretical.

During the Protestant Reformation, numerous radical reformers attracted large followings. One such enthusiast was John Matthys, a Dutch baker who, in 1534, gathered a revolutionary following in the German town of Münster. Local authorities assembled an army to suppress Matthys and his followers and besieged the town of Münster.

After Matthys was killed in a military skirmish, John Beukels took control of the movement. Beukels claimed to receive regular visions from God. Citing these visions, he justified harsh discipline on anyone who questioned his leadership. Beukels would not tolerate those who said they had a word from God that contradicted the messages he allegedly received. Many of Beukels's visions refuted Scripture's teachings. One such revelation allowed people in Münster to practice polygamy. Beukels assured his followers that God had given him a promise of victory for the people of Münster, but the besieging forces captured the city, killing Beukels and many of his cohorts.[5]

As a young boy, Vernon Howell was a devout follower of God. His grandmother reported often seeing him praying tearfully by his bedside for hours. Being reared in the Seventh-Day Adventist Church, he was thoroughly grounded in the Scriptures. As a young man, Howell gained the confidence of many as a committed Christian. However, Howell became increasingly dissatisfied with the traditional approach to Christianity. He began to claim

---

God was guiding him to a deeper level of spirituality. Howell joined a radical offshoot group of his denomination called the Branch Davidians and assumed the name David Koresh.

Koresh eventually gathered his disciples at a compound near Waco, Texas. Claiming unique spiritual insight into the Scriptures, he alleged that God had appointed him as his messenger to warn people about the imminent end of the world. Patterning himself after the biblical king David, the thirty-three-year-old kept a harem of women who made up the "House of David" while the men served as Koresh's "mighty men." After a February 28, 1993, shoot-out with federal agents, more than eighty Davidians barricaded themselves inside the compound to wait for the end. On April 19, federal authorities stormed the complex. It quickly caught fire and was soon a raging inferno. Still the commitment of Koresh's devotees to their leader and his cause was sorrowfully evident. One man, standing on a burning roof, refused to be rescued. A woman, her clothes on fire, attempted to run back into the burning compound rather than be saved.[6]

History brims with accounts of charismatic leaders who gathered gullible followers by citing divine visions. In recent years colorful, controversial televangelists have claimed outlandish revelations from God. Some have secured sizable donations for their ministries by promising certain favors from God. Others have justified their adultery with the claim that God told them they should be happy, even if this meant cheating on their wives—who no longer made them happy—in order to be with their mistresses—who did make them happy. Many have announced that God gave them specific details about future events. When those events did not occur, these red-faced "prophets" reported receiving a newer, fresher word from God even more dramatic than the first. Such confusing messages, all allegedly coming from God, obviously contradict his Word as clearly revealed in the Bible.

Tragically, delusional, paranoid cult leaders continue to gain followings by claiming to receive messages or visions from God. Even when the Word they purport God spoke to them completely contradicts what God has said in the Bible, people will often accept their leadership uncritically. As we will see in a later chapter, peoples' claims of divine revelation are never sufficient reason to automatically accept their message as coming from God.

The practice of citing a directive from God as an irrefutable argument to get one's way is not limited to the psychotic religious gurus of the world. Christians can be guilty of claiming a "word from the Lord" as an excuse for doing what they want to do. Many an attractive young woman has been surprised to learn that God has revealed to *several* ardent suitors that she is to be their future bride! We have known more than one pastor who "heard" from God that his church was to build a large, expensive new facility. When concerned church members noted the numerous problems such a project might encounter, their pastor charged them with resisting a word from God and lacking faith. Of course, the problems *did* materialize, just as the wise church members feared. That's when the chagrined pastor suddenly heard a new word from God advising him to accept the pastorate of another church, leaving a mountain of debt behind him! Such a misuse of God's Word is nothing less than spiritual anarchy. Abuses such as these have predictably caused sincere Christians to become skeptical of anyone claiming to hear a word from God.

Part of the problem today is that many Christians have a tenuous view of absolute truth. When Christians have been polled concerning whether they believe in absolute truth, their response has almost mirrored that of non-Christians. The result is that even when Christians read what God says in the Bible, they will not accept it as truth if it does not match their experience. Instead, many Christians reinterpret the Bible to match their experience. They say things like, "I know Jesus said to love our enemies, but that person doesn't deserve to be forgiven after what he did!" We must not take the words of Scripture and run them through the filter of our own beliefs and feelings in order to decide what the Bible verse means to us. Such an approach mistakenly elevates experience over the Word of God.

Sometimes, Christians have genuinely believed they were acting on God's initiative. Later, they became bitterly disillusioned after discovering they were wrong. What happened? They failed to verify from the Scriptures that the direction they were taking was from God. God will never lead people to act contrary to what he has set forth in the Bible. We will discuss this in greater depth later, but it is safe to say that whoever relies solely on a perceived word from God, while neglecting to validate it in the Scriptures, is doomed to inevitable error.

So far we've presented two extreme ends of a spectrum. On one end are people who view the Scriptures as God's only means of communicating with people. Those who follow this viewpoint discount the belief that God pursues an intimate, daily involvement in peoples' lives and that he speaks to people through a variety of means. Their position is that the Bible tells people all they need to know to live a victorious Christian life and that God leaves them free to apply these truths themselves. Others lean strongly the other way, emphasizing personal experience with little or no biblical verification. Those who adhere to this outlook lean much more toward their own personal interpretation of how to live the Christian life. In the more radical cases, the Scriptures, if consulted at all, are twisted and interpreted to fit the need of the day.

Christian Doctrine: An Impersonal Approach

Another school of thought influences the way people approach their relationship with God. This view elevates doctrine and diminishes Christian experience. It challenges the position that the Christian life is a dynamic relationship with a Person who communicates regularly with his people.

Since biblical times, some have seen Christianity as a theology, or a set of doctrines to be followed. The book *Experiencing God* describes the essence of Christianity as experiencing an intimate, personal relationship with Jesus Christ.[7] Some have refuted the assertion that God continues to speak to people today. They cite numerous examples where misguided zealots justified various atrocities with the claim that God "spoke to them." Indeed, as mentioned earlier, people throughout history have claimed direct access to God and then committed outrageous deeds in his name. Such misrepresentations have predictably created a wariness of anyone claiming personal communication with God. The unfortunate result has been that many have opted to throw the baby out with the bathwater. They find safety in theology, so they cling to dogma and facts *about* Christ rather than enjoying a vibrant relationship *with* him. They summarily reject the availability of God's personal guidance and opt instead for a lifeless set of doctrines.

The fact is, theology is extremely important in the Christian's life. We have both spent our lives studying theology; however, we contend that while theology should inform a Christian's relationship with God, it should never take its place. Theology is somewhat like an autobiography. As you read a person's autobiography, you can learn many important facts, including perhaps his or her age, family background, and work experience. You may also discover the person's opinions and feelings about certain issues.

Assuming the account is honest, you may reach the end of the book with considerably more knowledge about its subject than when you began. You may even feel as if you know the author. You may develop a greater desire to learn more about the author. You may even consider yourself an authority on the subject. Nevertheless, as fascinating as an autobiography may be, it is not the same as the actual person. Moreover, as much as you might want to, you cannot change the facts of the autobiography. Perhaps the author says she suffered a tumultuous home life, but you want to believe she had an idyllic childhood. You may choose to believe your version, but the truth remains unchanged. Doctrines are like that. They detail the known truths about the Person of God. They help broaden our understanding about God, but they are not God.

Doctrines are important because they depict a real God who relates to people in specific ways. Regardless of whether you are comfortable with certain doctrines, the facts remain the same. God is who he is. When you become a Christian, a collection of doctrines does not take up residence within you. Christ does (Gal. 2:20). The doctrine of salvation simply explains the process. When you are converted, you do not yield your will to a set of theological maxims but to the Lord of life. Your theology of Christ and his lordship describes the reality of this relationship. Doctrines do not save or transform lives. Christ does. Doctrines do not give specific guidance to lives. A divine Person does. You do not pray to a doctrine; you pray to a Person. Merely to believe and understand a doctrine is not to experience the abundant life Christ desires for you. In order to do that, you need to experience a Person. The doctrine can lead you to Christ, but it can never substitute for him.

Why would a person choose a static theology over experiencing the living Christ? Some people are more comfortable dealing with doctrines than they are with responding to a living, ruling, righteous God. Doctrines that make people uncomfortable can be ignored or reinterpreted. The Person of Christ must be obeyed. The Pharisees were diligent theologians who spent untold hours reading the Scriptures and debating minute aspects of theology. Jesus condemned them in spite of their theological acumen: "You pore over the Scriptures because you think you have eternal life in them, yet they testify about Me. And you are not willing to come to Me that you may have life" (John 5:39–40 HCSB).

Ironically, the same laws they scrutinized highlighted the grave error of their ways. Jesus did not condemn them for studying the Scriptures but for elevating the Scriptures above the Messiah to whom the Scriptures directed them. Those troubled by talk of God speaking to people today and those who dismiss the possibility of experiencing God personally are in danger of repeating the Pharisees' folly. The tragedy of many religious scholars has been that they immerse themselves in studies about Jesus while never coming to know him personally. They devote their entire lives to studying doctrine, and even teaching it, yet they miss the unmatchable joy of experiencing God personally.

A College Professor
(a personal example from Henry)

Not long ago, a middle-aged Bible college professor approached me at a conference and tearfully told me his story. For years, he said, his Christian life had been dull and lifeless. He was thoroughly educated in Bible knowledge, yet he did not sense God's presence in his life, nor did he hear God speaking to him. Nevertheless, year after year, he taught class after class of students preparing themselves for Christian ministry. He did not encourage his students to listen to God because he had not experienced God speaking to him. Then, through the study *Experiencing God*, he was challenged by the truth that the Christian life was not a set of doctrines but a relationship with a living person. He now enjoys a vibrant, daily walk with God. However, with tears in his eyes, he recalled the hundreds of students who had sat under his teaching while he espoused a lifeless theology to them.

Note the opposite portrayal in Andrew Bonar's description of the saintly Scottish pastor Robert Murray M'Cheyne: "There is a wide difference between preaching *doctrine* and preaching Christ. Mr. M'Cheyne preached all the doctrines of Scripture as understood by our confession of faith. . . . Still it was not *doctrine* alone that he preached; it was *Christ*, from whom all doctrine shoots forth as rays from the center."[8]

Matthew's Gospel brilliantly illustrates two opposite approaches to the Person of Christ (Matt. 2:1–12). The eastern Magi, having traveled to Jerusalem seeking the significance of an unusual star, asked the Jewish theologians where the Messiah was to be born. The religious pundits answered immediately—"*Bethlehem.*" They had studied the Scriptures; their doctrine of the Messiah's birth was impeccable. The Magi, on the other hand, were less schooled in Jewish holy writ. Nonetheless, these road-weary wise men continued their journey the final five miles to the Messiah's birthplace, while the doctrinally sound scholars remained in the comfortable confines of Jerusalem. Why had these pagan Magi traveled hundreds of miles to see a baby? They were wise enough to recognize something unusual happening that they must investigate for themselves. Why did the religious leaders not make the connection and go with them? Only God knows, but somehow, in spite of their accurate messianic doctrine, they completely missed the Messiah!

A half century later, Saul of Tarsus, better known in the New Testament as Paul, made the same mistake. He was a zealous Pharisee, an expert in religion, yet he was a stranger to God. After his dramatic personal encounter with Christ on the road to Damascus, he confessed: "But everything that was a gain to me, I have considered to be a loss because of Christ. More than that, I also consider everything to be a loss in view of the surpassing value of knowing Christ Jesus my Lord. Because of Him I have suffered the loss of all things and consider them filth, so that I may gain Christ. . . . My goal is to know Him and the power of His resurrection and the fellowship of His sufferings, being conformed to His death" (Phil. 3:7–8, 10 HCSB).

The Book of Revelation teaches that some people choose devotion to doctrine at the expense of developing a relationship with God. When the apostle John was exiled on the dreary Isle of Patmos, the risen Christ appeared to him. In that vision, Christ delivered a message to seven churches. To the church at Ephesus, he was both commending and condemning. He applauded this respected church for testing and rejecting self-proclaimed religious leaders who were actually false prophets:

"You hate the practices of the Nicolaitans, which I also hate" (Rev. 2:6 HCSB), said the risen Christ, for the Ephesian Christians were sticklers about doctrine. However, Christ was not finished. "But I have this against you," he went on, "you have abandoned the love you had at first" (Rev. 2:4 HCSB). Was it possible to oppose heretics, to maintain pristine theology, and yet no longer love Christ? Of course. James said the demons' theology is fundamentally correct, yet their allegiance to Christ is obviously lacking (James 2:19). How does doctrinal orthodoxy stand up against a neglected or nonexistent relationship with Christ? The Ephesian church couldn't be faulted doctrinally, yet here are the words Christ had for them: "Remember then how far you have fallen; repent, and do the works you did at first. Otherwise, I will come to you and remove your lampstand from its place—unless you repent" (Rev. 2:5 HCSB).

The necessity of doctrine cannot be overlooked because it points to Christ. The Ephesian church was wise not to tolerate false teachings. Doctrine explains truth. For Christians, doctrine ought to describe the reality of their personal experience with God. Andrew Murray illustrates it this way:

> There are two ways of knowing things. The one is in the mind by thought or idea—I know about a thing. The other is by living—I know by experience. An intelligent blind man may know all that science teaches about the light by having books read to him. A child who has never thought what light is knows more about light than the blind scholar. The scholar knows all about it by thinking. The child knows it in reality by seeing and enjoying it.[9]

Murray issues a warning reminiscent of Proverbs 3:5. He exhorts: "Do not trust your own understanding. It can only give you thoughts and ideas about spiritual things without the reality of them."[10]

Murray's words provide a fitting introduction to a fourth viewpoint—the one that will be the thesis for this book: God created us for fellowship with him (John 17:3; 1 John 1:1–4). He desires an intimate, personal relationship with us, so he *will* speak to us! Communication is essential to that relationship.

Experiencing God: A Personal Approach

When Jesus met the adulterous woman at the edge of a Samaritan village, he knew what she needed. It was not a theological discussion but a life-changing encounter with the Son of God. She, on the other hand, kept trying to engage him in a debate over whether Jewish or Samaritan theologians were correct. Jesus was certainly capable of debating doctrine, but instead he chose to give her what she needed—the opportunity to experience a personal relationship with a loving God (John 4:23–24).

Modern Christians sometimes struggle because they must relate to an invisible God. They do not hear his audible voice. They do not feel his physical touch. Many Christians conclude the only relationship they can have with God will be found in diligently obeying biblical commandments and teachings. So they invest their lives earnestly trying to follow the rules and admonitions they find in Scripture. This can lead to a ritualistic, legalistic religion. This stagnant approach to worship has no more life to it than worshiping idols. The psalmist said:

Their idols are silver and gold,
The work of man's hands.
They have mouths, but they cannot speak;
They have eyes, but they cannot see;
They have ears, but they cannot hear;
They have noses, but they cannot smell;
They have hands, but they cannot feel;
They have feet, but they cannot walk;
They cannot make a sound with their throat.

Those who make them will become like them, everyone who trusts in them."

(Ps. 115:4–8 NASB)

The psalmist issued a grave warning: You will become like that which you worship. Those who worship a lifeless, silent god embrace a lifeless religion that offers nothing but silence. The Christian life is meant to include so much more!

Jesus said, "If anyone loves me, he will keep My word. My Father will love him, and We will come to him and make Our home with him" (John 14:23 HCSB).

This sounds like a vibrant relationship, not a set of doctrines! It is difficult to imagine a relationship enduring in which the parties never communicate. The fundamental nature of Christianity is a relationship between God and people. People do not negotiate or invent this relationship to suit their tastes. It is prescribed by the truths found in Scripture. The relationship is with God, not the god of peoples' own creation but the true God who has revealed himself in Scripture. Anyone who claims to know a god other than the one described in the Bible is embracing heresy (Gal. 1:6–9).

Summary

Some people contend that God no longer speaks to people beyond what he has already said in Scripture. They are reluctant to believe God gives specific guidance to individuals today. Others act as if God's Word to them today overrides anything he has said in the Bible. Such people are experience driven. They tend to be controlled by their emotions.

Many Christians use alleged divine revelations as a means of manipulating others. Perhaps they are troubled by what they deem to be restrictive in the Scriptures, so they appeal to visions and dreams to release them from what they find too restraining.

A third approach to Christianity elevates doctrine *about* God over relating *to* God. This view can be adopted in reaction to the excesses of people who behave as if God constantly speaks to them in ways that contradict the Bible. Others who take this approach are uncomfortable with the idea of God being involved with people on a regular and intimate basis. They feel that God is above taking regular time to commune with ordinary people about seemingly ordinary things.

We contend that God *does* speak to his people. However, people must be prepared to hear what he is saying. It is crucial that Christians clearly understand what God is communicating to them and know how to respond appropriately. The question, then, is not *whether* God speaks to his people but *how* he does so.

Perhaps you have been confused about what God is saying to you. You may have been taught that God does not speak to people. Maybe you have grown disillusioned because of professing Christians who claim God speaks to them in excessive and unbiblical ways. If you have not heard God speak to you, perhaps you have come to assume your experience is normative for the Christian life. This book is written to help you clearly recognize God's voice.

When God speaks, he does not give new *revelation* about himself that contradicts what he has already revealed in Scripture. Rather, God speaks to give *application* of his Word to the specific circumstances in your life. When God speaks to you, he is not writing a new book of Scripture; rather, he is applying to your life what he has already said in his Word. Throughout the Bible, whenever God spoke to someone, that person's life was never the same again. The same is true today. Our prayer is that as you listen to what God is saying to you, you will respond in love and obedience and your life will be transformed as well.

Epilogue

The director of immunology did come to understand what God was telling him to do. In his case the call of God he had first heard as a teenager remained unchanged after all those years. Doug resigned his position at the research hospital and applied to be a foreign missionary. He was appointed and sent to serve in Uganda, Africa—a region with one of the highest concentrations of AIDS cases in the world. He currently administers a hospital, continues to conduct AIDS research, and has worked with the Ugandan government. He and his family are making a positive difference for God's kingdom in Africa as they jointly experience the joy of knowing they are in the center of God's will.

Be encouraged! God, who spoke to Adam and Eve in the garden and spoke to Moses at the burning bush, said to the disciples, "But your eyes are blessed because they do see, and your ears because they do hear" (Matt. 13:16). He said to the churches in Revelation, "Anyone who has an ear should listen to what the Spirit says to the churches (Rev. 2:7, 11, 17, 29; 3:6, 13, 22). He wants you to hear his voice, recognize it, and follow him too! Our prayer is that we can help you in the process.

Questions for Reflection

1. When was the last time you clearly heard God speak? What did he say?

2. Has God spoken to you in different ways in the past?

3. If you have not heard God speaking recently, why do you think that may be?

4. What are the times in your life when you feel you need to hear from God?

5. Are you more comfortable believing truths about God or relating to God personally?

6. What adjustments do you need to make in order to hear God's voice when he speaks to you?

FOR THE RECORD: GOD SPEAKS

CHAPTER TWO

Sometimes the odds are stacked against you. No matter what choice you make, it seems you can't win. Hezekiah, king of Judah, found himself in such a predicament. During his illustrious rule Israel had enjoyed a period of relative peace and prosperity. But now Assyria, the world superpower, was sweeping across the country like a fire over a prairie grainfield, consuming every city in its path. Naturally, Hezekiah felt the heat. He faced the most critical moment of his reign. A wrong move now, and all the accumulated success of his rule was a giant moot point. Assyria had already conquered the northern tribes of Israel and banished them to exile. Samaria, Israel's capital city, had been considered a formidable fortress. It proved to be no match for the Assyrians. Now the Assyrian army surrounded Jerusalem, determined to subjugate the nation of Judah once and for all. The enemy general, Rabshakeh, taunted King Hezekiah, arrogantly trying to solicit his nation's compliance with threats and lies:

> Hear the Word of the great king, the king of Assyria. Thus says the king, "Do not let Hezekiah deceive you, for he will not be able to deliver you from my hand; nor let Hezekiah make you trust in the LORD, saying, 'The LORD will surely deliver us, and this city will not be given into the hand of the king of Assyria.' Do not listen to Hezekiah, for thus says the king of Assyria, 'Make your peace with me and come out to me, and eat each of his vine and each of his fig tree and drink each of the waters of his own cistern, until I come and take you away to a land like your

own land, a land of grain and new wine, a land of bread and vineyards, a land of olive trees and honey, that you may live and not die. But do not listen to Hezekiah when he misleads you, saying, "The LORD will deliver us." Has any one of the gods of the nations delivered his land from the hand of the king of Assyria? Where are the gods of Hamath and Arpad? Where are the gods of Sepharvaim, Hena and Ivvah? Have they delivered Samaria from my hand? Who among all the gods of the lands have delivered their land from my hand, that the LORD should deliver Jerusalem from my hand?" (2 Kings 18:28–35).

Hezekiah had two choices: (1) Surrender, and be dethroned and enslaved. His family would undoubtedly be executed. (2) Refuse to surrender, and the Assyrians would inevitably conquer the city, precipitating a fierce blood-bath. If ever there was a rock-and-a-hard-place moment, surely this was it.

Then, God spoke to Hezekiah: "Do not be afraid because of the words that you have heard, with which the servants of the king of Assyria have blasphemed Me. Behold, I will put a spirit in him so that he shall hear a rumor and return to his own land. And I will make him fall by the sword in his own land" (2 Kings 19:6–7).

King Hezekiah heard God's message as spoken through the prophet Isaiah, and that changed everything! Now he knew what to do! God rescued Jerusalem just as he said.

Since Hezekiah's day the world has changed by quantum leaps, but one thing remains the same: God continues to communicate with people. Both the Old and New Testaments bear historical witness to the multiplicity of methods God has used to maintain his relationship with his people. The apex of that communication, of course, came in the person of Christ (Heb. 1:2).

God Speaks:
The Old Testament Record

Virtually every Christian can cite a few notable Old Testament examples when God spoke to people. Most would mention angels and prophets. Many might recall the burning bush. A close study of the Old Testament produces a multifarious list of ways God clearly revealed his will, his pleasure, and his displeasure. To gain a sense of how God communicated in biblical times, and to lay a foundation for further consideration, the following is a brief summary of twenty-four Old Testament examples in which God communicated with people.

Creation

The psalmist proclaimed: "The heavens are telling of the glory of God; and their expanse is declaring the work of His hands. Day to day pours forth speech, and night to night reveals knowledge" (Ps. 19:1–2). According to the Bible, all of nature carries God's fingerprints. God speaks in a general way through the majesty of the cosmos he created.

The whole world admires the rainbow's beauty. But the Scriptures indicate God created the rainbow specifically to remind people of his promise to them (Gen. 9:11–17). Charles Spurgeon, the famous English pastor said: "God seems to talk to me in every primrose and daisy and smile at me from every star, and whisper to me in every breath of morning air, and call aloud to me in every storm."[1]

Angels

Angels have experienced a groundswell of popularity lately. They are everywhere—chubby cherubs on stationery, jewelry, and calendars. People are fascinated with angels. The word *angel* means "messenger" or "one who is sent." The Old Testament sometimes depicts angels as spectacular, terrifying creatures. At other times angels appeared to be like ordinary people. Surely this is what prompted the writer of Hebrews to caution believers to treat strangers kindly, in case they were unknowingly entertaining celestial guests (Heb. 13:2).

The Bible depicts angels as heavenly beings sent by God to relay messages to people. An angel was sent to comfort and instruct Hagar about her son Ishmael (Gen. 16:7). Angels were dispatched to warn Lot of the imminent doom of the city of Sodom (Gen. 19:1–13). An angel instructed Joshua on how to capture the city of Jericho (Josh. 5:13–18). The angel Gabriel comforted Daniel and helped him interpret the events of his day (Dan. 9:20–23; 10:10–21). Angels were such trustworthy heavenly messengers that the Scriptures sometimes say, "The Lord said . . ." when referring to a message delivered by an angel (Gen. 18:1–15). A message communicated by an angel was obviously one of extreme importance! (Judg. 6:12; 2 Kings 1:3; Dan. 9:21).

Prophets

We generally think of prophets as foretelling the future. That is not always the case. Like angels, prophets relayed God's messages to people. At times such messages included foretelling future events, but the role of a prophet was to proclaim God's Word to people whether it concerned the present or the distant future. In numerous Old Testament examples, God chose to send word to people through a human servant (Deut. 18:18–22; 2 Sam. 12:7; 24:10–12; 1 Kings 12:22–24, 20:42, 21:23; 2 Kings 1:4).

The role of prophet was obviously a tremendous honor. Amos declared, "The Lord God does nothing unless He reveals His secret counsel to His servants the prophets" (Amos 3:7). God said of Samuel, one of the earliest prophets mentioned in the Bible, that he would "do what is in My heart and soul" (1 Sam. 2:35).

The true prophet knew what was on God's heart and mind and he declared it to others. To despise a prophetic message was to reject a word from God (Isa. 7:13). True prophets were not to be taken lightly. Neither were false prophets. At times deceivers would arise and seek to mislead people (1 Kings 22:6; Jer. 28:15–17). God gave clear guidelines on identifying false prophets (Deut. 18:20–22). God also specified the penalty for false prophets—death.

Dreams

The most famous Old Testament dream arguably belonged to Joseph. As a boy, the second youngest of twelve brothers, Joseph learned through a divine dream of his future as a political leader (Gen. 37:5–11). Joseph's brothers chose not to believe the dream was from God because they didn't like the plot, but time proved the authenticity of Joseph's claim. Likewise, through dreams God revealed to a baker and a cupbearer what their fates would be (Gen. 40:12, 18). God used a dream to warn Pharaoh of an impending famine (Gen. 41:16). Interestingly, after first communicating to Joseph through a dream, God then used Joseph to assist others in interpreting the dreams he gave them. Through a dream God assured Jacob of his presence in the desert and of his prodigious plans for Jacob's future (Gen. 28:10–16). God revealed the future to King Nebuchadnezzar of Babylon by way of a dream, interpreted through Daniel (Dan. 2:1–45). Two common factors about the dreams are mentioned in the Old Testament: First, they were never sought by the recipients but came at God's initiative at unexpected moments. Second, the dreams were not about minor affairs but usually involved matters of great significance.

Visions

Visions were similar to dreams, except those receiving them were awake. God appeared to Abraham in a vision, confirming his promise to grant him a son (Gen. 15:1). In the temple Isaiah experienced an amazing vision where he saw the Lord seated on his heavenly throne (Isa. 6:1–13). Standing on the banks of the Chebar River, the exiled prophet Ezekiel witnessed a spectacular vision of God. God gave Ezekiel several other visions during his ministry (Ezek. 1:1ff; 8:1ff; 9:1ff; 10:1ff; 37:1ff; 40:1ff; 43:1ff). The prophet Daniel interpreted a disturbing vision for King Nebuchadnezzar concerning the monarch's future (Dan. 4:4ff). Daniel received his own terrifying visions of the future (Dan. 7–12). At times, the Bible does not clearly distinguish whether someone received a vision or a dream, or a combination of both, but it is clear that God visited the person in a visual manner that was unforgettable (Dan. 7:1–2).

Lot-Casting

Strange as it sounds in light of the modern gambling epidemic, lot-casting was used during Old Testament days to determine God's will. Casting lots was generally done reverently with the assumption that God wanted to reveal his will on a matter. For example, priests would sometimes cast lots to determine which animal God wanted them to sacrifice (Lev. 16:8). The land of Canaan was distributed among the twelve tribes by lot-casting (Num. 34:13). Joshua cast lots to discover whose sin caused the Israelite's defeat by the city of Ai (Josh. 7:14). By casting lots pagan soldiers determined that Jonah was the culprit who had offended God and caused a lethal storm (Jon. 1:7). Those casting lots trusted God to guide the results as he communicated his will (Prov. 16:33).

Urim and Thummin

The Urim and Thummim were special objects used as a sacred means of determining God's desire in matters critical to the Israelite nation (Num. 27:21; Neh. 7:65). They were kept securely in the breastplate of the high priest (Exod. 28:30; Lev. 8:8; Deut. 33:8). Some people consider them to be another form of casting lots. This particular method of seeking God's will was not used by individuals but was a special method God reserved to reveal his will corporately to the nation of Israel.

Gentle Voice

Many times God spoke softly, but audibly, to individuals. Young Samuel heard God calling him in the middle of the night (1 Sam. 3:4). So unmistakably real was God's voice that the boy assumed it was the priest, Eli, beckoning him from an adjoining room.

A beautiful story, found in the Book of 1 Kings, relates a time when the discouraged prophet Elijah was refreshed by God's voice during a difficult period in the prophet's life. The passage describes God's comforting visit to Elijah. First there was a strong wind, but God was not in the wind. Then there was an earthquake, but God was not in the earthquake. A fire followed, but God was not in the fire. Last came a gentle wind blowing, and through that gentle breeze came God's soothing voice, restoring the weary prophet (1 Kings 19:11–14).

Fire

Sometimes God spoke gently and quietly. At other times he communicated in a dramatic, spectacular fashion. He spoke to the children of Israel through fire (Deut. 4:33, 36). When Gideon was afraid and needed reassurance, God confirmed his Word to him by sending an angel with fire (Judg. 6:17–21). Likewise, God's response to Elijah's prayer on Mount Carmel was a consuming fire (1 Kings 18:37–39). When King Solomon dedicated the temple to the Lord, God responded by sending down fire to incinerate the offerings on the altar (2 Chron. 7:1–2). God's presence was so tangible that day in the intense inferno that the priests could not enter the temple building without losing their lives.

Burning Bush

As Moses tended sheep in the desert, a strange phenomenon caught his attention. He hurried over to take a closer look because a bush was on fire, yet it was not consumed by the blaze. Within the flames, Moses saw an angel of the Lord. As he approached, Moses heard God's voice from within the bush, calling him by name (Exod. 3:1–4).

Preaching

"Repent or face God's wrath." This warning, preached so often through the generations, hearkens back to the early days of Old Testament history. Though he was a reluctant evangelist, Jonah delivered God's admonition to the sinful Ninevites: "Yet forty days and Nineveh will be overthrown" (Jon. 3:4). Fortunately, the people in the debauched imperial city listened to Jonah, believed his message was from God, and renounced their wicked ways (Jon. 3:5–10).

Thus, God spared them the judgment that was their due. Other preachers mentioned in the Old Testament through whom God communicated include Noah and Ezra.

Judgments

In the days before Christ, God expressed his displeasure with people by judging them. Deuteronomy 28 records the covenant God established with his people in which he forewarned punishment should they violate the terms of their relationship (Deut. 28:15–68). For example, God revealed to King Solomon that military defeat, drought, famine, pestilence, and various plagues and illnesses were all to be viewed as God communicating his offense at peoples' sin (2 Chron. 6:24–31; 7:13–14). God expected people to make the connection between their circumstances and his voice (Amos 4:6–12).

Symbolic Actions

Symbolism is a common thread woven throughout the Bible. God communicated through his prophets using symbolic actions. For instance, he commanded Isaiah to walk around naked and barefoot as a sign of the impending shameful fate awaiting Egypt and Ethiopia (Isa. 20). God instructed Jeremiah to purchase a plot of land as a symbol for the people of Jerusalem that, though they faced imminent defeat, they could still have hope for the future (Jer. 32:6–15).

The prophet Hosea's life became a touching symbol for his nation: "The LORD said to Hosea, 'Go, take to yourself a wife of harlotry and have children of harlotry; for the land commits flagrant harlotry, forsaking the LORD'" (Hos. 1:2 NASB). The righteous prophet obeyed and, in doing so, made himself vulnerable to the inevitable heartache of Gomer's blatant adultery. The anguish caused by her unfaithfulness and the beautiful act of selfless love wherein Hosea purchased her back from the slavery block provide a vivid picture of God's unfathomable love for his wayward people.

Signs

We see bits and pieces. God sees everything. Therefore, God gives us signs, or events with divine meaning, to help us understand the bigger picture.

When God parted the Jordan River, allowing the children of Israel to cross into the promised land, that was a sign to them of God's provision for them. God commanded them to build a stone monument on the riverbank to serve as a physical reminder of his miraculous intervention on their behalf. Future generations of Israelites would view the monument and be reminded of God's power to provide for those who obey his will (Josh. 4:1–24). The birth of a child also served as a sign from God as did the names of a prophet's children (Isa. 7:3, 14; 8:3–4; Hos. 1:4, 6, 9).

Miracles

A rod transformed into a snake. Then it turned back into a rod. Moses' hand became leprous as he reached inside his cloak. Then it was restored to healthy flesh (Exod. 4:1–8). Moses witnessed several amazing, miraculous signs from God. Such miracles helped build his confidence as he reluctantly stepped into the leadership role God called him to perform. But Moses was not the only one seeing the wondrous acts. God also gave the Egyptians the opportunity to experience miraculous events. They, too, witnessed Moses' staff turn into a snake, but Pharaoh's heart was hardened, and he would not be persuaded to obey God's Word (Exod. 7:8–13). Subsequently, God sent ten plagues on Egypt to compel Pharaoh to free the Hebrew slaves. Still, to his peril, Pharoah steadfastly refused to accept God's message (Exod. 7:14–11:10). Supernatural events were often God's means of getting people's attention and showing them his power. Depending on the person witnessing the miracle and the condition of their heart, the experience could be either reassuring or terrifying!

Writing on the Wall

There was an instance when God literally communicated with someone by writing on a wall. Belshazzar, king of Babylon, received an ominous warning etched on his palace wall (Dan. 5). Daniel interpreted the inscription for Belshazzar: God was going to judge the king for his wickedness. Before the night was over, the king was dead.

Donkey

In a famous biblical episode, God used a donkey to speak to the wayward prophet Balaam (Num. 22:21–35). This event may give hope to some Christian public speakers, but it is the only time recorded in the Scriptures where God used this unusual method of communication.

Trumpet

In a spectacular moment on Mount Sinai, God's presence was announced with trumpet blasts so loud the Israelites trembled (Exod. 19:16, 19). Numerous times, the sounding of a trumpet introduced an important message from God for his people (Jer. 4:5; 6:1; Joel 2:1, 15; Zeph. 1:16).

Thunder and Lightning, Smoke and Storms

On Mount Sinai, God spoke dramatically to the Israelites through thunder, lightning, and smoke (Exod. 19:16; 20:18). The Bible records that God's cosmic communication terrified the Israelites. They knew it was God, and they implored their leader, "Speak to us yourself and we will listen—but do not have God speak to us or we will die" (Exod. 20:18). In Samuel's day, God sent thunder and rain to communicate his intolerance for his peoples' sin (1 Sam. 12:17–18). On another occasion the Bible indicates ". . . the Lord answered Job out of the storm" (Job 40:6).

Fleece

God graciously chose to strengthen Gideon's faith through a fleece of wool (Judg. 6:36–40). Seeking a sign from God that would confirm his promise to save Israel, Gideon set a fleece on the ground overnight. He awoke to find the fleece drenched but the surrounding ground completely dry. He repeated the exercise that evening, and the next day he found the ground soaked but the fleece totally dry. By communicating with the hesitant deliverer this way, God strengthened Gideon's resolve and prepared him to lead the Israelite forces against their enemies. The Scriptures do not record anyone putting God to such a test again.

Sound of Marching in the Treetops

God used an equally unusual method to help David know when to advance on his enemies. God directed David to attack when he heard the sound of marching in the tops of the balsam trees. This sound was to be David's cue that God was going before him to assure him victory (2 Sam. 5:22–25; 1 Chron. 14:14–17). Once again this is a one-time event that is not mentioned elsewhere in the Bible.

Face-to-Face

The Bible says, "The LORD used to speak to Moses face-to-face, just as a man speaks to his friend" (Exod. 33:11). The larger context of this passage makes it clear that Moses did not physically look on the face of God, for God said, "You cannot see My face, for no man can see Me and live" (Exod. 33:20). It is clear, however, that Moses communed with God in an extremely intimate and personal manner.

Personal Guidance

As Nehemiah sought to rebuild the wall around Jerusalem, he received God's guidance several times. Nehemiah declared, "What my God was putting in my mind to do" (Neh. 2:12). He also said, "Then God put it into my heart" (Neh. 7:5). God promised the prophet

Jeremiah that one day he would put his Word in peoples' hearts and minds (Jer. 31:31–34). God also put his words into the heart of the prophet Ezekiel (Ezek. 3:3–4, 10). It is not clear exactly what this means, except that these people had a clear impression in their hearts and minds and they knew it was from God.

Various Unspecified Ways

Obviously God used a variety of ways to communicate throughout the Old Testament. We have mentioned several specific examples. However, the majority of the time, the Bible does not specify exactly *how* God spoke, only *that* he spoke. Thus, we read, "God spoke to Noah . . ." (Gen. 8:15); "the LORD said to Abraham . . ." (Gen. 12:1); "the LORD said to Moses . . ." (Exod. 24:12); "the LORD said to Joshua . . ." (Josh. 7:10); "the LORD said to Samuel . . ." (1 Sam. 16:1); "Then the word of the LORD came to Isaiah . . ." (Isa. 38:4); "the word of the LORD which came to Hosea . . ." (Hos. 1:1); "The word of the LORD which came to Zephaniah . . ." (Zeph. 1:1). Were these instances referring to an audible voice? Were they dreams? Were they visions? We are not told specifically how God spoke, but the Bible is clear that when God spoke, the people knew it was God, they knew what he was going to do, and they knew what their response should be.

God Speaks:
The Old Testament Record

- Creation
- Angels
- Prophets
- Dreams
- Visions
- Casting Lots
- Urim and Thummim
- Gentle Voice
- Fire
- Burning Bush
- Preaching

- Judgments
- Symbolic Actions
- Signs
- Miracles
- Writing on the Wall
- Donkey
- Trumpet
- Thunder and Lightning, Smoke and Storms
- Fleece
- Sound of Marching in the Treetops
- Face-to-Face
- Personal Guidance
- Various Unspecified Ways

God Speaks:
The New Testament Record

When Jesus came to earth, nothing changed and everything changed. God continued to reach out to people, often in ways that mirrored Old Testament ways. Yet now there was a new dimension to his communication. The writer of Hebrews said, "Long ago God spoke to the fathers by the prophets at different times and in different ways. In these last days, He has spoken to us by His Son, whom He has appointed heir of all things and through whom He made the universe" (Heb. 1:1–2 HCSB). The coming of the Lord Jesus was not merely another means by which God expressed his Word. Jesus was—and is—God's word. The apostle John wrote, "The Word became flesh and took up residence among us " (John 1:14 HCSB). Jesus spoke to people throughout his earthly ministry, but only a fortunate few understood they were having an encounter with God's Son. Since Jesus' earthly ministry God has chosen to communicate with people in a variety of ways.

Risen Christ

The Gospels record numerous occurrences of Jesus speaking directly to men and women in the days immediately following his resurrection. He first appeared at the empty tomb, speaking words of life to those who had come expecting to find a corpse (John 20:14–18). He joined two bewildered men as they walked the dusty trail to Emmaus discussing the days' bizarre events. Only after he departed did they realize they had just conversed with the risen Christ (Luke 24:13–35). Jesus joined the Eleven in the upper room, reproaching them for their collective faith deficit, but also giving them a second chance (Mark 16:14–18). And later, so Thomas could allay his doubts, Jesus appeared and spoke to him as well (John 20:24–29). The New Testament mentions more than one occurrence of the risen, ascended Christ speaking to people. Saul of Tarsus had a profoundly humbling encounter with the risen Christ (Acts 9:3–5). The aging apostle John was spending his days as a prisoner on the dreary isle of Patmos when the risen Christ personally delivered a message to him for the churches in Asia (Rev. 1:9–16).

Nature

The New Testament corroborates the Old Testament teaching that God's divine character is revealed in his creation. Paul said nature so clearly testifies to God's existence that those who reject God's message as expressed in his creation are "without excuse" (Rom. 1:18–20).

Angels

As in the Old Testament, angels appear throughout the New Testament as God's appointed messengers (Matt. 1:24; 2:24; John 20:12; Acts 5:19; 8:26; 10:30–33). The angel Gabriel delivered particularly epochal messages (Dan. 8:16; 9:21; Luke 1:19, 26). While Paul was lost at sea, God sent an angel to comfort him and to tell him about God's plans for him (Acts 27:23–25).

Dreams

God used a dream to warn the eastern Magi not to return to Jerusalem (Matt. 2:12). An angel also appeared in a dream to alert Joseph to King Herod's evil intentions (Matt. 2:13).

Visions

After Saul's dramatic encounter with the risen Christ, Ananias received a vision sending him to find Saul and to heal his blindness (Acts 9:10–12). Meanwhile, God gave Saul a vision preparing him for Ananias's coming (Acts 9:12). Peter received a vision that transformed his attitude toward Gentiles and subsequently his entire ministry (Acts 10:9–17). The apostle Paul's first missionary journey to Europe was initiated by a vision (Acts 16:9). Likewise, a vision inspired Paul's bold preaching in Corinth (Acts 18:9–10).

Prayer

While Paul was praying in the temple, God spoke to him, warning him to flee his enemies and instructing him to evangelize the Gentiles (Acts 22:17–21). In the Scriptures, prayer is often presented as a two-way conversation wherein people hear God respond to their prayers.

Prophets

Prophets are usually associated with the Old Testament, but God continued to use prophets in the New Testament as well. The Holy Spirit directed Agabus to predict the famine that would sweep across the known world (Acts 11:28). Agabus also prophesied Paul's arrest if he went to Jerusalem (Acts 21:10–11). Prophecy is listed as one of the gifts of the Spirit (Rom. 12:6; 1 Cor. 12:10; Eph. 4:11).

Lot-casting

The disciples cast lots to determine who would take Judas's place as an apostle (Acts 1:23–26). After Pentecost the Bible does not record any more instances of lot-casting as a way to determine God's will.

Signs and Wonders

Signs were events that pointed people to God. Sometimes these were miracles. Other times they were world events (Matt. 24:3). John's Gospel indicates the miracles Jesus performed were signs to convince people that he was the Christ (John 20:30–31). Jesus condemned those who witnessed his miracles but refused to repent of their sin and believe in him (Matt. 11:20–24). He also rebuked the scribes and Pharisees for seeking signs because he knew their treacherous motives: "An evil and adulterous generation demands a sign, but no sign will be given to it" (Matt. 12:39 HCSB).

Preachers

God continued to use preachers, such as Peter, Paul, and Apollos to proclaim his truth (Rom. 10:14–15). In fact, the Bible indicates that preachers are essential for people to hear God's word (Rom. 10:14). Paul's letter to the Thessalonians explains that God used human messengers to proclaim his gospel to others and that the power of the message, not the messenger, transformed lives: "For this reason we also constantly thank God that when you received from us the word of God's message, you accepted it not as the word of men, but for what it really is, the word of God, which also performs its work in you who believe" (1 Thess. 2:13).

Scripture

It is obvious the Scriptures guided Jesus throughout his life. When Satan tempted Jesus in the desert, the Father supplied strength through his Word. Jesus knew the Scriptures so well Satan could not trap him with lies or half-truths (Matt. 4:4, 7, 10). After the resurrection, Jesus opened his disciples' minds so they too could understand the Scriptures (Luke 24:27, 45). The Book of Acts repeatedly mentions the disciples basing their actions on the Scriptures (Acts 1:20; 2:16–21; 7:2–53).

An Unbeliever

God demonstrated his sovereignty when he elected to use Caiaphas, an enemy of Christ, to communicate his truth to others (John 11:49–53).

The Church

Jesus walked on earth as God in the flesh. When the risen Christ returned to his Father's side, God established the church to be the visible manifestation of his presence. Though Jesus was no longer bodily present as a man, he was, and is, still present as spiritual head of the newly established church (Col. 1:18). Therefore, the Book of Acts says, the early church was empowered to "speak the word of God with boldness" (Acts 4:31).

God designed the church to function as a unified group whereby each individual part contributes beneficially to the whole. When the early church sought to understand God's will, they determined it corporately (Acts 11:1–18; 15:1–35). The Corinthian church was torn by problems of division and disunity, so Paul used the brilliant metaphor of the human body to explain how a church should function (1 Cor. 12). The church is a collection of diverse people to whom God grants a variety of gifts and insights. But although the membership is varied, there is only one God. His Spirit will accomplish what only God can do, and he will guide the members to work together as one healthy body clearly understanding and carrying out the Father's will.[2]

A Direct Word from the Father

Those present at Jesus' baptism heard the Father praise his Son for his obedience (Luke 3:22). At the Mount of Transfiguration, the Father's voice was again audible, but this time it was in rebuke. God chastised Peter for suggesting they build three tabernacles—one for Moses, one for Elijah, and one for Jesus (Luke 9:33). Before Peter had even finished expressing his misguided suggestion, a cloud overshadowed him and his companions. God's disapproving voice came from the cloud, commanding Peter to keep his opinions to himself and to listen to Jesus (Luke 9:35).

Poor Peter! Why was the heavenly Father so hard on him when his intentions were clearly honorable? Peter should have known better in light of recent events. Eight days earlier Jesus had commended Peter for correctly identifying him as the Messiah. However, Peter had not come to this profound conclusion by his own reasoning. Jesus pointed out that Peter should consider himself blessed not because of his superior wisdom but because the Father had revealed this truth directly to him (Matt. 16:17).

The Holy Spirit

Those who walked physically with Jesus obviously had a unique opportunity. Yet Jesus told his followers it was to their advantage that he leave them (John 16:7). As Jesus returned to the Father, he promised his disciples the Holy Spirit. This third member of the holy Trinity would do his divine work within the hearts and minds of *all* believers. Through the Son, God brought salvation. Through the Spirit he would enable believers to experience that salvation. The Spirit would guide Christians in numerous ways, convicting them of sin, revealing God's truth, teaching God's ways, and reinforcing Christ's words. The Spirit would help Christians testify to the truth of Christ to unbelievers by giving them God's words to say. He would reveal the Father's thoughts and help believers know how to pray (Matt. 10:19–20; John 14:26; 16:7–8, 13; Rom. 8:26; 1 Cor. 2:9–16).

The Book of Acts wonderfully expresses the way God's Spirit guides his church. The Holy Spirit led Philip to evangelize the Ethiopian eunuch (Acts 8:29). The Spirit also instructed the church at Antioch to send out Paul and Barnabas as missionaries (Acts 13:2).

Various Unspecified Ways

Like the Old Testament, the New Testament often reveals *that* God communicated but not *how* he did so. We know that God spoke to Philip, because Acts 8:29 tells us, "The Spirit said to Philip, 'Go up and join this chariot.'" We are not told whether the Spirit communicated in an audible voice, through a vision, or through other means. Similarly, we read that Paul and Timothy were "forbidden by the Holy Spirit to speak the Word in Asia." Jesus' Spirit also prevented them from entering Bithynia (Acts 16:6).

The details of these messages are not provided, but clearly Philip and Paul both knew who was guiding them, and they knew exactly what God was saying.

God Speaks:
The New Testament Record

- Risen Christ
- Nature
- Angels
- Dreams
- Visions
- Prayer
- Prophets
- Lot-casting
- Signs and Wonders
- Preachers
- Scripture
- An Unbeliever
- The Church
- A Direct Word from the Father
- The Holy Spirit
- Various Unspecified Ways

Conclusion

This concludes a survey of ways God has communicated with people throughout Scripture. We can infer from the epilogue of John's Gospel that this list, though it is lengthy, is not exhaustive (John 21:25). No doubt God spoke in countless other ways as well, ways we do not read about in the Scriptures. Obviously the key is not how God spoke. God steadfastly refused to limit himself to only one way of communicating. The significant point was that almighty God chose to communicate with people in unmistakable ways. In the next chapter we will see that although God used a variety of methods in relating to people, there are several factors in his communication that are consistent.

Questions for Reflection

1. What did you notice about the ways God spoke to people during biblical times?

2. Which of the ways God spoke that are mentioned in this chapter have you experienced personally?

3. Are there ways God might speak to you that you have not considered before?

GOD SPEAKS: HIS WAY
CHAPTER THREE

O swald Chambers is best known for the widely read devotional book *My Utmost for His Highest*, a collection of his teachings assembled and published by his devoted wife Biddy after his death. Generations of Christians the world over have grown closer to the Lord because of this classic book and the wisdom contained within it.

Chambers served during World War I as a chaplain for the British forces. When he was sent to Egypt, he initially went alone, considering the circumstances too dangerous to bring his family. Biddy was as eager to join him as he was to have her come. But as a husband and father, Chambers wanted to avoid an unwise decision that could endanger his family. So Chambers did what he always did—he sought God's specific guidance in the matter. He read Mark 9:8 as well as Psalm 37:4: "Delight yourself in the LORD and, He will give you the desires of your heart." God spoke to him through his Word, confirming to Chambers that he should invite his family to join him immediately.[1] Chambers observed: "No man by mere high human wisdom would dare undertake a step for Jesus' sake unless he knows that the Holy Spirit has directly spoken to him."[2]

As it turned out, Oswald Chambers died during the war. However, Biddy had spent many evenings sitting in the tent listening as her husband shared God's Word with the soldiers. She had taken fastidious notes, which eventually helped serve as the basis for several books. Those writings have in turn affected millions of lives. Had she not been there, much of what Chambers said would have been lost.

Plenty of biblical evidence shows that God communicates with people and that he has done so throughout the generations. But what does this mean to those of us who seek his voice today? Should we start a personal list, based on the ways God has communicated in the past, then consider it incomplete until he speaks to us through a donkey and a piece of lamb's wool? The Bible makes an intriguing distinction: "He made known His ways to Moses, His acts to the children of Israel" (Ps. 103:7). The Israelites could cite many instances when the Lord spoke to their forefathers. They had personally experienced several compelling encounters with him. However, they apparently viewed these as random events. They did not learn about God himself from their experiences. Moses, on the other hand, saw beyond the act of God speaking. He was enlightened to understand the purpose behind the words. This distinction between God's acts and his ways is a significant one. Chapter 2 listed numerous acts of God as he spoke to people, examples of when and where he spoke, and the various means by which he communicated his message (how he spoke). This chapter examines the way, God spoke and the implications they has for us as we seek to hear his voice today.

God's Pattern

God Speaks Uniquely

Saul of Tarsus was a Pharisee—zealous, self-righteous, and proud. Are we surprised that he met Christ in a sensational and humbling fashion? God's first words to young Samuel, on the other hand, were spoken in a quiet, gentle voice in the stillness of the night. Encounters between God and individuals matched not only the person's character but also the circumstances. Saul's was a dramatic public experience. Samuel's was a gentle, private one. Still, each heard the Lord calling him by name.

God Speaks Personally

We are creatures of convenience. We love to find formulas that work and apply them everywhere we can. This helps to simplify our lives, and that's not a bad thing. But God does not limit himself to a formula. Were today's mind-set prevalent in Balaam's day, he might be tempted to get published after hearing God speak through a donkey. He could detail his experience for those who had not yet heard from their donkeys, perhaps dubbing his work *Donkeys for Dummies*. Smart marketing could net him a small fortune, and people everywhere would be well prepared should God ever choose the donkey-speaking experience for them. But, of course, the method wasn't the main thing. Hearing God's voice through a donkey might sound incredible, but the really mind-boggling fact is that God spoke to Balaam—period. How often people say, "If God would just speak to me in an audible voice, then I would believe him!" Hebrews 11:6 explains, "Without faith, it is impossible to please God" (HCSB). God's choice to communicate in so many diverse ways forces us to put our faith in him, not a method. We do not seek a word from God to prove he is real so we can have a relationship with him. Rather, as we seek to develop an intimate relationship with him, we will hear him speak to us (James 4:8).

God Speaks Progressively

The Bible reveals a progressive pattern in the way God communicated with people. In Old Testament times the heavenly Father spoke in multiple ways. The Gospels tell us God fulfilled the Old Testament prophecies and deepened his relationship with his people by sending his Son. After Christ's ascension, God sent the Spirit and established the church, continuing to communicate with his people. Jesus said it was to his disciples' advantage that he leave them so they would receive the Holy Spirit.

God also relates to individuals in a progressive way. In the Bible, someone's first meeting with God is often more dramatic than later encounters. The original discourse between God and Moses was the burning bush experience. A bright light literally blinded Saul of Tarsus when the risen Christ first confronted him. Likewise, Ezekiel's first encounter with God was unforgettable as he saw a great cloud with fire flashing and heavenly messengers within it

(Ezek. 1:4–21). However, as each of these men grew in his relationship with God, God did not always need to use such dramatic means to gain their attention and to communicate his will. For example, the apostle Paul mentions hearing from God often, but apart from a couple of exceptions, the manner he describes seems to indicate an intimate, daily communication, not a string of earth-shattering events. Many people seek a series of spectacular experiences with God, but biblically the dramatic seems to be the exception rather than the norm.

God seeks a dynamic, growing relationship with his people, so he speaks progressively to individuals. He guides people step-by-step, day-by-day, each new word building upon what he said previously. When God first spoke to Abraham, it was to tell him to leave his homeland and to go to a different place. At first, God didn't even tell him where his new home would be. After following God for almost forty-five years, Abraham received the command to sacrifice his only son (Gen. 22:1–3). It is doubtful Abraham would have been prepared for such a difficult word at the outset of his walk with God.

Likewise, Jesus taught his disciples in a progressive way. He did not speak to them about the cross, for example, until they had first come to understand that he was the Christ (Matt. 16:13–21). They simply were not ready for such a stunning revelation before then.

God Speaks Consistently

We must be cautious when we say "God always . . ." or, "God never . . ." because God is God. He can do what he chooses, when he chooses, and how he chooses. But some things are safely stated in the absolute. One of those truths is that God will never say anything inconsistent with his character. God is holy. Therefore, he does not speak to people in an unholy manner (Ps. 60:6; 65:5). Nor does he guide people in ways that would cause them to act unethically. David heard from God often, but he knew better than to claim his adultery with Bathsheba was in response to God's directive. David realized when he sinned it was because he did not *heed* God's voice. God's nature is also love, so his words always reflect perfect love (1 John 4:7–8). Even the Lord's harshest words are spoken in love. John 3:16 lays out the hard reality that people who reject God will perish, but the same verse assures us that God will give people ample opportunity to prevent their self-destruction.

God Speaks Faithfully

"Surely, as I have planned, so it will be, and as I have purposed, so it will stand" (Isa. 14:24 NIV). Those are God's words. From the beginning of creation God established the pattern for his Word: "God said . . . It was so . . . (Gen. 1). The Bible consistently demonstrates the reliability of God's Word. If God predicts a certain event, that event will happen exactly as he said, "For the Lord Almighty has purposed, and who can thwart him? His hand is stretched out, and who can turn it back? (Isa. 14:27). When God makes a vow, he keeps it (Isa. 55:10–11). God's promise of military success for the Israelites was a certainty, no matter what condition their army was in or how fierce their opponents were. Victory was a given—all that remained was to see how God worked out the details.

God Speaks Unmistakably

The Bible testifies that, despite the numerous times and ways God spoke to people, they ultimately knew it was God speaking. They also knew what God was saying. From Adam and Eve through to the exiled apostle John, the question was not, Is God speaking to me? but, How will I respond to what God is telling me? Our problem so often is not that we don't know what God is saying to us. The problem is that we *do* know, but we don't always want to hear what he is telling us.

God Speaks Diagnostically

Since creation, people have responded to a word from God in one of two ways. They either rejected his message, or they accepted it—some more graciously than others. According to Luke's Gospel, Zacharias was a righteous man. He prayed and prayed for a child, though his wife's biological clock had long since ticked past the time for childbearing. Yet, when the angel Gabriel revealed God's answer, that Elizabeth was going to bear a son, Zacharias did not believe him. Because of his unbelief, God rendered him mute until the day John was born (Luke 1:19–20).

Gabriel's message to Mary, namely that she was to bear the Messiah, was equally inconceivable (excuse the pun). It was a physical impossibility, as Mary knew, yet her humble response has been a model for generations of believers: "Consider me the Lord's slave, May it be done to me according to your word" (Luke 1:38). When God speaks, neutrality is not an option. A response is unavoidable, and the condition of peoples' hearts is revealed in that response.

God's Pattern

1. God Speaks Uniquely.
2. God Speaks Personally.
3. God Speaks Progressively.
4. God Speaks Consistently.
5. God Speaks Faithfully.
6. God Speaks Unmistakably.
7. God speaks Diagnostically.

God's Purpose

People do not "figure God out." God reveals himself to people. Without the presence of God's Spirit, no one would understand God's will (Rom. 8:5–8). God's Spirit not only reveals his will but also enables us to respond in obedience. God reveals at least three primary things to us when he speaks. He reveals his character, his purposes, and his ways.

God Speaks to Reveal His Character

The Bible records many different names for God. These names reflect the multifaceted nature of his character as revealed to men and women in a variety of personal encounters. For example, when God provided a sacrifice to take Isaac's place on the altar, Abraham learned that God is Jehovah-Jireh (Provider) (Gen. 22:14). Earlier Abraham came to know God as "Everlasting God" (Gen. 21:33). Through firsthand encounters with God, Abraham gained much more than head knowledge that God is a provider or that God is everlasting. He gained experiential knowledge. It is one thing to be told God is holy; it is quite another to experience his holiness. The former might impress you, but the latter will compel you to live a holy life yourself. You are not likely to attempt the impossible until you know experientially that the God who commands you to do so is all powerful. You will struggle to forgive others until you truly grasp the incredible price God paid to forgive you. A relationship with God does not grow out of head knowledge. It may begin there, but it becomes vibrant by personal experience.

God Speaks to Reveal His Purposes

When we listen for God's voice, what are we seeking? Is it answered prayer in which God merely grants our request? Is it his praise for the Christian services we perform? Is it guidance to help us carry out the plans we're making?

Certainly God does bless us beyond our due. He also affirms his children and gives us wisdom when we need it. But God's purposes are not the same as ours. We want him to indulge us; he wants to transform us (Rom. 8:29).

God is on mission to redeem a lost world. His purposes are to draw us to himself and to help us become increasingly more like his Son. When he speaks, it is against this backdrop. Therefore, when we seek to promote ourselves or when we ask God to make our plans successful, we will not always hear what we want to hear in response. However, when we ask him for guidance according to what is on *his* heart and when we ask how we can adjust our lives to *his* plans, the Bible says we will hear him clearly.

God Speaks to Reveal His Ways

The way something is done reveals volumes. David prayed, "Show me your ways, O LORD; teach me your paths" (Ps. 25:4 NIV). He was acknowledging that his ways were not necessarily God's ways. How often do people do things in God's name that holy God would never sanction?

The apostle Paul, before his conversion, demonstrated the extremes of such erroneous thinking. He thought he was honoring God by hunting down Christians and punishing them for their blasphemy. God set him straight in a huge—not to mention humbling—way.

Peter was basically a bigot who considered all races other than his own to be unclean. His views were socially acceptable in his culture, and they merely reflected what he had been raised to believe. But, like Paul, Peter was wrong. And as he had done with Paul, God corrected Peter (Acts 10:15).

God will speak to people, teaching them how to do things according to his ways. God's ways are perfect.[3] He will never ask his people to do anything in an unholy way. For example, God will never lead you to cheat on your income tax so you'll have more money to give to missions. That may sound absurd, but countless Christians have justified their blatant sin with the disclaimer, "It's for a good cause." No matter how honorable the end, it doesn't justify dishonorable means. And yes, God does notice: "For a man's ways are in full view of the LORD" (Prov. 5:21 NIV). God will not allow his name to be dishonored. He will make his ways clear so they can be followed.

God's Purpose

1. God speaks to reveal his character
2. God speaks to reveal his purposes
3. God speaks to reveal his ways

God's Focus

The Reverend Robinson was to meet the famed English pastor F. B. Meyer at the Canadian National Railway station in Montreal on the morning of August 31, 1927. Riding to the Montreal station by taxi, Robinson suddenly sensed he should go to the Canadian Pacific Railway station instead. As Robinson was getting out of his car, he spied Reverend Meyer. Meyer had been inadvertently placed on the wrong train, and he knew that his host was planning to meet him at a different station. As Meyer explained to Robinson, "I told God about it, and said, 'Please, Father, let Mr. Robinson meet me in Montreal,' and I knew it would be all right. Oh! God is so good, so good, my friend."[4]

In a matter as simple as picking up a visiting speaker at a train station, the Holy Spirit had given clear and specific guidance. Robinson had no way to know Meyer had boarded the wrong train. But God knew. Does God guide people this specifically? Does he intervene this directly into people's everyday affairs? This is a hotly debated question among Christians today. The biblical record is that God does give specific guidance.

God Speaks: Disclosing Specifics

As mentioned in the opening chapter, some people claim God does not speak to people specifically. They argue that God has given his commandments and biblical teachings. People are to follow God's laws and apply biblical principles to their lives. As long as they do these things, they will be guided sufficiently to lead a victorious Christian life. The problem with this teaching is that does not align with Scripture. The Bible is a collection of accounts that reveal God speaking to people to give them specific instructions they would never have known otherwise.

No matter where you look in the Old Testament, you will find God's specific instructions to his people. When God told Noah to build an ark, God didn't say, "Noah, it's going to rain for forty days and nights. You'd better take whatever action seems appropriate to you." Not only did God command Noah to build the ark, but he was also meticulously specific about the details for its construction. It was to be made of gopher wood. It was to measure three hundred cubits in length, fifty cubits in width, and thirty cubits in height. There were to be three decks. It was to have a solitary window, positioned exactly one cubit from the top of the ship (Gen. 6:13–16).

God wanted the children of Israel to build a tabernacle. He could have said, "I want a place to manifest my presence where you can offer sacrifices to me. Brainstorm over the kind of place you think would honor me and then construct it in whatever way seems expedient." Rather, God gave specialized instructions for the tabernacle, just as he did for the ark of the covenant, the mercy seat, the golden lamp stand, the curtains of linen, the curtains of goat's hair, the veil, and the bronze altar. God directed the Israelites with great attention to detail concerning the garments the priests were to wear as well as instructing them on how to offer each type of sacrifice (Lev. 25–30). God painstakingly described exactly how he wanted his people to worship him. Chapter after chapter in the books of Exodus and Leviticus are devoted to describing, in minute detail, such things as the order and type of stones found on the breastplate of judgment or the number and size of curtains in the tabernacle.

Gideon was raising an army to rid his nation of the occupying Midianite soldiers. His first move was to issue a call for all able-bodied men to assemble for battle. This was standard military logic. But what God had Gideon do next completely defied common sense. Thirty-two thousand troops had gathered. God instructed Gideon to send twenty-two thousand of them home. Then God whittled Gideon's army down further. Though the Israelites were going up against a vastly superior army, God instructed Gideon to send home all but three hundred fighters. What must these troops have thought when God's next instructions were for Gideon to have his tiny group of men surround the enemy with trumpets and empty pots! (Judg. 7:2–18). This is not a strategy a general would ever have contrived! And that was the whole point. The victory that followed for the Israelites could only have come from God.

God's pointed guidance is not limited to the Old Testament. God continued to provide specific leadership for people throughout the New Testament. Philip the evangelist was enjoying remarkable success proclaiming the gospel in the city of Samaria. Large crowds were listening to him. Unclean spirits were being exorcized from people whom they had held captive. Leading community figures were turning to Christ. In the midst of Philip's enormous success, an angel of the Lord instructed him to leave Samaria and to travel into the desert

(Acts 8:4–13, 26). It didn't make sense. Church growth books would never instruct you to leave crowds who were enthusiastically responding to your message and retreat into a wilderness. But that's what God told Philip to do. Of course, on that dusty road Philip met the Ethiopian eunuch. Through this convert the gospel may have entered the continent of Africa.

Ananias was a believer whom God visited in a vision. He was told to go to a street called Straight. There he was to inquire at the house of a man named Judas, asking for Saul of Tarsus who would be praying there (Acts 9:11). Pretty detailed instructions! Would Ananias ever have gone to that particular street, to that particular house, to call on that particular man had he not been directed by the Holy Spirit?

As Peter prayed, three strangers knocked on his door. Immediately the Holy Spirit instructed Peter, "Three men are here looking for you. Get up, go downstairs, and accompany them with no doubts at all, because I have sent them" (Acts 10:19–20 HCSB). Again, God spoke specifically to a disciple, this time to minister to the God-fearing centurion Cornelius, along with his family and friends.

It would be hard to read the Scriptures and miss the obvious specificity in the way God communicates. The Bible is a reliable record of how God has related to people in the past. It is also our guide for how God will speak to us today. To say "I've never heard God speak specifically to me that way" does not negate the fact that God does speak that way. Our experience cannot be the measure by which we understand Scripture. Scripture must be the standard by which we evaluate our experience. Those who have been used mightily by the Lord have been people who determined to gain God's guidance in every area of their lives.

George Muller

George Muller would not preach a sermon until he knew he had received specific guidance to do so from God. Muller explained:

> Rather than presuming to know what is best for
> the hearers, I ask the Lord to graciously teach me the

subject I should speak about, or the portion of his word I should explain. Sometimes I will have a particular subject or passage on my mind before asking him. If, after prayer, I feel persuaded that I should speak on that subject, I study it, but still leave myself open to the Lord to change it if he pleases.

Frequently, however, I have no subject in my mind before I pray. In this case, I wait on my knees for an answer, trying to listen for the voice of the Spirit to direct me. Then, if a passage or subject is brought to mind, I again ask the Lord if that is his will. Sometimes I ask repeatedly, especially if the subject or text is a difficult one. If after prayer, my mind is peaceful about it, I take this to be the text. But I still leave myself open to the Lord for direction, in case he decides to alter it, or if I have been mistaken.

Sometimes I still do not have a text after praying. At first I was puzzled by this, but I have learned to simply continue with my regular reading of the Scriptures, praying while I read for a text. I have had to read five, ten, even twenty chapters before the Lord has given me a text. Many times I have even had to go to the meeting place without a subject. But I have always obtained it, perhaps, only a few minutes before I was going to speak. The Lord always helps me when I preach, provided I have earnestly sought him in private.[5]

What a magnificent testimony of relying on God for guidance in such an important task. Wouldn't it be wonderful if *all* preachers followed Muller's example?

Billy Graham

Billy Graham wisely avoided a subtle yet sinister trap that has befallen many evangelists. That is the snare of success. As Graham's ministry rapidly accelerated and more and more people accepted the gospel, Graham knew he and his team members could inadvertently allow themselves to be guided by factors other than the Holy Spirit's leadership. He wanted to be certain their decisions were based on God's clear leading, not on where they thought they would enjoy success. He confessed, "I did not want numerical success to become our standard for discerning the will of God. We did not dare go forward without his direction."[6] Surely this is why Graham's ministry has remained fruitful while evangelistic ministries all around fell like card houses.

God Speaks: Requiring Faith

Do you recall the story in Acts where the disciples were praying fervently for Peter's release from prison? When God answered their prayers and the servant told them Peter was at their door, their reaction was, "You're crazy!" (Acts 12:1–15 HCSB). If they really believed God was going to answer their prayer, would they have reacted this way when he did? Surely one reason some do not hear God speak specifically to them is because they don't really believe he will do so. Then, when God does speak, they refuse to acknowledge who it is. Jesus prepared the twelve disciples for his departure with this disclosure:

"If you love Me, you will keep My commandments. And I will ask the Father, and He will give you
another Counselor to be with you forever. He is the
Spirit of truth, whom the world is unable to receive
because it doesn't see Him or know Him. But you do
know Him, because He remains with you and will be
in you. I will not leave you as orphans; I am coming
to you. . . . The one who has My commandments and
keeps them is the one who loves Me. And the one
who loves Me will be loved by My Father.
I also will love him and will reveal myself to him. . . .
If anyone loves Me, he will keep My word. My Father
will love him, and We will come to him and make
Our home with Him. The one who doesn't love Me
will not keep My words" (John 14:21, 23–24 HCSB).

The measure for determining if someone really loves Jesus is the way that person receives God's Word. Those who listen closely to the Lord and subsequently do as he directs obviously love him. Conversely, people who constantly resist God's directions are demonstrating their lack of love for God. Some adamantly argue that they *do* love

God; they just struggle to obey him. According to Jesus, a failure to follow God's Word is a failure to love him. The willingness to obey every word from God is critical to hearing God speak. Those who do not believe God speaks specifically will simply ignore or explain away the times when God communicates with them. However, those who spend each day in the profound awareness that God does speak are in a wonderful position to receive his Word. There's not a person on earth who does not desperately need to receive such a word.

Recognizing God's Answer

A friend was serving as student director on a large university campus. He tells an amusing story about the day a concerned student came to see him in his office. She was deeply troubled about her financial situation. She explained, "I am in desperate need of a part-time job if I am to stay in school. I have prayed and asked God to help me, but every place I have applied is not hiring." She asked, "Do you really believe God can help me find a job?"

Just then a fellow student passed by the open doorway and saw her meeting with the director. The friend apologized for interrupting, and said, "I've been looking for you! After your meeting we need to talk. My boss asked me today if I knew anyone who needed a part-time job. I told him about you, and he wants to talk to you right away!" The anxious student thanked her friend, then turned back to the student director and continued where she had left off, "So do you think God can help me find a job?" It's a good thing there were no two-by-fours within reach! Unbelief can render a person stone deaf to God's voice.

God Speaks: Step-by-Step

Catriona LeMay Doan is one of Canada's most decorated athletes. She is also a fine Christian woman and a gracious spokesperson for Christ. Being Canadians ourselves, we both watched with keen interest when she competed in the last Olympics. LeMay Doan is a speed-skating phenomenon. She breaks world records regularly, usually her own. Her specialty is the sprint, as her nickname "the

Cat" implies. She trains relentlessly, conditioning her body to cover five hundred meters of ice in an unbelievably short time. And it pays off on the podium. During the 2002 Olympics, the Cat skated away with the gold medal, as expected, in the sprint. A couple of days later, she competed in the longer one-thousand-meter race. The gun went off, and two skaters darted off the line. LeMay Doan easily shot ahead of her opponent. By five hundred meters a significant gap separated the two skaters. Then things changed. The Cat started to lose her lead. Her face etched in obvious pain, she drove as hard as she could, but by the final stretch she had fallen well behind her rival skater. Why? Was she not a good speed skater? Of course she was! But she had trained for the sprint. Her body was a powerful machine, but her lungs and her muscles could not sustain sprint speed in such a long race.

Why do we share her story? The Christian life is not a sprint. It's a long race. The way we begin is important. The way we end even more so.

At times people get an assignment from God, then they race off to do it without waiting for the specifics of how and when he wants them to carry it out. For example, over the years we have been dismayed to see a number of men and women receive God's call to the ministry; but in their impatience to "get at it," they neglected to seek God's further direction regarding how to prepare for a lifetime of ministry. Instead they dashed out of the starting block, eager to serve God but not prepared for the long race ahead. These people have generally encountered discouragement and failure. When it comes to following Christ, what God wants you to do is obviously important, but so is how he wants you to do it. Those who want to remain in the race for its entirety must be willing to linger long enough to receive God's specific guidance.

God instructed Abraham, "Leave your country, your people and your father's household and go to the land I will show you" (Gen. 12:1 NIV). At first, God didn't offer Abraham many details. Abraham was not privy to the exact location God had in mind for him and his descendants. Nor was he yet aware that God's promise of a son would involve twenty-five years of waiting. The impending judgment of Sodom and Gomorrah and the invasion of enemy kings were events known only to God when Abraham first began following him. It was to be a long pilgrimage for Abraham, the specifics of which would unfold over time. But Abraham *did* know for certain what was required of him each step of the way.

Moses also walked with God step-by-step. He knew his assignment—go to Egypt and deliver the children of Israel from their bondage—but the details were sketchy at first. God told Moses that Pharaoh would initially reject his request. God didn't tell him that Pharaoh would increase the Israelites' burden until they bitterly blamed Moses for their hardship (Exod. 5:21). God did not reveal which plagues he would send. Moses was not told in advance about the Egyptian army pursuing them to the Red Sea with the intent to annihilate them. But, like Abraham, Moses walked faithfully with God over a lifetime as God guided him specifically.

J. Edwin Orr

God used J. Edwin Orr mightily around the world in the area of spiritual revival. He was an ordinary man who experienced God working repeatedly in his life in extraordinary ways. God invited him to travel across Europe, preaching and spreading awareness of the need for revival. Orr was not a wealthy man, but he concluded that if God called him, God would provide. As he obeyed his calling, Orr witnessed a tremendous response. Wherever he went, people united together to pray for revival.

He arrived at Londonderry late in the evening of January 29, 1934. His funds were exhausted and so was he, but he knew of no place to spend the night. A Christian man at the YMCA told Orr he would take him to a comfortable lodging place. When they arrived at a luxurious hotel, Orr felt uneasy because he knew he could not afford such first-class accommodations. Nevertheless, the proprietress set a hearty meal before him, then ushered him into a spacious room.

The next morning Orr prayed silently all the way to the front desk, prepared to be shocked by the extent of his bill. To his surprise (and great relief) he was told there would be no charge. The owner explained that she was a Christian. That morning during her devotions the Lord had clearly instructed her that she was not to charge her guest for his stay because he was God's servant. She had resisted at first, planning to charge just enough to recoup her costs. However, the Holy Spirit so convicted her of this attitude that she relented and chose not to ask for a penny.[7]

In Ireland, Orr went to the train station without the funds for a ticket, yet convinced God was directing him to a nearby city. As he neared the ticket booth, a stranger suddenly appeared and handed him a ticket to his destination![8] On another occasion Orr was in Glasgow, Scotland, when he was encouraged to attend a rally that was taking place in Stirling, thirty miles away. Orr sensed God leading him to attend, but he barely had enough money to purchase a one-way bus ticket. Since he was committed to preach in Glasgow that evening, Orr knew it was imperative that he make the return trip that same day. At the close of the afternoon service, people began to leave the meeting place until Orr was left almost entirely alone. He began to pray that God would provide for his need.

Suddenly a stranger approached him and introduced himself as Austin Stirling, pastor of the Baptist church in Cumnock. When Orr introduced himself, the man's face lit up. He had been praying that God would allow him to meet Orr! Stirling urged Orr to accompany him home but was informed of Orr's commitment in Glasgow that evening. Suddenly, his new friend had an idea. "I simply must have an hour's conversation with you," he declared. "Would you mind not using your return ticket to Glasgow? I've got a car around the corner. I'll motor you to Glasgow, and then we shall have our talk."[9] God had provided yet again, and again the provision came after Orr proved his faithfulness by obeying God's specific directive.

God Speaks: Heeding Specifics

God expects us to take his word seriously. If he chooses to mention a specific detail, he intends for us to heed it. When God led the Israelites to construct the ark of the covenant, he commanded them to transport it by using poles. He warned them that anyone touching the ark would die (Num. 4:15).

Many years later King David decided to bring the ark to Jerusalem. Ignoring God's directions, his men placed it on a cart. A cart would make it easier for those carrying it than using the two poles. But that was not how God had specifically instructed his people to treat the symbol of his holy presence. During the journey the cart was shaken, and the ark began to teeter. Instinctively, a man named Uzzah, who was walking beside the cart, reached out to steady the sacred cargo. He died instantly (2 Sam. 6:6).

Were the specific details of God's will important? They were to Uzzah! Such consequences seem unusually harsh, yet God was teaching his people to take his Word seriously. After that event we can only assume the Israelites paid careful attention to every point of God's instructions.

King Saul's grave mistake was assuming some details of God's instruction were not critical to the overall outcome. God told Saul he should not go into battle with the Philistines until Samuel had offered a sacrifice on the altar at Gilgal. But Samuel was delayed in coming. As the ranks of the Philistine army swelled each day, the Israelite soldiers became increasingly fearful, and there were numerous desertions. Saul waited seven days, then assumed the role of priest himself and offered a sacrifice to God. Saul undoubtedly thought the important thing was for a sacrifice to be offered so they could commence the battle. So he did the reasonable thing. This act of impatience cost Saul his kingdom. God not only meant what he said, but he also held King Saul strictly accountable for not adhering to his word.

A Ten O'Clock Meeting

During the great revival led by Duncan Campbell in the Hebrides, many people heard God speak to them in unusual ways. A non-Christian schoolmaster lived fifteen miles from where Campbell was preaching. He was looking over some papers at 10:00 one evening. Suddenly he was overcome with an urgent compulsion to travel to the island of Barvas. His wife chastised him for his intentions, suspecting it was an excuse to go drinking with his friends. He replied that he didn't know why he needed to go to the island, but he had a hunch he would not be drinking any more. The schoolmaster took a ferry to the island of Barvas and came upon a late-night meeting Duncan Campbell was holding in a farmhouse. As soon as the man heard Campbell speaking, he was overcome with conviction for his sin. He asked Christ to forgive him and was soon singing praises for his newfound salvation![10]

Confirmation of the Specifics

One of the great stories of the modern mission movement was the partnership for a time of two great missionaries, Hudson Taylor and William Burns. Burns had been used mightily in revival in Scotland. Taylor had undertaken the challenge to evangelize China. For seven months the two served together in the region around the great city of Shanghai. However, Taylor began to sense a growing impression from the Holy Spirit that he was to shift the focus of his ministry to the southern port city of Swatow where no missionaries had gone. Taylor was ready for the challenge, but he dreaded leaving his godly friend Burns.

For some time Taylor delayed telling Burns that they would have to part company. Finally, Taylor knew he was being disobedient to God and must tell Burns what God was leading him to do. As Taylor began telling Burns his plans, rather than a look of disappointment, there was a broad smile on Burns's face! Burns informed Taylor that God had placed an identical burden for the city of Swatow on his heart. The only reason he had not already departed was his reluctance to separate from his dear friend

Hudson. Burns confessed that he, too, had determined on that very day to tell his friend of his plans to depart immediately for the new mission field. How exciting for these two saintly comrades to receive such a confirmation of God's word.[11]

God's Focus

1. God Speaks: Disclosing Specifics
2. God Speaks: Requiring Faith
3. God Speaks: Step-by-Step
4. God Speaks: Heeding Specifics

Conclusion

The Bible is the guidebook for the Christian life. It demonstrates how God walks with people. The overwhelming testimony of Scripture is that God speaks in specific ways. It is imperative that people respond obediently to what he says. If you are not presently hearing God's voice, take time to examine your relationship with Christ. Are you faithfully seeking God's guidance for your life? Are you alert and ready for what he will say? Have you obeyed the last direction he gave you? God's Word is your life. Be extremely careful that you do not miss it.

Questions for Reflection

1. Do you believe God keeps his word? Are you presently waiting for God to fulfill a promise? What is it?

2. Do you agree that the problem most often is not that people don't know what God is saying to them but that they are unwilling to obey what they do know God is saying? Why or why not?

3. What has God been revealing to you about his character, his purposes, and his ways?

4. Has God spoken to you specifically? What did he say?

5. When you ask God to guide you, do you really believe he will? Why or why not?

6. Could it be that God has been speaking to you but you have not recognized his voice? Why or why not?

7. Have you been diligent to obey everything you know God has told you to do to the letter?

8. What are some specific directions you are presently seeking from God? What are you doing to find God's will in the matter? Are you prepared to do whatever he tells you?

THE HOLY SPIRIT: GOD'S PRESENCE IN OUR LIVES
CHAPTER FOUR

The impassioned young missionary couldn't wait to set sail for India! Settling into his cabin on the ship, John Hyde found a letter waiting for him. It was from a friend, who wrote, "I shall not cease praying for you, dear John, until you are filled with the Holy Spirit."[1]

Hyde was furious! Here he was devoting his life to missions in India, and his friend thought he lacked the Spirit! He crumpled the letter and flung it across the room.

As time passed, however, Hyde became more and more uneasy. He grew increasingly convinced that his friend had been right. He was painfully aware of recurring sins and ungodly attitudes in his life. Finally Hyde reached a crisis point: "I was led to tell the Lord I was willing even to fail in my language examinations in India, and be a missionary working quietly out of sight, that I would do anything and be anything but the Holy Spirit I would have at any cost."

God's answer came, assuring Hyde the Holy Spirit would indeed free him from his sins and use him to carry out his divine work in India. From that moment, John Hyde began to learn what it meant to walk in the Spirit. He spent extended periods of time in prayer, sometimes praying the entire night. And his were no ordinary prayers—when Hyde prayed, others in the room would break into tears because they, too, keenly sensed the Holy Spirit's presence. Like George Muller, Hyde only preached a message when he knew the Spirit had given him one. When he did preach, the entire congregation was often embraced by the Spirit's overpowering presence.

The Spirit gave Hyde deep compassion for those who did not know Christ. Hyde prayed for the privilege of leading one person each day to become a Christian. By year-end, Hyde had guided more than 366 people to give their lives to Christ! The next year Hyde boldly asked God to grant him *two* souls every day. Eventually, at least five people per day put their trust in God because of Hyde's testimony and his faithfulness to pray. "Praying Hyde" as he was called, became known as the most deeply spiritual man in India. He enjoyed the Holy Spirit's presence in dimensions he could not have imagined on that ship. And the friend? The one who penned the disturbing letter saw his prayers answered in a truly phenomenal way!

The Holy Spirit: Identity Revealed

The Holy Spirit is probably the most misrepresented member of the Trinity. Older Bible translations used the term "Holy Ghost." Of course, that term conjures up all manner of discomforting and uninviting images. Modern opinions vary greatly on exactly who the Holy Spirit is and what role he plays in the Christian's life. Some view him as a power source that energizes Christians. This greatly diminishes the Spirit's identity, stripping him of personal qualities and regarding him as a force rather than a person. Others separate the Holy Spirit from the other two persons in the Trinity. They see the Spirit as a maverick who guides people independently of the Father and the Son. As such, his alleged directions sometimes contradict what the Father and Son say in the Scriptures. A lot of people don't really know *what* to do with the Holy Spirit, so they ignore him altogether. They concentrate on the other two-thirds of the Trinity because *father* and *son* are concepts they understand, but *spirit* is beyond their experience.

The best way to understand how God relates to people is to focus on the unique role each member of the Trinity plays in the relationship. The Father is sovereign. He has designed a perfect will for his people. The Father planned for the atonement for sin through the redeeming act of the cross. The Son accomplished the Father's will when he took on physical form and was crucified for humanity's sin. The Son continues to intercede for people with the Father (1 John 2:1). The Spirit takes the will of the Father and the work of the Son and seeks to make them a reality in the believer's life.

The Old Testament reveals the heart and mind of the Father and the plans he has for his people. The Gospels relate the Son's role in bringing about the Father's plan of redemption. The Book of Acts, the rest of the New Testament, and church history demonstrate the Holy Spirit working in individuals' lives to help them respond to the Father's will and the atoning work of the Son. People who wish to recognize God's voice must understand not only the Father's purpose and the Son's redemptive role but also the crucial influence the Holy Spirit must have in their lives.

The Holy Spirit: The Old Testament Record

The Holy Spirit did not join the Trinity on the day of Pentecost. The Bible bears witness to the Holy Spirit's activity from Genesis to Revelation. The Trinity has been active in human affairs throughout history (Gen. 1:2; John 1:1–4).

The Old Testament speaks of the Holy Spirit visiting people to help them accomplish the specific task the Father had for them. The Holy Spirit gave Moses wisdom for judging the children of Israel (Num. 11:17). When God appointed seventy judges to assist Moses in administering the people, the Bible indicates God gave his Spirit to them (Num. 11:25). First, God commanded his people to build a tabernacle in which they could worship. Then, he filled Bezalel, a craftsman, with his Spirit, providing the knowledge and skill to construct a place fitting for God to reside (Exod. 35:30–36).

God placed his Spirit upon Gideon and used him to deliver the Israelites from their enemies (Judg. 6:34). When God chose Saul to be Israel's first king, Samuel told him: "Then the Spirit of the LORD will come upon you mightily, and you shall prophesy with them and be changed into another man" (1 Sam. 10:6). Likewise, when God chose David as king, the Spirit of God empowered the heir apparent in a mighty way (1 Sam. 16:13). God called Ezekiel to be his prophet, but it was the Spirit, which God placed within him, that helped him understand God's message for the people (Ezek. 2:2). All true prophets, whether from ancient or modern times, were enlightened to God's message by the Holy Spirit. The apostle Peter wrote, "No prophecy was ever made by an act of human will, but men moved by the Holy Spirit spoke from God" (2 Pet. 1:21).

The Old Testament reveals a pattern wherein the Holy Spirit helped people, as needed, to carry out the Father's will. When the assignment was finished, or if the person disobeyed God, the Father withdrew his Spirit. After Bezalel constructed the tabernacle, we are not told that he continued to enjoy the Spirit's presence. When King Saul sinned against God, the Holy Spirit departed from him (1 Sam. 16:14). King David witnessed the terror that Saul experienced when God withdrew his Spirit from him. So, when David committed his own grievous sin, he pled with his Lord, "Do not cast me away from your presence, and do not take Your Holy Spirit from me" (Ps. 51:11). In times before Pentecost, the key to the Spirit's presence was God's assignment. With God's call came the enabling presence of his Spirit. Once the assignment was accomplished, God's Spirit was withdrawn.

The Holy Spirit: The New Testament Record

With Christ's birth and the dawning of the New Testament, the Holy Spirit's role assumed an added dimension. The Spirit's assignment is still to help believers carry out the Father's purposes, but now *all* believers need the Spirit's presence because every believer is called to function as God's priest (1 Pet. 2:9). Jesus' final command to his followers was "Go, therefore, and make disciples of all nations, baptizing them in the name of the Father and the Son and the Holy Spirit, teaching them to observe everything I have commanded you" (Matt. 28:18–20 HCSB). Along with the assignment Jesus promised every believer God's continual presence: "And remember I am with you always, to the end of the age" (Matt. 28:20 HCSB). Though he was rejoining his Father in heaven, Christ promised his disciples he would ask the Father to send them another Counselor, one who would never leave them (John 14:16). As Jesus was about to ascend to heaven, he left this parting injunction: "But you will receive power when the Holy Spirit has come upon you; and you will be My witnesses in Jerusalem, and all Judea and Samaria, and to the ends of the earth" (Acts 1:8 HCSB). Since Jesus' followers were all to be his witnesses, they would all require the Holy Spirit's presence. So Jesus further commanded them to wait in Jerusalem until the Spirit came upon them (Acts 1:4).

Once the disciples received the Holy Spirit at Pentecost, a fresh vibrancy defined their lives. Peter, for example, spoke with new boldness, demonstrating a profound understanding of the Scriptures. People responded by the thousands! (Acts 2). No wonder Paul urged Christians to be filled with the Spirit (Eph. 5:18). The Book of Acts details the dramatic difference the Holy Spirit makes!

The Holy Spirit: Active in Believers

The Holy Spirit continues his divine work today. He did not go into retirement after he helped the disciples launch the early church. He is still involved in the life of every believer. Even before people place their faith in Christ, the Holy Spirit is active, convicting them of their sin and convincing them of their need for God (John 16:8–11).

Before Conversion

God's persistent desire for people is that they put their faith in him (1 Tim. 2:4). To that end, the Spirit's role is twofold: to make unbelievers aware that their sin separates them from their Creator and to draw them by God's redemptive love as expressed on the cross. We often have people tell us they do not believe God exists because he doesn't answer their prayers. They are looking at the matter backwards. Why is there silence when some people pray? Proverbs says: "The Lord is far from the wicked, but he hears the prayer of the righteous" (Prov. 15:29). What non-Christians need most is not to have their wish granted but to become children of God. One who is destined for eternal separation from God has a spiritual need that far surpasses God's providing a new job or even healing a disease. Therefore, the Spirit will communicate with non-Christians primarily to convict them of their sin. Until people reach a point of repentance and acknowledge their need for Christ, the Spirit's role is to draw them to a relationship with the Savior. Then, as part of the relationship, prayers are answered.

Pursued by God

Charles Spurgeon, the most famous London pastor of his day, describes the way God's Spirit worked relentlessly in his life, pursuing him until finally Spurgeon was compelled to repent of his sin and to yield his life to Christ: "I must confess . . . that I never would have been saved if I could have helped it. As long as ever I could, I rebelled, and revolted, and struggled against God. When he would have me pray, I would not pray, and when he would have me listen to the sound of the ministry, I would not. And when I heard, and the tear rolled down my cheek, I wiped it away and defied him to melt my soul. But long before I began with Christ, he began with me."[2]

At Conversion

The miracle of conversion, as the Spirit testifies to each new believer, is that although the individual was always God's *creation*, now he is God's *child*. There is a significant difference between the two identities. As God's adopted child, the Christian is a fellow heir with Christ (Rom. 8:14–17). God's children possess a unique spiritual perception that non-Christians do not have. Speaking to unbelievers, Jesus said: "Why don't you understand what I say? Because you cannot listen to My word. You are of your father the Devil. . . . If I tell the truth, why don't you believe Me? The one who is from God listens to God's words. This is why you don't listen, because you are not from God. . . . My sheep hear my voice" (John 8:43–44, 46–47; 10:27 HCSB).

Jesus was surrounded by multitudes of people—men, women, and children—for much of his earthly ministry. Some were wealthy; others were poor. Some were sick; others were healthy. There were bright people and not-so-bright people, nice people and nasty people. Why did some believe Jesus was the Messiah and others reject him as an imposter? Even more puzzling, why were the ones who did believe Jesus those whom you would least expect to do so—people such as the tax gatherers and harlots? It was not for lack of opportunity. Jesus lamented the fact that many were given the invitation to follow him, yet they chose to reject him (Matt. 23:37). Nor, it seems, did it depend on people finding Christ on their own (Rom. 3:10–18). The key was the Holy Spirit. He was the one at work in sinners' hearts, drawing them to the Father.

To those who did recognize him as the Christ, Jesus said, "But your eyes are blessed because they do see, and your ears because they do hear!" (Matt. 13:16).

Jesus said genuine Christians hear his voice as he leads them (John 10:4–5, 14). Those who never hear God speak should examine whether they have been born again.

After Conversion

After conversion the Holy Spirit's role changes, but it is no less important. New Christians are just that—new Christians. They need the Holy Spirit's guidance to mature in their faith. Those just beginning their relationship with Christ are like newborn babies (1 Pet. 2:2). Babies have eyes and ears. They can see visual images, and they can hear sounds. However, they are not yet capable of interpreting everything their senses tell them. Babies quickly learn to recognize their parents' voices. It takes longer for them to understand what those voices are saying. Likewise, new believers are capable of hearing God speak, but they must learn by experience how to understand what he is telling them.

The Holy Spirit is absolutely essential in helping believers grow in their understanding of what God has purposed for them. God wants every believer to experience what Jesus called the abundant life (John 10:10). Therefore, the Holy Spirit leads Christians into a deeper and deeper knowledge of him. It is a planned, deliberate process. It is inconceivable that God would draw people to give their lives to him, only to abandon them to live out their Christian lives independent of his direction. God cares about each of his children, and he takes an active part in guiding them to experience his will to the fullest.

In several distinct ways the Spirit works in the lives of believers:

The Holy Spirit: Brings Assurance

"The Spirit Himself testifies with our spirit that we are God's children" (Rom. 8:16 HCSB).

Once you become a Christian, you may occasionally have doubts that you are truly God's child. Satan will use whatever means he can to entice you to question your salvation. Can you know for certain that you are God's child? Absolutely! God is not the author of confusion. He will dispel your doubts and assure you of your inheritance with Christ.

The Holy Spirit: Convicts of Sin

"Those whose lives are in the flesh are unable to please God. You however, are not in the flesh but in the Spirit, since the Spirit of God lives in you" (Rom. 8:8–9).

Sin separates us from God. Therefore, when we sin, God's Spirit will convict us so we return to God. If we ignore his voice, he will persist in convicting us, because God wants the relationship restored. This is the great hope of the Christian—that God does not abandon us to our own debauchery. Rather, his Holy Spirit persistently works in our hearts to bring us to repentance. With repentance comes forgiveness and restoration. What greater gift could the Holy Spirit give us than conviction of sin?

The Holy Spirit: Brings Understanding

"But a natural man does not accept the things of the Spirit of God, for they are foolishness to him; and he cannot understand them, because they are spiritually appraised" (1 Cor. 2:14 HCSB).

Our ways are not God's ways (Isa. 55:8–9; Rom. 3:10ff). We do not naturally think the way God does. People can pick up a Bible and begin reading, even studying it, but they will not understand its spiritual truths unless the Holy Spirit opens their spiritual understanding.

Augustine

Augustine confessed the futility he experienced in seeking to understand Scripture through his own wisdom: "When I turned to those Scriptures . . . they seemed to me undignified, in comparison to Ciceronian dignity; for my swelling pride shrunk from their humble method, nor could my sharp wit penetrate their depths. Yet were they such as would grow up in a little one. But I disdained to be a little one; and, swollen with arrogance, took myself to be a great one."[3] Only after the prideful scholar was humiliated to tears was he able finally to comprehend the breathtakingly simple yet profound truths of Scripture.

Emmaeus Travelers

The Gospel of Luke relates the amazing event that occurred after Jesus' resurrection. Cleopas and a companion were walking along the road to Emmaeus, seven miles from Jerusalem. Suddenly Jesus joined the two men, but they could not recognize him. The men were confused and disoriented to the days' events. They had apparently been followers of Jesus but had been stunned when Jesus was brutally crucified. Then some women reported seeing him alive. This report bewildered them.

Jesus challenged these men, exhorting them by saying: "'O how unwise and slow you are to believe in your hearts all that the prophets have spoken! Didn't the Messiah have to suffer these things and enter into His glory?'" Then we read: "Beginning with Moses and all the prophets, he interpreted for them in all the Scriptures concerning himself" (Luke 24:25–27 HCSB). Once Jesus had left these men, they said to one another, "Weren't our hearts ablaze within us while he was talking with us on the road and explaining the Scriptures to us?" (Luke 24:32).

At the close of the Gospel of Luke, we find Jesus appearing to his followers who had gathered together. Scripture indicates that Jesus "opened their minds to understand the Scriptures" (Luke 24:45 HCSB). Apparently even when Christians gather together, they cannot understand the Scriptures apart from the work of God in opening their hearts and minds. Since Pentecost, the role of the Holy Spirit is to help people understand what the Bible has to say to them.

The Holy Spirit: Guides to Truth

"When the Spirit of truth comes, He will guide you into all the truth" (John 16:13 HCSB).

Have you ever received a phone call from a telemarketer? (If you haven't, please share your secret!) First comes the greeting: "Hello Mrs. [grossly mispronounces your name], this is your lucky day! You have the opportunity to win a dream vacation!" Your heart momentarily begins to race as you contemplate your wonderful prize. "You might as well begin packing your suitcase, Mrs. ____. All you have to do is . . ." Your heart sinks. What initially sounded like something too good to be true turned out to be exactly that. Or you answer the doorbell to find a door-to-door salesman grinning at you. The salesman proceeds to inform you that using your present vacuum cleaner could lead to dire consequences for your carpets, your children's health, your pet's life span, your home insurance rates, and your reputation in the neighborhood.

The world is filled with voices seeking to convince you that reality is what they say it is. How do you know what is true? What if the way you are raising your children will ultimately cause them to reject your values? What if your career decision is going to cause you lifelong regret? How do you make critical life decisions? You must rely on the

Spirit of truth. He knows the future. He's been there. He knows the facts. He knows the truth.

The Holy Spirit: Brings Comfort

"I will not leave you as orphans; I am coming to you" (John 14:16 HCSB).

The great thing about having parents is the sense of security they give. Even when you're older, you always know your parents are in your corner. If everyone else gives up on you, at least your mother still loves you and thinks you're special. Orphans are on their own. They must look out for themselves. There is no mother to comfort them in times of sorrow, no father to look out for their interests.

The picture Christ gave his disciples when he promised a Comforter is one of pure love and devotion. God loves you. He knows you intimately. He knows how to pick you up when you fall. He wants to comfort you when you grieve. Even your best friends may not know what to say in times of deep heartache, but the Holy Spirit can reach the deepest recesses of your soul and bring comfort as no one else can.

The Holy Spirit: Exalts Christ

"No one speaking by the Spirit of God says, 'Jesus is cursed,' and no one can say 'Jesus is Lord,' except by the Holy Spirit" (1 Cor. 12:3 HCSB).

To an atheist the claims of Christ may seem foolish. God's Word does not make sense to the unbeliever because it is not written according to the world's wisdom. It is written with God's wisdom (1 Cor. 1:18–25). New Christians have much to learn about Christ. As they begin to study the Scriptures, the Holy Spirit will open their minds to discover amazing truths. God's Spirit will teach new believers, expanding and enriching their understanding of God's Word. The Spirit gives God's children the assurance in their hearts that what they are reading in the Bible is absolutely true. The Holy Spirit continually seeks to exalt and magnify Christ. People cannot discover what Christ is truly like on their own. God must reveal the depths and multifaceted nature of his character to them (Matt. 16:17; John 15:26). The Holy Spirit leads Christians into a deeper knowledge of their Savior and Lord.

Revealed through Prayer

We mentioned Praying Hyde at the beginning of the chapter. Pengwern Jones, a friend of Hyde's, relates an experience that took place during a convention meeting when the pair shared a room. Hyde rose at dawn and began to pray. Jones left for breakfast and returned to find Hyde still praying. At lunchtime Hyde was still beside his bed, deep in prayer. Throughout the afternoon as Jones came and went, Hyde remained by his bed absorbed in divine communion. At 6:30 that evening, his face glowing, Hyde rose from his knees and began to tell Jones the insights the Spirit had revealed to him about the person and work of Christ. Jones recounts, "I shall never forget his words as they gave me a new vision of Christ. . . . I could not keep the tears back. At times I felt that it could not be true, that Christ had never suffered so much for me. . . . How I wish I could repeat it as Hyde brought me step by step to see Christ that evening."[4]

The Holy Spirit: Reveals God's Will

"Now we have not received the spirit of the world, but the Spirit who is from God, in order to know what has been freely given to us by God" (1 Cor. 2:12 HCSB).

Only the Holy Spirit knows all the riches of Christ and what the heavenly Father has purposed in his heart for each believer. Christians, especially new believers, are not fully aware of what it means to be God's adopted heir. We know we are children of the king, yet we can barely begin to plumb the depths of that reality. What a tragedy to live our lives in turmoil when God wants us to experience his infinite peace or to remain tightly in sin's grip when God wants us to enjoy the absolute freedom of victory over sin. The Spirit works to enlighten us to the spiritual wealth that is ours, so we don't continue unwittingly to live in spiritual poverty.

The Holy Spirit: Calls into Service

"As they were ministering to the Lord and fasting, the Holy Spirit said, 'Set apart for me Barnabas and Saul for the work that I have called them to.' Then, after they had fasted, prayed and laid hands on them, they sent them off" (Acts 13:2–3 HCSB).

From the day the Holy Spirit sets someone aside for God's service, that person's life is never the same again. When the Spirit invites someone to a career of Christian ministry, that person has two options—to obey the inner compulsion of God's call or to spend a lifetime resisting it. It takes an enormous amount of energy to continue holding out against the Holy Spirit.

Christians sometimes talk about "wrestling with God." What an absurd concept! People who choose to fight God over their calling do not understand whom they are resisting. Nor do they realize the incredible blessing they are forfeiting. Some of the most miserable people we have known were those who received God's call to full-time Christian service but spent a lifetime rejecting it. Conversely, as we have both experienced, no joy can surpass that of embracing the undeserved privilege of God's call!

Another category of life's most miserable people must include those who languish for years in career ministry to which they were never called in the first place. The Book of Acts demonstrates that the Holy Spirit's call was clear and specific. The response of those in the early church also shows that they took God's call extremely seriously.

Callings

On a sweltering Alabama day in July 1925, a sandy-haired teenager named Bill Wallace was in the family garage working on a partially dismantled Ford. Wallace was adept at mechanical work. In fact, he planned to attend trade school and embark on a mechanical career. Suddenly the Holy Spirit spoke powerfully to him, asking him what he intended to do with his life. Wallace paused for a moment, then continued his work. The question came back a second time so forcefully it caused Wallace to make a mistake in what he was doing.

When the question came the third time, Wallace stopped working and reached for his New Testament that was lying nearby on the workbench. Wallace was soon certain God was calling him to be a medical missionary. There, alone in his garage, he scrawled his commitment into his grease-stained New Testament. As a seventeen-year-old, he had settled one of the most important issues of his life. Bill Wallace went on to become one of the missionary heroes of his day, ultimately giving his life in China as a martyr for the cause of Christ.[5]

One of the most widely known preachers in the world experienced God's call on his life while he was a college student. In his own words here is Billy Graham's account of his calling:

> But did I want to preach for a lifetime? I asked myself that question for the umpteenth time on one of my nighttime walks around the golf course. The inner, irresistible urge would not subside. Finally, one night, I got down on my knees at the edge of one of the greens. Then I prostrated myself on the dewy turf. "O God," I sobbed, "if you want me to serve you, I will." The moonlight, the moss, the green, the golf course—all the surroundings stayed the same. No sign in the heavens. No voice from above. But in my spirit I knew I had been called into the ministry. And I knew my answer was yes. From that night in 1938 on, my purpose and objectives in life were set. I knew I would be a preacher of the Gospel.[6]

Sometimes God reveals his call to people early in their Christian walk. Charles Finney, for example, was enlisted to Christian service shortly after his conversion. Others receive their call later in life. The experience is as unique as the individual. But regardless of when and how the call comes, when God speaks, there is no mistaking it, and there should only be one response.

The Holy Spirit: Protects from Sin

"Walk by the Spirit and you will not carry out the desire of the flesh" (Gal. 5:16 HCSB).

Over the years we have heard of innumerable instances where the Spirit of God protected people from sin. A woman was tempted to commit adultery and was waiting one evening for her suitor to call at her home. At that moment a Christian friend was prompted to call, and the two women talked at length. As a result the woman chose to remain faithful to her husband. She says the Spirit used that phone call to help her realize the gravity of what she was considering.

A man was contemplating sin as he drove down the highway. Suddenly he noticed a billboard along the roadside with a Scripture verse on it. Using words directly from the Bible, the Spirit convicted him of his sinful intentions.

The Spirit provides numerous and timely warnings to help us resist temptation. If we are alert to his prompting, he will protect us from sin.

The Holy Spirit: Knows the Future

"When the Spirit of truth comes, He will guide you into all the truth. For He will not speak on His own, but He will speak whatever He hears. He will also declare to you what is to come" (John 16:13 HCSB).

Life is a mystery. Who knows what triumph or tragedy lies on the horizon? God does. God is not bound by time as we are. He is in the future, just as he is in the present. He knows your personal future. He is the only one who can guide you safely and securely through your life.

God's Leading
(a personal example from Richard)

I was raised in Canada. When I was eighteen, I accepted God's call to the ministry. I earned my undergraduate degree from the University of Saskatchewan in Saskatoon. For years I had dreamed of being a pastor in Canada, but when the time came for my seminary training, my wife Lisa and I moved to Texas. We could not get our remaining education in Canada because our denomination had no Canadian seminary at that time. For a number of reasons, including the poor health of my wife's parents and the desperate shortage of Canadian pastors, I planned to fast-track through the master of divinity program and return to a church in Canada within two and one-half years.

Everything was racing along according to my plan when the Holy Spirit began prompting me to consider staying in Texas to pursue a Ph.D. This made no sense to me. I had my heart set on being a pastor. I didn't need a doctorate for that. I had no desire to teach at a Bible college or a seminary. Even if I did, there were no schools of my denomination in Canada. Pursuing more studies would involve several more years away from Canada, where the spiritual need was greater than ever.

Nonetheless, Lisa and I both clearly sensed God leading us to stay. I enrolled in the doctoral program. Our educational pilgrimage stretched to seven years instead of two and one-half. Lisa's father passed away during that time, and her mother was diagnosed with the cancer that would eventually take her life. My sixteen-year-old sister was stricken with Hodgkin's Disease. Those were difficult years to be so far from home. Yet the Spirit continued to confirm that we were following God's will.

While I was still in the doctoral program, our denomination finally established a seminary in Canada. Several years later, while I was pastor of a wonderful church in Manitoba, the seminary began to look for its second president. I was asked to consider the position. Once again, a change in our plans made no sense. And once again, though we were extremely happy at our church and terribly reluctant to leave, we knew without a doubt that God was calling us. That was nine years ago.

God has confirmed over and over again that this was his plan for us all along. Before the seminary existed, God knew there would be a need for a Canadian with a Ph.D. to serve as its president. And what about those caveats?

The dire need for Canadian pastors? My heart's desire to be a pastor? God has graciously used my life to help prepare hundreds of students from all across Canada to serve in our churches. He has allowed me the privilege of serving as a pastor to our students—men and women not only from Canada, but from around the world.

Recently, a colleague made a peculiar comment to me: "Richard, you were so lucky to be a Canadian with a Ph.D. right when the Canadian seminary was looking for a president!" It wasn't luck. It was the Holy Spirit, who knew the future and who knew far better than I did how to prepare me for it. God is good!

The Holy Spirit: Produces Fruit

"Now those who belong to Christ Jesus have crucified the flesh with its passions and desires. If we live by the Spirit, we must also follow the Spirit" (Gal. 5:24–25 HCSB).

What does it mean to "live by the Spirit"? Once we have experienced salvation, the Holy Spirit's primary role in our lives is to make us like Christ. When we follow the Spirit's lead, we cast off the "fruits of sinful flesh." That was Paul's euphemistic phrase for all sorts of sins: "sexual immorality, moral impurity, promiscuity, idolatry, sorcery, hatreds, strife, jealousy, outbursts of anger, selfish ambitions, dissensions, factions, envy, drunkenness, carousing, and anything similar" (Gal. 5:19–21 HCSB). These are the practices the Spirit crucifies in our lives when we live according to his guidance. They will be replaced by the following qualities the Spirit works into our lives: "love, joy, peace, patience, kindness, goodness, faith, gentleness, self-control" (Gal. 5:22–23 HCSB). God wants us to be like Christ. If we are not loving, we do not resemble Christ. The Holy Spirit will show us that we are not a loving person. He will convict us of our unloving nature and enable us to love others with Christ's love. He will persist in his work, reminding us to love others and helping us to do so in his strength. Ditto for joy, peace, patience, and all the other spiritual fruits that characterize Christ.

Some people excuse their un-Christlike behavior with comments such as, "Well that's just the way I am!" How tragic! Christ died so they would not have to remain the way they were. If we will open our lives to the Spirit's transforming work, everything in our lives can be changed to be like Christ. As God builds the fruits of the Spirit into our lives, his reward is seeing us enjoy the fullness of life he intended for us all along.

Determined to Produce

When our family moved to Canada in 1970, the children discovered a garden in the backyard. It was springtime, and they were curious to see what would emerge from the ground once the snow melted. They were disappointed. Only one plant survived the winter. It was a strange-looking species with large leaves and a red stalk. As young boys they suspected it might be poisonous. So they decided to conduct extensive "scientific" experiments on it to determine if it was dangerous to the general public. Their "research" consisted of pulling off its leaves, stepping on it, and hitting it with sticks. After concluding it *was* poisonous, they decided to destroy the offensive weed immediately. (Actually, by that point they had already pummeled it to a pulp!)

To their surprise several weeks later they discovered that the plant had not died, and it was once again lush and full. At this point they decided to consult their parents. They learned that it was not a poisonous plant but a delicious fruit named rhubarb! With our family's limited income, we could not afford to purchase many desserts, but their mother became an expert rhubarb pie maker! Without that plant the children would have grown up practically dessertless! On many days they thanked God for the tenacity of that rhubarb plant. Even when they did everything they could to destroy it, it had persisted in its effort to produce fruit!

The Holy Spirit is tenacious. He is determined to produce spiritual fruit in your life until you are like Christ. You would have to purposefully resist the work of the Spirit for him not to produce fruit in your life.

The Holy Spirit: Places Members

"But now God has placed the parts, each one of them, in the body just as He wanted" (1 Cor. 12:18 HCSB).

The Bible says the church, like the body, is made up of many distinguishable parts, yet it functions as one unit. Paul said the Holy Spirit is the one responsible for placing each person in the church to serve where God knows is best (1 Cor. 12:18). The Spirit also equips each member to carry out his or her role in the body for the common good (1 Cor. 12:7). The Spirit's goal for the church is that it function in a way beneficial to all members. Strong members lend strength to weaker ones. Those who are joyful comfort those who grieve. The wise share their wisdom, and so it goes, all for the building up of the whole body.

The Spirit will guide you to the church in which he wants you to serve; then he will direct you to where he wants you to serve within the church. Finally, he will equip you for that service. In this way the Lord builds his church according to his divine purposes. Individual church members can sometimes feel they are dispensable and that their role is unimportant. They are nearsighted. A church is like a body. It must be viewed as a whole. Every person who contributes to the functioning of the church is crucially important. Paul said, "On the contrary, all the more, those parts of the body that seem to be weaker are necessary. And those parts of the body that we think to be less honorable, we clothe these with greater honor" (1 Cor. 12:22–23 HCSB). This being so, churches would do well to pay attention to *all* members, not just those with the higher profiles.

God Added to the Body
(a personal example from Richard)

While I was a pastor, I took seriously the fact that God adds people to the church. As soon as I arrived at my church, church members began asking me what I was going to do to provide programming for the children. The church had once conducted weekly programs for boys and girls, but through a long period of decline, all of them had been abandoned. Now that a fresh, young pastor had arrived on the scene, parents were eager for me to fix the problem! My response to them was always the same: "I will pray that God will add someone to our church who has the heart for that work." Before long some men rose up and volunteered to work with the boys in our church, but no one felt capable of working with the girls.

Several months later a young family visited our church. They had three little girls. As I visited them in their home, they told me they had never belonged to a church of our denomination before. Nevertheless, they felt strongly that God was leading them to join our church body. I asked them to share the passion Christ had given them. The wife looked somewhat sheepish for a moment and said, "Well, I know girls, and I love doing crafts." I smiled and said, "Christ is *indeed* adding you to our church and let me tell you why!" Phyllis began a ministry to young girls that blossomed and flourished. In fact, the children's ministry grew to the point that ultimately we had eight different age-group ministries taking place every Wednesday evening at our small church. The Holy Spirit knew exactly what our church needed, and he met the need perfectly.

The Holy Spirit: Produces Unity

"For we were all baptized by one Spirit into one body—whether Jews or Greeks, whether slaves or free—and we were all made to drink of one Spirit" (1 Cor. 12:13 HCSB).

How important is unity within the church? The apostle Paul wrote the early churches urging them to diligently guard the "unity of the Spirit with the peace that binds us" (Eph. 4:3 HCSB). How likely is unity within the church? Without God's help it's no more likely than world peace. But thanks to the Holy Spirit, it's not only possible—it ought to be normative.

Unity Brought Revival
(a personal example from Henry)

In the seventies, when I was a pastor in Saskatoon, Canada, I became friends with Bill McLeod, pastor of Ebenezer Baptist Church. Ebenezer Baptist had many good, faithful members. The church was running fine programs, but there were problems within the body.

Two leaders in the church, Sam and Arnold, were brothers who had been feuding for thirteen years. Both brothers continued to serve in the church, but they had not spoken to each other for two years. If Sam's family sat on one side of the auditorium, Arnold's family could be found on the opposite side. Many people were unaware of the enmity between the two siblings, but their pastor knew, and it grieved him.

Then, during a special week of meetings, the Holy Spirit led McLeod to bring the two brothers together. At first both were reluctant to concede they had been wrong. Then the Spirit broke them and revealed to each of them the sin of their stubbornness. Both began to weep over the condition of their hearts. They knew they should confess their sin to the rest of the church, but this would be difficult since both men were respected church leaders. Yet, humbled by the Holy Spirit, they went to the body and shared their story.

A miracle began to unfold. Others began confessing their sin too. When the time came for the meetings to end, they did not end. God continued to bring person after person to repentance. The meetings were extended. Night after night more people came. Night after night more people repented. Soon the assemblies grew too large for the church's auditorium, so they moved to a larger facility. Swelling crowds meant the meetings had to be moved four times over the course of the next seven weeks. Finally, the expansive civic auditorium downtown was rented. Revival swept across western Canada, the United States, and Europe. God alone knows the extensive impact the Holy Spirit had that year on thousands of lives. But it all began with a pastor, two brothers, and the Holy Spirit.

The Holy Spirit: Gives Words

"But when they hand you over, don't worry about how or what you should speak. For you will be given what to say at that hour, because you are not speaking, but the Spirit of your Father is speaking in you " (Matt. 10:19–20 HCSB).

It's intriguing to read the Bible and note the long list of reluctant preachers. Moses suffered a severe lack of confidence and rightly so. He stood before the burning bush and shared his doubts with God: "Who am I that Pharaoh should listen to me?" "What if the Israelites should ask a tough question I can't answer?" Moreover he was not an eloquent speaker. He called himself "slow of speech and tongue." God's answer was definitive: "I am the one sending you, and I will be with you" (Exod. 4).

Gideon showed no more self-confidence than Moses: "But Lord, how can I save Israel? My clan is the weakest in Manasseh, and I am the least in my family." Again, the Lord replied, "I will be with you" (Judg. 6:15–16).

Jonah's eagerness to preach God's message was obvious by his reaction to the call—he promptly ran away and hid. King Herod, on the other hand, apparently enjoyed pontificating before a crowd. As the Book of Acts relates, he was quite happy to share a message. The problem was, it was Herod's message, not God's: "So on an appointed day, dressed in royal robes and seated on the throne, Herod delivered a public address to them. The populace began to shout, 'It's the voice of a god and not of a man!' At once an angel of the Lord struck him because he did not give the glory to God, and he became infected with worms and died. Then God's message flourished and multiplied" (Acts 12:21–24 HCSB).

Throughout the Bible and still today, those most eager to speak are not always the ones with God's message. But, to those whom God calls to speak on his behalf, he promises the words to say.

The Holy Spirit: Reminds Us

"But the Counselor, the Holy Spirit, whom the Father will send in My name, will teach you all things and remind you of everything I have told you" (John 14:26 HCSB).

As Jesus was preparing the disciples for his imminent departure, he assured them that the coming of the Holy Spirit would be greatly to their benefit. Not only would the Holy Spirit be their teacher and counselor after Jesus ascended to heaven, but he would also bring to the disciples' remembrance everything Jesus had said to them. Some Bible commentators claim this promise was only meant for the eleven disciples in order to enable them to write Scripture. However, it would seem that just as Jesus' Great Commission was for the succeeding generations of disciples, so this promise of the Holy Spirit's activity in the lives of disciples pertains to contemporary followers of Jesus as well.

The role of the Holy Spirit today is not to write Scripture. It is to apply Scripture. The Spirit does not give new revelation; he reminds believers of what God has already revealed and then applies those truths to their lives. For instance, a man might read Ephesians 4 during his morning devotions. At the close he might comment to himself how good he feels after he reads Scripture at the beginning of each day. Later that evening, after a particularly difficult day at the office, he and his wife have a disagreement that escalates into anger. As the man gets into bed that night, he is still fuming and refusing to speak to his wife. In awkward, painful silence the two pull the covers up over their heads and desperately try to will themselves to sleep so they no longer have to be aware of the other's existence in the bed.

In the stillness of the night, the man suddenly recalls a verse he read in his quiet time that morning: "Don't let the sun go down on your anger" (Eph. 4:26). The man instantly becomes uneasy, knowing that he is blatantly disobeying a direct command of Scripture. Yet in his self-righteous state, he assures himself that he is in the right and his wife in the wrong.

A still, small voice silently asks, "Why would you knowingly disobey what God commands in the Bible?" The man is smitten by the hardness of his heart. Regardless of whether his wife is in the wrong, he realizes that he is responsible for his own anger. He interrupts the silence with a sincere apology to his wife. His wife immediately forgives him and tearfully asks him to forgive her. They end the day content in the knowledge that their relationship with each other is restored and so is their relationship with God.

What happened? Where did that verse come from? Why, at that critical moment, did that particular verse come to mind? It was the Holy Spirit taking God's Word and applying it specifically to life.

The Spirit's Work

1. Brings Assurance
2. Convicts of Sin
3. Brings Understanding
4. Guides to Truth
5. Brings Comfort
6. Exalts Christ
7. Reveals God's Will
8. Calls into Service
9. Protects from Sin
10. Knows the Future
11. Produces Fruit
12. Places Members
13. Produces Unity
14. Gives Words
15. Reminds Us

The Holy Spirit: Our Reaction

Resisting the Spirit

"You stiff-necked people with uncircumcised hearts and ears! You are always resisting the Holy Spirit" (Acts 7:51 HCSB).

The Holy Spirit's work in your life can be like that of a surgeon. He systematically removes the sin that impedes a vibrant spiritual life. The Spirit will challenge your selfish actions and confront your sinful attitudes. He'll guide you to avoid temptation. He will convict you of changes you need to make to live a holy life. Like surgery the Spirit's work can be temporarily painful, but the result is worth the discomfort. Of course it's tempting to forego the Holy Spirit's work and thus avoid the unpleasantness of correction. This unwise response can bring devastating results.

The Holy Spirit will never force God's best on you if you are unwilling to receive it. Like those who live with a chronic health problem, you can become so used to the symptoms of your sin that you forget what it's like to be spiritually healthy. This doesn't have to happen. If you will allow him, God's Spirit will remove the sins in your life that are hurting you (and others) and restore you to a healthy relationship with him.

Grieving the Spirit

"And don't grieve God's Holy Spirit, who sealed you for the day of redemption" (Eph. 4:30 HCSB).

To understand what it means to grieve the Holy Spirit, you must have a solid grasp on what sin is. If you consider your sin to be nothing more than rule-breaking, you may console yourself with the rationalization that no one is perfect. If you view your sin as a failure to live by certain principles, you may deal with it by resolving to strive harder in the future. But when you realize that your sin is an absolute betrayal of the Person who loves you deeply and sacrificially, it throws a whole new light on your transgression (Ps. 51:3–4).

What grieves the Holy Spirit? Sin does. Paul urged Christians to avoid lying to one another, acting in anger toward one another, stealing from one another, and holding unwholesome conversations among themselves (Eph. 4:25–29). Christ went to immeasurable lengths to free you from your sin. Continuing by choice to live in sin is an affront to God, a blatant rejection of his grace.

Let's revisit the account of Hosea and Gomer (Hos. 1–3). When the godly prophet Hosea obeyed God by marrying Gomer, she had nothing to offer him. He loved her anyway. Still Gomer rejected his love and offered herself to anyone who cared to take advantage of her. How devastating for Hosea to watch his beloved plummet deeper and deeper into degradation! He stood by, willing and able to help, but by her behavior she continued to mock his love. To continue in sin when you know God wants you to return to him is not rule-breaking. It's heartbreaking.

Quenching the Spirit

"Don't stifle the Spirit" (1 Thess. 5:19 HCSB).

Pour enough water on a fire, and you'll eventually douse the flames. Paul used the word *stifle*, or *quench*, meaning "suppress" or "extinguish," to describe what we can do to the presence of the Holy Spirit in our lives. As we increasingly allow sin to fill our lives, we are, in essence, smothering the flames of the Spirit's presence. God's Spirit will not cohabit peacefully with sin. There is to be only one master (Matt. 6:24). We are free to choose sin, but we must understand that our choice sends a clear message to God's Spirit.

Blaspheming the Spirit

"Blasphemy against the Spirit will not be forgiven" (Matt. 12:30 HCSB).

One of the most controversial sins in Christendom concerns this offense. Jesus warned: "Because of this, I tell you, people will be forgiven every sin and blasphemy, but the blasphemy against the Spirit shall not be forgiven. Whoever speaks a word against the Son of Man, it will be forgiven him. But whoever speaks against the Holy Spirit, it will not be forgiven him, either in this age or in the one to come" (Matt. 12:31–32 HCSB). These words can strike terror in the hearts of Christians. Is it possible to commit an unforgivable sin? If so, what is it?

The context of the above passage reveals that Jesus had just miraculously freed a man from the demons that possessed him. The Spirit was using this occasion to disclose who Jesus was to the watching crowds. However, rather than recognizing and accepting the Word as coming from God, the Pharisees attributed Jesus' work to the power of Satan. By refusing to accept the testimony of God's Spirit, the Pharisees were doing more than shunning Jesus. Their hearts were so evil that they were rejecting a clear, unmistakable word from God. What's worse, they were attributing God's activity to demons. In so doing, the Pharisees revealed hearts that completely denied who Christ was.

Genuine Christians don't do this because to become a Christian, one must acknowledge the absolute lordship of Jesus Christ. Defying God's Spirit openly and repeatedly indicates a person has not truly submitted to Christ's lordship. Genuine Christians do not blaspheme the Spirit. However, if you are not experiencing the powerful, liberating presence of the Holy Spirit in your life, you should examine your heart to see if you have been resisting, grieving, or stifling the Holy Spirit.

Filled by the Spirit

John Hyde came to understand what it means to be filled with the Spirit. When Paul urged Christians to "*be filled*" with the Spirit (Eph. 5:18 HCSB), the way he said it was significant. The verb Paul used was in the present tense, indicating the need for a fresh, daily renewal of the Spirit's filling. His words were given as an imperative, implying the necessity for Christians to be Spirit filled. The word was also in the plural form, meaning that every Christian should be filled. Finally, his verb choice was passive. He said "be filled" not "fill yourself." You can't fill yourself with the Spirit. It is God's gift. John Hyde's friend was wise to pray for him that God would fill Hyde with the Holy Spirit. Every Christian should humbly ask God for the same privilege.

Duncan Campbell, a young British soldier, was severely wounded in battle during World War I. His life hanging in the balance, he turned to God. Campbell was already a Christian, but he described being completely overwhelmed at that moment by the Holy Spirit's presence. Campbell called this experience a "baptism of the

Spirit." Many of his fellow soldiers were converted due to his testimony in the hospital. He recovered from his injuries, and from that point on he dedicated his life to Christ's service.

Years later, God called him to minister in the Hebrides Islands in northern Scotland. There, God used his life in astounding ways. Once Campbell went to lead a two-week evangelistic mission on the Isle of Lewis. It ended up lasting two years! On another occasion, along with thirty other devout Christians, Campbell met in a barn to pray. They prayed together until 2:00 A.M. When they dismissed their meeting, they discovered the entire village awake and in the streets seeking to respond to God! People were heading to the church in droves, terribly convicted over the sin in their lives.

Duncan Campbell was an ordinary man whom God chose to use in extraordinary ways. John Hyde was a normal missionary whose life was used powerfully because he sought to be an instrument in the hands of the Holy Spirit. The presence of the Holy Spirit changes ordinary lives into extraordinary ones.

Homer, the legendary Greek poet, said, "There is nothing worse for mortals than a wandering life." He was so right. God has a plan for each person. When people yield their will to God and allow his Spirit full control of their lives, God will do miraculous things! God knows what he wants to do through each person. He will speak by his Spirit to each person, alerting his children to the necessary adjustments they need to make. Those who hear his voice and respond obediently will experience God's mighty power working through them.

Questions for Reflection

1. In what ways is the Holy Spirit presently working in your life?

2. Is the Holy Spirit convicting you of changes he wants to make in your life? Are you resisting him?

3. Would you describe your life as being filled with the Spirit?

4. Are there currently sins in your life that grieve the Holy Spirit?

5. What attitudes or behaviors could be quenching the Holy Spirit in your life?

6. What spiritual fruit is the Holy Spirit producing in your life?

7. Is anything happening in your life that could only be explained by the working of the Holy Spirit?

THE BIBLE: GOD'S WORD

CHAPTER 5

The city of London was frozen to a halt by a hostile blizzard. It was January 6, 1850—a Sunday morning—that alleviated the necessity for many people to brave the elements for work. Few attempted the trek to church. One young man, however, felt powerfully compelled to find a house of worship. At his mother's suggestion, the fifteen-year-old set out for a church in Colchester. He was unsuccessful; the storm was too fierce.

He stumbled upon the Artillery Street Primitive Methodist Church. Only a handful of hardy members—fifteen to be exact—had successfully forged their way there. The pastor had been unable to navigate the streets. When it became apparent this group would constitute the congregation, a thin, angular man agreed to share a few words from the pulpit. He took as his text Isaiah 45:22, "Look unto me, and be ye saved, all the ends of the earth."[1] The unlettered layman stumbled over the passage for several minutes. Then he focused his gaze on the troubled teenager trying to sit inconspicuously in the balcony. Pointing his long, bony finger at the startled boy, he shouted, "Young man, you're in trouble! Look to Jesus Christ! Look! Look! Look!" Young Charles Spurgeon did turn to Christ in that unexpected moment. From that cumbrous message emerged a convert who would become one of the greatest preachers in the modern era.

God speaks when he chooses. Storms don't stop him. Neither do novice speakers. The Holy Spirit is not restricted to polished outreach programs and silver-tongued orators. God had something to say to a

British teenager that day and that message, directly out of God's Word, was hand-delivered to Charles Spurgeon.

The Bible—God's Plumb Line

Many people underestimate God's Word. It is far more powerful than many realize. From Genesis to Revelation God's Word has the power to speak directly to a person's heart. By the Holy Spirit, God takes his written Word and applies it specifically to people's lives. Charles Spurgeon did not simply hear a verse from the Bible that inspired him to live a better life. He heard directly from God. The Bible is not merely one option for discovering God's will. God's written Word is the plumb line for our lives as we walk daily with him (Amos 7:7; Rev. 22:18–19; Deut. 4:2).

God speaks through his written Word. The Bible is the standard by which everything else is to be measured. For example, if a person says that he or she "feels led by the Spirit" to commit adultery (and yes, we have had several people tell us exactly that), we know that person is mistaken. We know because God's Word commands fidelity within marriage. When we examine God's written Word, it's imperative that we understand why it was written. The Bible records people's actions, but more importantly it is primarily the revelation of God's activity. To read the Scriptures from people's perspective is to miss the point. Four chapters into Genesis, people are already committing murder. Fast forward to Revelation, and the early church is being chastised for its sin. The focus of the Bible is not people. It is God.

How do we know how to live the Christian life? We look to the Bible but not to get ideas from what people did for God. We look to see what God did in peoples' lives. Having said that, let's examine God's written Word to see what it reveals about the way he spoke through both the Old and the New Testaments.

God's Word: Produces Results

"God spoke. It was so. It was good" (Gen, 1:3–4, 6–7, 9–10, 11–12, 14–15, 20–21, 24–25, 26, 31).

One word from God and the galaxies were immediately in place. One word from God and the earth was teeming with life. God spoke and the earth was divided into land and water. Whatever God speaks comes to pass. Through the prophet Isaiah, God said:

For as the rain and the snow come down from heaven,
And do not return there without watering the earth,
And making it bear and sprout,
And furnishing seed to the sower and bread to the eater;
So will My word be which goes forth from My mouth;
It will not return to Me empty,
Without accomplishing what I desire,
And without succeeding in the matter for which I sent it" (Isa. 55:10–11).

Every word God speaks is powerful. Every word accomplishes God's intention. Significantly, the final result of what God's Word produced was always "extremely good" (Gen. 1:31).

God's Word: Carries a Cost

God created humanity to experience abundant life in the paradise he designed. He left nothing to chance. He warned Adam of the only thing that would cost him paradise (Gen. 2:15–17). The danger, of course, was not so much in the fruit. The forbidden tree tested Adam and Eve's resolve to obey God's command. Would they choose to abide by God's Word, or would they reject it? In the most tragic moment in history, Adam and Eve chose to disregard God's Word. The consequences were disastrous (Gen. 3:14–19). Genesis 3 provides the painful details of the aftermath effectuated by their sin. A sobering reality is painstakingly clear in the opening chapters of the Bible. God's Word brings life. Rejecting his Word leads to suffering and death. The rest of the Bible, and all of history, bears witness to this truth.

Next Door to Death

Adoniram Judson was the oldest son of a Congregational minister in Plymouth in the early nineteenth century. He entered Brown University at the age of sixteen and quickly established himself as a brilliant student. Judson made a friend there, another bright, talented pupil named Jacob Eames. However, whereas Judson was a Christian, Eames was an ardent critic of Christianity. He fervently challenged the beliefs that Judson's parents had taught him from birth. By graduation, Adoniram Judson had abandoned the teachings of Christianity. Eventually he confessed to his parents that he had rejected their faith and embraced his friend's philosophy of deism. Having decided that his parents had cloistered him from life, Judson set out for New York City to discover the world.

His pilgrimage led him through a small village where he sought lodging for the night at the local inn. The only available space was next to the room of a dying man. Judson had no choice but to accept the room and to try to ignore the grim noises emanating through the adjoining wall. Throughout the night Judson endured the moans of the dying man and the footsteps of people coming and going as they vainly tried to save his life. The ominous situation gave Judson cause for reflection. Was *he* prepared for what lay on the other side of death's door?

When morning dawned, however, Judson collected himself. He wondered what his friend Eames would think of the momentary lapse in his atheistic resolve. As he paid his bill, he inquired of the dying man. "He is dead," replied the innkeeper, "a young man from the college in Providence. Name was Eames. Jacob Eames." Judson rode away certain that God had delivered him a dire warning. To reject God's Word was to embrace death. He turned his horse toward home and returned to his parents and to their faith. Adoniram Judson devoted the rest of his life to spreading the gospel. He and his wife Ann served as missionaries to Burma and were influential in the establishment of numerous mission organizations that continue to this day.[2]

God's Word: Brings Life

Just as rejecting a word from God inevitably leads to death, accepting and obeying God's Word brings abundant life. As the people of Israel prepared to enter the promised land, Moses gathered them together and reminded them of all God had promised:

"See, I set before you today life and prosperity, death and destruction. For I command you today to love the LORD your God, to walk in his ways, and to keep his commands, decrees and laws; then you will live and increase, and the LORD your God will bless you in the land you are entering to possess" (Deut. 30:15–16 NIV).

The promise was there. All they had to do was choose, by their obedience, to accept it. Moses, prevented by his own earlier disobedience from entering Canaan himself, exhorted the people to do the right thing: "Choose life, so that you and your children may live and that you may love the LORD your God, listen to his voice and hold fast to him. For the LORD is your life" (Deut. 30:20 NIV).

Once inside the promised land, the people were assembled again, this time by Joshua in the valley between two mountains, Mount Ebal and Mount Gerizim (Josh. 8:30–35). Half of the crowd stood on Mount Gerizim. The other half gathered on Mount Ebal. There, they dramatically portrayed the difference between rejecting God's Word and following him. From the valley the Levites pronounced the curses that would accompany disobedience to God's Word. The people on Mount Ebal responded by shouting a loud "Amen!" (Deut. 27). Then the Levites declared the blessings for obeying God's Word, to the enthusiastic chorus of "Amen!" from those positioned on Mount Gerizim (Deut. 28).

Modern visitors to this region will notice a dramatic contrast between the two mountains. Mount Ebal, the one identified with God's curses, is barren. It *looks* cursed. Mount Gerizim, from which the blessings were pronounced, is covered in lush vegetation. It's an intriguing observation. Whether the setting looked this way in

Joshua's day we don't know, but it certainly conveys a vivid picture now of the two choices—life and death.

A lot of messages are inspirational. But only God's message is inspired. Paul said, "All Scripture is inspired by God and is profitable for teaching, for rebuking, for correcting, for training in righteousness, so that the man of God may be complete, equipped for every good work" (2 Tim. 3:16–17 HCSB). The Greek word for inspired is literally "God breathed." It means "life-giving." Indeed, countless millions of people have found life in God's Word.

History bears witness to the work of the Holy Spirit in opening the minds of even the most calloused sinners so they received and understood God's Word. As a young man, Augustine, one of the esteemed early church fathers, indulged himself in every immoral whim and cruelly mocked his mother's Christian beliefs. Then God spoke to him through Romans 13:13–14, convicting him of the gravity of his carnal ways, and he was converted.[3]

Jonathan Edwards, towering figure of the First Great Awakening and preacher of the famous sermon, "Sinners in the Hands of an Angry God," turned to Christ after reading the apostle Paul's testimony (1 Tim. 1:17). Edwards said of his experience:

> The first instance that I remember of that sort of inward, sweet delight in God and divine things that I have lived much in since, was on reading those words "Now unto the King eternal, immortal, invisible, the only wise God, be honour and glory for ever and ever, Amen." As I read the words, there came into my soul, and was as it were diffused through it, a sense of the glory of the Divine Being; a new sense, quite different from any thing I ever experienced before. Never any words of Scripture seemed to me as these words did.[4]

Charles Finney, the powerful revival preacher of the Second Great Awakening, described his conversion this way:

> Just at that point this passage of Scripture seemed to drop into my mind with a flood of light: "Then shall you go and pray unto me, and I will

hearken to you. Then shall you seek me and find me, when you shall search for me with all your heart." I instantly seized hold of this with my heart. I had intellectually believed the Bible before, but never had the truth been in my mind that faith was a voluntary trust instead of an intellectual state. I was as conscious of trusting at that moment in God's truthfulness as I was of my own existence. . . . I knew that it was God's word, and God's voice, as it were, that spoke to me. . . . The Spirit seemed to lay stress upon that idea in the text, "When you search for me with all your heart." . . . I told the Lord I would take him at his Word, that he could not lie, and that therefore I was sure that he heard my prayer and that he would be found by me.[5]

A profound example of the earth-shattering effect that God's Word exerts on people is Martin Luther's testimony.

A Tower Experience

Luther was a devout Augustinian monk who had been given the task of teaching the Book of Romans at the University of Wittenberg. In studying Scripture, Luther carried with him all the prejudices he had inherited from his medieval upbringing. Luther had been taught to view God as a harsh monarch who exercised his righteousness by punishing sinners. Luther feared God and dreaded the thought that he might forget to confess a sin for which God, in his wrath, would severely punish him.

As the studious monk began to prepare his lectures on the Book of Romans, however, Paul's words seized hold of him. Luther later recounted:

I greatly longed to understand Paul's Epistle to the Romans and nothing stood in the way but one expression, "the justice of God," because I took it to mean that justice whereby God is just and deals justly in punishing the unjust. My situation was that, although an impeccable monk, I stood before God as a sinner troubled in conscience, and I had no confidence that my merit would assuage him. Therefore I did not love a just and angry God, but rather hated and murmured against him. Yet I clung to the dear Paul and had a great yearning to know what he meant.

Night and day I pondered until I saw the connection between the justice of God and the statement that "the just shall live by his faith." Then I grasped that the justice of God is that righteousness by which through grace and sheer mercy God justifies us through faith. Thereupon I felt myself to be reborn and to have gone through open doors into paradise. The whole of Scripture took on a new meaning and whereas before the "justice of God" had filled me with hate, now it became to me inexpressibly sweet in greater love. This passage of Paul became to me a gate to heaven. . . .

If you have a true faith that Christ is your Saviour, then at once you have a gracious God, for faith leads you in and opens up God's heart and will, that you should see pure grace and overflowing love. Thus it is to behold God in faith that you should look upon his fatherly, friendly heart, in which there is no anger nor ungraciousness. He who sees God as angry does not see him rightly but looks only on a curtain, as if a dark cloud had been drawn across his face."[6]

Martin Luther's encounter with God through his Word was so magnificent that his life was forever changed. Even more significant, Luther shared God's revelation with others and launched the Reformation. Millions of people across Europe responded to the life-changing truths revealed in the Bible. History was forever changed because one man believed what the Holy Spirit revealed to him in Scripture. That's the power of God's holy Word.

God's Word: Changes Lives

Some people characterize the Bible as a collection of helpful insights and pithy sayings that can motivate readers as they live their busy lives. It's like the Christian version of the horoscope, providing beneficial information about the day or days ahead. Scripture never portrays itself in such an anemic way. Jesus emphasized the divine nature of his words: "The words that I have spoken to you are spirit and are life" (John 6:63 HCSB). Paul likened the Word of God to a sword wielded by the Holy Spirit (Eph. 6:17 HCSB). The writer of Hebrews gave notice: "For the Word of God is living and active and sharper than any two-edged sword, and piercing as far as the division of soul and spirit, of both joints and marrow, and able to judge the thoughts and intentions of the heart" (Heb. 4:12). God's Word lays bare all human pretense. The Holy Spirit cuts through our behaviors and attitudes to expose our motives. As we meditate on the Scriptures, a supernatural process takes place; God peels back our protective layers of hypocrisy until we see what he sees. Then it becomes obvious whether our lives are pleasing to him.

A woman reads her Bible one morning as is her custom. Her devotional guide points her to the verse for the day, so she looks up the passage and reads: "Let no unwholesome word proceed from your mouth, but only such a word as is good for edification according to the need of the moment, so that it will give grace to those who hear" (Eph. 4:29). She might say to herself, *That's a great thought for today. I'm probably guilty of unwholesome words. I'm going to pray that God will help me get through the whole day without uttering a single unwholesome word.* After a brief prayer, she sets out for work, planning to be mindful all day of what she says.

Another woman reads her Bible that morning, as is her custom. Her devotional guide points her to the verse for the day, so she looks up the passage and reads: "Let no unwholesome word proceed from your mouth, but only such a word as is good for edification according to the need of the moment, so that it will give grace to those who hear" (Eph. 4:29). As she meditates on God's Word the Holy Spirit grips her with a profound realization: that verse is meant for her. She recalls the unkind words she said to her own family the previous evening when she was tired and cranky. It strikes her that her exaggerating and gossip blind her coworkers to the truth about her boss, while making *her* look like a saint.

She knows she has a sharp tongue and a penchant for sarcasm. "But God," she justifies, "I'm that kind of person—not afraid to speak my mind. People understand that. They just accept me for who I am." She doesn't get away with it. The Spirit gently reminds her of her Savior's words: "I tell you that on the day of judgment people will have to account for every careless word they speak" (Matt. 12:36 HCSB). By this point she is broken. She sees her sin for what it is. It's not a problem with her tongue. It's a problem within her heart. She recalls the words of David and prays them as her own: "Create in me a pure heart, O God, and renew a steadfast spirit within me" (Ps. 51:10 NIV). She pleads with the Holy Spirit not to let her forget God's cleansing word to her that day. It's time to go to work. She doesn't skip out the door, determined to try for a whole day to guard her tongue. She goes to work a changed person. Her spirit is renewed, and her heart is thankful because her God loves her enough to deal with the sin that was poisoning her life.

God's Word: Tests Us

Whenever God speaks, what we do next exposes the condition of our hearts. The Old Testament provides several glimpses of this truth. When God met the children of Israel at Mount Sinai and gave them his law, it was a time of testing for the people. God spoke through thunder, lightning, smoke, and trumpet blasts. The Israelites pleaded with Moses: "Speak to us yourself and we will listen; but do not let God speak to us, or we will die."

Moses assured them, "Do not be afraid; for God has come in order to test you, and in order that the fear of Him may remain with you, so that you may not sin" (Exod. 20:19–20). The children of Israel had not walked with God as closely as Moses had, so they were not prepared when God spoke as is evident by their response. On another occasion God promised Abraham and Sarah a child one year later. Sarah's response of spontaneous laughter clearly revealed that she was not ready to believe (Gen. 17:9–15).

Tested in Canada

Henry's third son, Mel Blackaby, was called as pastor of a small church in Alberta, Canada. The church soon experienced significant growth, and even with two Sunday morning services, the small auditorium became inadequate to hold the growing number of people in attendance. Excited about the growth and wanting to welcome each new person God added to their body, the church searched the Scriptures and prayed to determine what they should do.

The membership collectively sensed God leading them to expand the current facility by adding a larger auditorium. However, a respected architect informed them they could not build the size facility they needed on their present location. Yet they unanimously sensed God was telling them to do exactly that. They were at an impasse. What they did next would reveal what they believed about God. They moved ahead. Soon afterward they discovered the architect was mistaken. But the testing was just beginning!

As the church prayed, the people were convinced God was telling them to pay off their existing mortgage of $450,000 before starting construction on the new auditorium. Considering they were a relatively small congregation, this seemed ludicrous. Not only that, but God gave specific instructions about how they were to collect the funds. They were not to ask for outside help in eliminating their debt. Nor were they to launch a fund-raising campaign. They were simply to take up an offering among themselves.

The church now averaged about three hundred people on Sundays, but over half of those were children, students, and new believers. Not a person among them would be considered wealthy. Furthermore, because the growth had come rapidly, the members had not been preparing for the expense of a building program so soon. Yet God spoke to them, and they knew what he said. Mel preached only one message, summarizing what the church had heard from God and challenging the people to obey. The church set aside September 30, a Sunday only two months away, for a special offering. In the meantime families and individuals sought God's guidance for the specific amount they were to contribute.

On September 30, or Loaves and Fishes Sunday as they called it, the offering was taken. Families and individuals came to the front of the church and laid their offerings before the Lord. Teenagers submitted their contributions—earned by odd jobs and saved allowances. One small child dragged a bag filled with rolled pennies to the front and laid it there.

For that evening, a picnic was scheduled to celebrate God's faithfulness, even before the offering was counted. You could have heard a pin drop as the church awaited the news that evening. Overwhelmed by God's faithfulness, Mel stood before his congregation and thanked the people for their obedience. "God spoke to us, and we obeyed as best we knew," he said, "and as a result our church is now debt free!"

The church had received a clear word from God. He had been specific as to how they were to obey. No fundraising. No soliciting donations from wealthy Texas oil tycoons. Just bring in the offerings, and watch what God could do with them. They knew it was impossible—almost half a million dollars on one Sunday. But they responded to God's Word with joy and faithfulness. After that day story after story came out, telling how God had guided the members in determining their donation. Teenagers told of giving all the money they had, only to receive the exact amount from a completely unexpected source shortly afterwards. In all, the church had raised $450,000, exactly what was needed. The people's hearts had been tested, and they proved faithful. As a result they experienced the blessing of seeing their Lord do a miracle in their midst.

God's Word: Requires Understanding

Some refer to God's Word as a mystery. It's not a mystery. God always provides a way for people to understand what he has said. In Old Testament days, God went to great lengths to ensure that priests, scribes, and prophets recorded his words so people could have them for centuries to come. God sent prophets to proclaim his messages to people (Amos 3:7). God said: "I have also spoken to the prophets, and I gave numerous visions, and through the prophets I gave parables" (Hos. 12:10). The New Testament records the Holy Spirit sending Philip to explain Scripture to the Ethiopian traveler (Acts 8:26–40). God provides Bible teachers, pastors, and godly friends today to those seeking to understand God's Word.

Helped by a Layman with a Book

John and Charles Wesley lived in England during the eighteenth century. Both were devoutly religious young men, but neither knew what it meant to be a Christian. While in college at Oxford, the two brothers habitually met with a group of students, including George Whitefield, to encourage one another to live holy lives. Their classmates dubbed them the "Holy Club." Incredibly, as devoted as they were to living pure lives, neither knew Christ.

Charles became a Christian after William Holland visited him while he lay recuperating from an illness. Holland read to Charles from Martin Luther's commentary on the Book of Galatians. The apostle Paul's words, "who loved me and gave Himself up for me" (Gal. 2:20 NASB) repeated themselves over and over in Charles's mind until on May 21, 1738, he believed these words were meant for him. He gave his life to Christ.

Upon graduation, John served for a time as missionary to the American colony in Georgia. When he returned to England, John was in turmoil. He knew that despite his missionary service for God, he did not have a personal relationship with Christ. On Sunday evening, May 24, 1738, John attended a small Moravian mission church on Aldersgate Street. The layman, William Holland, was reading from the preface to Martin Luther's commentary on the Book of Romans. While Holland read Luther's description of the change that takes place in people when they trust Christ, Wesley claimed, "I felt my heart strangely warmed. I felt I did trust in Christ, Christ alone for salvation; and an assurance was given to me that he had taken away *my* sins, even *mine*, and saved *me* from the law of sin and death."[7]

Within a few days God spoke to both brothers. In both instances the same messenger read the words of someone who had struggled two centuries earlier with the salvation issues the Wesleys were now seeking to understand. Through the witness of William Holland and the words of Martin Luther, God spoke to the Wesleys. Through John and Charles Wesley, God launched a tremendous revival across England through which thousands of people found salvation for their souls.

God's Word: Contains Promises

"For His divine power has given us everything required for life and godliness, through the knowledge of Him who called us by His own glory and goodness. By these He has given us very great and precious promises, so that through them you may share in the divine nature, escaping the corruption that is in the world because of evil desires" (2 Pet 1:3–4 HCSB).

God's written Word overflows with his promises to his children. The apostle Peter realized that when you become a Christian you become an heir to all the promises of the Father. Notice a few of those promises:

"Keep asking, and it will be given to you. Keep searching, and you will find. Keep knocking and the door will be opened to you" (Matt. 7:7 HCSB).

"Whatever you ask in my name, I will do it, so that the Father may be glorified in the Son" (John 14:13 HCSB).

"And my God will supply all your needs according to his riches in glory in Christ Jesus" (Phil. 4:19 HCSB).

"And God is able to make every grace overflow to you, so that in every way, always having everything you need, you may excel in every good work" (2 Cor. 9:8 HCSB).

The apostle Paul described Christ as the fulfillment of God's every promise: "For every one of God's promises is 'Yes' in Him" (2 Cor. 1:20 HCSB). To abide in Christ is to have access to all of God's promises. God's promises are gifts of his grace, but they sometimes come with a stipulation. For example, James 4:8 promises: "Draw near to God and He will draw near to you." This Scripture says that if we draw near to him, then he will make his presence tangible in our lives. How do we draw near to God? The rest of verse 8 tells us: "Cleanse your hands, sinner, and purify your hearts, double-minded people!" (HCSB). God makes every promise accessible by clearly directing us on what we should do to claim it.

A Caution

At times people will exhort Christians to "claim" the promises of God. It is good to believe God will abide by his Word, but there are connotations to "claiming God's promises." God's promises are his wonderful gifts of grace to us. They are entirely undeserved. We should be extremely careful that we receive them in humility rather than expecting their fulfillment as though they are our just due. As we discover the incredible promises God makes to us, we should do everything we can to meet the requirements God sets forth in order to receive these marvelous gifts. It is an enlightening exercise to review the great promises of God and systematically ask, "Am I presently experiencing the full reality of this promise?" If not, what adjustments are required in my life so I can enjoy all God has intended for me?

God's Word: Gives Guidance

George Muller was burdened about the plight of hundreds of homeless children in his city of Bristol. It was the late nineteenth century, and there were insufficient social means to provide for the swelling ranks of homeless children. The need was obvious, but Muller had no money. Nonetheless, he began praying about whether he should be the one to establish a home for orphans. In his own words, here's what he did: "I have been praying every day this week concerning the orphan house, entreating the Lord to take away every thought of it if the matter is not of him. After repeatedly examining the motives of my heart, I am convinced that it is of God."[8]

Then he sought counsel from godly friends.

> Brother Craik and I have talked about the orphan house. I wanted him to show me any hidden corruption of my heart or any other scriptural reason

against engaging in it. The only reason I could doubt that it is of God for me to begin this work is the numerous responsibilities which I have already. But if the matter is of God, he will, in due time, send suitable individuals so that comparatively little of my time will be taken up in this service.[9]

Three days later Muller noted in his journal: "This Scripture came alive to me today: 'Open thy mouth wide, and I will fill it' (Ps. 81:10). I was led to apply it to the orphan house and asked the Lord for a building, one thousand pounds, and suitable individuals to take care of the children."[10] The success of Muller's orphanage is legendary.

Did you notice anything about the process through which God spoke to George Muller? First, Muller saw a need. There would have been countless other needs around him as well. Yet Muller sensed a personal burden about this particular situation. So he prayed. He opened his heart to the Lord for a thorough examination. Muller wanted to be sure that what he did next was out of pure motives, in response to God's directions. He sought advice from a trusted Christian friend. Finally, the word came to him through the Scriptures. That's when he knew for certain what he should do.

Throughout the New Testament, God used Scripture to guide people specifically. When reporting on Jesus' actions, the Gospel writers would often add, regarding the Scriptures, "In order that it might be fulfilled . . ." (Matt. 8:17; 12:17–21; 13:14–15, 34–35; 21:4–5; 26:24, 31, 54, 56; 27:9, 34–35, 46; Luke 4:17–21; John 19:36–37). Jesus based everything he did on God's Word. When Satan tempted him, he resisted by quoting God's Word (Matt. 4:1–11; Luke 4:1–13). When his opponents maligned him, he answered with Scriptures (Matt. 9:13; 12:40; 21:16). When he encountered money changers in the temple, he was angered because they were disregarding his Father's word (Matt. 21:13).

The disciples learned to follow Jesus' example as they made decisions. After Jesus ascended to heaven, the early church was left with God's Word and God's Spirit. The eleven bewildered disciples, trying to understand how

Judas could have betrayed their Master, found their answer in Scripture (Acts 1:20). Amid the astounding events of Pentecost, God's Holy Spirit spoke through Peter as he used Scripture to explain what was happening (Acts 2:16–21). Early Christians were regularly required to defend their faith publicly. The Holy Spirit gave them the words of Scripture (Acts 2:25–36; 4:11; 7:1–53; 23:5). God performed many miracles through the early church, the purpose for which they came to understand through the Scriptures (Acts 3:11–26). The early church praised God for answered prayer by using the words of Scripture (Acts 4:24–26). Christians in the early church saw thousands come to know Christ not because of their words but because of God's words (Acts 2; 8:30–35). Like the modern church, the early church faced theological issues. They turned to Scripture for their resolution (Acts 15:15–19). As believers in the early church faced rejection, they found perspective in the words God spoke through the prophet Isaiah (Acts 28:25–28).

God's Word and Land Mines

Many countries today are dangerous places because of antipersonnel land mines that were planted during wartime. Some places harbor so many buried explosives that no one knows where it is safe to walk anymore. Suppose you had to pass through a region littered with land mines. You would enter the territory with dread. One false step and you could be maimed or killed. However, if a military commander gave you an accurate map pinpointing every trap, you would be greatly liberated. With map in hand, you would be free to travel everywhere the map said it was safe to do so. You could walk or run or roll across the safe fields, knowing your life was not in peril. You could wisely avoid the danger zones and escape harm.

However, the general would not force you to take the map. You would be perfectly free to live on the edge and feel your way across the land. You could decide you don't like being told where to walk. If you wanted to, you could exercise your freedom to travel where you pleased. You would be within your rights. You would be a fool, quite possibly a dead one. But you would be within your rights.

God's Word is a map to help us avoid the land mines of sin. Sin has the potential of tearing us apart, but we have the map that accurately leads us along the safe path. We can choose to reject God's Word and live free from the "constraints" of the map. We can ignore God's guidance and make our own way through life as best we can. But why would we want to do that?

God's Word: Requires Meditation

Christians face the constant temptation of treating God's Word lightly. It is incredible to think that Almighty God speaks to us through his Word, yet we casually skim the Bible before racing off to our first appointment! Meditation is God's invitation to take his Word seriously. God's Word is clear, yet it is deeply profound. God's Word is multidimensional. It holds so much truth that it takes significant time to digest it. This requires meditation. Why do some people achieve a depth of understanding of God's Word that others do not? Some people are unwilling to spend an extended length of time contemplating God's Word.

When God promised that if we seek him we would find him, he was not talking about a lackadaisical, half-hearted search. God said: "You will seek Me and find Me when you search for Me with all your heart" (Jer. 29:13; cf. Deut. 4:29). Meditation invites God to explain his Word to you and to open your heart, mind, and soul to what he wants to communicate with you. Meditation means staying with a passage of Scripture until the Holy Spirit enlightens your understanding to its meaning and its application.

George Muller on Meditation

George Muller is best known for his praying in faith, but he was also diligent to meditate on God's Word. In one of his journal entries he noted:

It often astonished me that I did not see the importance of meditation upon Scripture earlier in my Christian life. As the outward man is not fit for work for any length of time unless he eats, so it is with the inner man. What is the food of the inner man? Not prayer, but *the Word of God*—not the simple reading of the Word of God, so that it only passes though our minds, just as water runs through a pipe. No, we must consider what we read, ponder over it, and apply it to our hearts.

When we pray, we speak to God. This exercise of the soul can best be performed after the inner man has been nourished by meditation on the Word of God. Through His Word, our Father speaks to us, encourages us, comforts us, instructs us, humbles us, and reproves us. We may profitably meditate, with God's blessing, although we are spiritually weak. The weaker we are, the more meditation we need to strengthen our inner man. Meditation on God's Word has given me the help and strength to pass peacefully through deep trials. What a difference there is when the soul is refreshed in fellowship with God early in the morning! Without spiritual preparation, the service, the trials, and the temptations of the day can be overwhelming.[11]

How to Meditate on God's Word

Meditation is savoring each word God places before you. When you meditate you need to:

1. Take your time. You cannot meditate in a hurry!

2. Choose a reasonable amount of Scripture to meditate on at a time so you can devote your full attention to every word.

3. Choose verses as God leads. He may lead you to a particular passage such as Isaiah 53, which vividly portrays the Suffering Servant, or he may draw you to verses that will have particular relevance to your current circumstances.

4. As you read, take time to consider each word. At times the placement of a simple conjunction such as *but* can have profound implications.

5. As you ponder the passage, consider each phrase. Read it several times. Phrases can be read in various ways with different emphases. At times you can read a familiar passage and immediately conclude you know all there is to know about it. Taking time to meditate on each phrase invites the Spirit to open your understanding to deeper truths in the verse.

6. Carefully consider the context. Examine how the various phrases are connected to one another. If you are studying the life of Jesus, for example, notice how his teaching is connected to the events happening around him.

7. As you meditate, look for two things. First allow the Spirit to help you understand the greater truth of the words you are reading. Second, seek the Spirit's application of this passage for your life. You will emerge from your meditation a changed person.

8. Understand that the Bible is not merely a book to be studied and conquered. God's Word is living. You will never in a lifetime plumb the depths of its riches. To assume you've read it all is to grossly overestimate your capacity to think like God. When you read a passage of Scripture, God will reveal the truth he knows you are capable of understanding and responding to at that time. As you mature in your faith, God will know when you are ready for further insights into the same passage. There will always be great value and joy in meditating on passages more than once.

God's Word:

- Produces results
- Carries a cost
- Brings life
- Changes lives
- Tests us
- Requires understanding
- Holds promises
- Gives guidance
- Requires meditation

Conclusion

The best way to hear God speak to you is to spend regular time reading, studying, and meditating on his Word. God speaks through the Bible in clear, understandable language. The first step in knowing God's will for your life is to carefully obey every revelation of his that you find in the Bible. For example, 1 Thessalonians 5:18 expresses the command: "Give thanks in everything, for this is God's will for you in Christ Jesus" (HCSB). This verse clearly directs us to have a thankful heart toward God regardless of our circumstances. Likewise, the Scriptures command us to forgive others and to serve one another. If we are angry at God because of perceived unfairness, if we refuse to forgive someone, or if we turn our back on a friend who needs us, we are hardly in a position to receive a further word from God. We already know God's will for us. Be thankful! Forgive! Serve!

At times the Bible describes God as a potter and his people as clay (Jer. 18:1–12; Rom. 9:19–26). God is seeking to shape us into the image of his Son. The Holy Spirit will use the Word of God to address our sin. We are only clay. We have no right to challenge the wisdom of the Potter or to second-guess what he is doing. Ours is only to obey what God tells us in his Word.

Those who are willing to immerse themselves daily in God's Word will find that he reveals enough to keep them busy for the day at hand! It is foolish for someone to seek God's will but neglect the regular reading of his Word. There God most clearly speaks to people. Wise Christians will regularly fill their minds with God's words, allowing the Spirit ample opportunity to impress particular Scriptures on their minds as he directs them to obedience.

Questions for Reflection

1. Are you presently spending ample time reading and studying God's Word?

2. Do you read through each section of Scripture?

3. What passage of Scripture has God recently drawn to your attention? What might God be trying to say to you through those verses?

4. Do you meditate on Scripture?

5. Are you obeying all you know God has already told you through his Word?

6. Is there a particular truth in Scripture that you have not incorporated into your life? If so, why not?

7. What command in Scripture are you having difficulty obeying right now? Take that verse to God in prayer. Ask God to help you apply it to your life. Be prepared to do whatever God tells you to do next.

PRAYER: WHAT IT IS AND WHAT IT ISN'T

CHAPTER 6

Divine Calls and Phone Calls
(a personal example from Richard)

While I was in university, God began to impress on me the magnitude of his call on my life. One afternoon I decided to spend extensive time with the Lord, to settle some issues, and to seek his guidance. I retreated to my room, and I carefully read Isaiah 53, the profound portrayal of the Suffering Servant. As I meditated on the prophecy of Jesus suffering for my sins, I was smitten by Christ's unfathomable love for me. I was overcome by his commitment to be wholly obedient to the Father even to the point of a cross. I knelt beside my bed and earnestly prayed to God, promising that I, too, would be willing to do anything he asked me to do.

My vow had barely escaped my lips when the phone rang. I winced, hoping the call was not for me. I was having such a sacred moment with God; I was reluctant to tarnish the moment by talking to a mere mortal. The call was for me. What's worse, it was a guy named Kyle. Kyle was a social misfit who lacked the essential social graces to make friends. He would systematically call every student from our church. Kyle did not know how to initiate or maintain conversation, so he would sit in silence while the "callee" tried to pry a conversation out of him. It was always an exercise in futility. Now, during one of the most profound encounters I had ever had with God, Kyle was calling to ease his loneliness!

"Tell him I can't come to the phone right now. I'm in the middle of something important," I told my roommate. Then I returned to my bedside and continued my prayer of submission to my Lord: "Lord, whatever you want me to do, I will do. Wherever you want me to go, I will go. Whomever you want me to minister to, I will." God had spoken, but I was too busy saying my prayers to hear!

What if you climbed a tall mountain to speak with a wise guru at the top? But once you reached the summit, you sat at the white-haired gentleman's feet and proceeded to do all the talking? Then you began your descent. Would that be a worthwhile endeavor? Did the wise man need to know all you had to say? Would you reach the bottom of the mountain wishing you had asked a question or two? Incredibly, many people enter God's awesome, holy presence in prayer and then do all the talking!

What God has to say to us is infinitely more important than what we have to say to him, yet we generally monopolize the conversation. God already knows everything we are telling him, yet we continue talking rather than allowing him to tell us things we do not know.

What is prayer, and what is it not? It is a relationship. It is not an activity. Prayer is two-way communication, but it is not communication between two equal parties.

What Is Prayer?

The single greatest reason to pray is to take the focus away from us and turn it to God. As our lives are swallowed up in the problems and details of living in this world, we often become overwhelmed. We are finite, weak creatures. It is quite possible to exhaust our limited strength and knowledge. What we need is proper perspective. God gives this to us when he draws our minds away from our needs and toward his holiness. We are not the center of the universe; God is. God is not our creation, existing to serve us. We are his creation. We exist to serve him. God may choose to bless us continually and protect us from harm, but he is not obligated to do so. On the contrary, we may choose to dishonor God, but our obligation is to bring him glory. Prayer is the process by which God helps us rearrange our priorities.

"The Isle of Patmos" has a nice sound to it. It conjures images of a tranquil, tropical paradise. This is where the aging apostle John spent his last days. But Patmos was anything but a peaceful retirement venue. Exiled to this desolate island, teeming with the most hardened convicts in the Roman Empire, prospects for the aging saint were grim. On the Lord's Day, John was "in the Spirit." No doubt John had many burdens that day. He was probably unsure about his own welfare. He must have been distressed about his family and friends who were facing persecution on the mainland. He would most certainly have been troubled about the young Christians suffering torment and cruel death at the hands of the Roman authorities. In the midst of John's time with God, the risen Christ suddenly appeared. The sight of Christ in his glorified state was terrifying. John, the one "whom Jesus loved," had known Jesus well (John 13:23; 19:26; 20:2; 21:7, 20). He had leaned against Jesus during the last supper. Jesus had entrusted the care of his mother Mary to his dear friend John. Nevertheless, when John saw Jesus as he was in his resurrected glory, it absolutely paralyzed him with fear. In fact, John fell to the ground like a dead man (Rev. 1:17).

John needed to be reminded that Jesus, for whom Christians were suffering and dying, was the Supreme Ruler of the universe. John had walked with the incarnate Son of God for over three years. He knew Jesus well. John also had the Scriptures that testified to God's greatness. What John experienced now was the astounding visual confirmation that the two were one and the same. Surely this fresh revelation gave him renewed strength to face his dismal circumstances. So it is with us. Although the joy and wonder of our first encounter with Christ may linger with us for a lifetime, we still need fresh encounters with Christ so our darkened world never obscures the glory of the risen Christ.

John R. Sampey was a seminary professor for sixty years. As a young parent he suffered the agony of watching his two-year-old daughter Anita waste away from an illness she contracted on her second birthday. It was an excruciating time but at the same time an enlightening one for him and his wife.

One day as I stood looking into the face of our little daughter as she lay helpless in her crib, there suddenly flashed into my mind a verse from Psalm 103, "Like as a father pitieth his children, so the Lord pitieth them that fear him." I said aloud, "O Lord, is thy pitying love like this thing tugging at my heart? If so, it will never fail us." I felt such pity and compassion that I would have gladly taken the place of the dear child, if she could go free.

Toward the end all hope of her recovery left us. One day as my wife and I hovered over the wasting form of our only child, she said; "Mr. Sampey, God evidently means to take our little one; let's just give her to him." We clasped hands over the crib, and I tried as best I could to tell our Heavenly Father how grateful we were that he had sent this little flower to bloom in our garden and cheer our hearts, but now that it was fading we begged him to transplant it in the heavenly garden where it could grow and flourish. Before we had finished our prayer a great Presence seemed to flood the room in which we stood praying, and we felt that the Heavenly Father would care for our dear one in his own beautiful way."[1]

Throughout the time of the Sampey's praying, they never did receive what they initially asked for, the healing of their only daughter. However, they came to experience God in a new and deeper dimension. God communicated to them that he was someone they could trust with the most precious person in their lives. They saw how he loved them as a parent loves his child. That's why we pray, not necessarily to obtain what we want but to know God more intimately. Prayer enables us to see and experience God as he really is.

Why Pray?

The motivating impulse of our praying should not primarily be what is on our heart but what is on God's. Jesus taught us to pray, "Give us today our daily bread," but the crux of the Lord's Prayer is, "Your will be done on earth as it is in heaven" (Matt. 6:10–11 HCSB). It is understandable for us to pray from the honesty of our hearts, "My Father! If it is possible, let this cup pass from Me." But our ultimate conclusion when we pray must be, as it was with Jesus, "Yet not as I will, but as You will" (Matt. 26:39 HCSB).

Prayer does not come naturally. The apostle Paul described our inherent inability to pray: "In the same way the Spirit also joins to help in our weakness, because we do not know what to pray for as we should, but the Spirit Himself intercedes for us with unspoken groanings. And He who searches the hearts knows the Spirit's mind-set, because He intercedes for the saints according to the will of God" (Rom. 8:26–27). Clearly we do not know what to pray unless the Holy Spirit helps us. In fact, we are foolish to begin asking God for things before seeking what is on his mind. If we do, we will invariably ask God for the wrong things. Ephesians 3:20 indicates that Christ "is able to do above and beyond all that we ask or think." The great danger many Christians face is in assuming we know what's best and immediately "praying in faith" that God will hear and do what we want him to. Some Christian leaders teach that if we persist in our prayers, God will ultimately give us what we are asking. The tragedy is that often our persistency is in asking for the wrong thing. Were God to concede to our misguided prayers, the results could be disastrous.

Sometimes the hardness of our hearts drives us to demand things of God. God may give us what we ask as a form of discipline upon us. Consider the fascinating account of the grumbling, faithless children of Israel. They complained incessantly to God, "So He gave them their request, but sent a wasting disease among them" (Ps. 106:15). They complained long enough and vigorously enough that God gave them what they asked for, but it cost them! Seeking our will rather than God's always comes at a price.

The biblical pattern is that God related to people so he could share what was on his heart. While Abram lived in Ur, his prayers to God might have been, "Lord, bless me and my wife Sarai. Comfort Sarai since she cannot have children. Help us to be a witness to our next-door neighbor in Ur." Then God came to Abram and told him his plans for Abram and Sarai. They were leaving Ur for Canaan. They would have a child, and their descendants would be as numerous as the stars. Because of what God would do through Abram and Sarai, all the families of the earth would be blessed. This revelation from God would radically affect Abram's prayer life! Whatever he had been praying before was completely irrelevant, now that God had revealed what was on his heart. Abram could not know God's plans apart from God telling him. He needed to know God was speaking, to know what God was saying, and to know clearly what God wanted him to do. All of this was God's responsibility, and he led Abram through this process until everything was in place. God left no loose ends as he unfolded, one day at a time, what Abram was to do next.

As Moses herded sheep for his father-in-law in the wilderness, his prayers might have gone something like this: "Lord, please comfort my relatives in Egypt that their slavery will not be too unbearable. Help me not to lose too many sheep as I work for my father-in-law. Please keep me safe from any Egyptian official who might discover my whereabouts and have me arrested for that murder I committed when I lived in Egypt." Then Moses encountered God through the burning bush. God revealed his agenda. He was planning to use Moses to set every Hebrew slave in Egypt free. Moses would stand before Pharaoh himself to deliver God's message. After that encounter with God, Moses' prayers could never be the same again!

Jesus set the pattern for our praying. He did not determine his own agenda, then ask his Father to bless it. Rather, whatever the Father told Jesus to do, that became

Jesus' course of action. Whatever the Father told the Son, Jesus then told the disciples. Jesus prayed, "Now they have come to know that everything You have given Me is from You; for the words which You gave Me I have given to them; and they received them and truly understood that I came forth from You, and they believed that You sent Me" (John 17:7–8). The pattern is there for us. As we abide in Christ today, the Holy Spirit reveals to us what is on the Father's heart. That revelation should become the overriding agenda for our life.

Reoriented

Randy Bond was fuming. He had been hired by the Canadian Southern Baptist Seminary to enlist new students. One weekend Randy planned a recruiting trip to another province. He would drive to a city seven hours away and visit with several university students who were considering seminary enrollment. The local student director had assured Randy there would be almost forty prospective seminary students lined up to meet with him. But when the time came, not one person showed up! As Randy drove the seven hours home, frustration ate away at him. His wife and three small children were ill, and he had left them alone all weekend for this!

That Wednesday, Randy attended the weekly prayer meeting at church. He was still vexed. After all, he was doing everything he knew to do to enlist seminary students, men and women who would plant churches and spread the gospel across Canada. Randy was working hard, but God did not seem to be blessing his efforts. Why wasn't God doing his part? Didn't God care? Didn't God want the millions of unchurched Canadians to be reached with the good news of Jesus Christ? During the prayer time Randy began to pray with a small group. Suddenly, God laid his heart for Canada upon Randy's heart. It was as though Randy temporarily felt the enormous weight God felt for every person in Canada who did not know Christ. The reality of God revealing his heart to Randy was almost more than he could bear. Suddenly Randy began to cry out in prayer, "I need your Spirit! I need your Spirit!"

Through that prayer time God radically reoriented Randy's perspective. Randy understood that God's love for Canadians was deeper than he could fathom. In fact, God cared so profoundly for them he would not entrust their eternal salvation to Randy's best plans and efforts. Why did Randy make that "fruitless" trip? It wasn't to enlist a student or two. It was to initiate a transformation in Randy's own life. Through prayer God revealed his heart to Randy, and from that moment on, God began to do unusual and powerful things through Randy's life. Randy would readily tell you there is a vast difference between recruiting his way and doing it God's way.

Prayer is God's way of adjusting his people to him. It is not a time for us to ask God to adapt to our plans and desires. He loves us too much to do that.

To Whom Do We Pray?

Prayer is communication between two persons. Prayer does not involve reciting a wish list to a cosmic ombudsman. It is not a means of tapping into a supernatural power source. It is not a ritual formula we recite with the hope of stumbling upon the right words that will mysteriously open the vaults of heaven.

When Jesus taught his disciples to pray, he instructed them to begin their prayers, "Our Father" (Matt. 6:9). Jesus' concept of father was that of a perfect father (Luke 11:10–13). This father always relates to his children in perfect love. This father is never absent. He is never disinterested. He is never preoccupied. He is never unable to respond to a need. This father's children know before they ask that they'll receive his loving best every time. This father is so kind his children enjoy being around him even when they don't need anything. There is pure joy in his presence. Sadly, many Christians never experience this level of relationship with God. For many, prayer is simply an avenue to inform God of their concerns and desires. Yet God desires far more as he communes with his children. Like an earthly parent, there are times when he is seeking to communicate his love for us (Isa. 65:1–3). There is much that we can miss if we do not take time to listen while we pray!

James Stewart was a twentieth-century evangelist who saw God do a mighty work across Europe through his life. He describes one particularly memorable prayer experience:

> On the very first evening when I arrived, tired and weary, I knelt at my bedside just to have "a little talk with Jesus." I meant to spend only a few minutes on my knees. Suddenly, however, the heavens opened and I had a glorious sense of the divine Presence. Waves and waves of divine love flooded and filled my soul. So overwhelmed was I with sweet communion and revelation that all my weariness was forgotten. This sweet sense of the Lord's presence continued for the space of more than three hours, though it seemed to me only three minutes! All I could do was weep quietly as the joy of the Lord was poured into my soul. This was a "Song of Solomon" experience for me. My "Beloved" had manifested Himself to me, as if to put His sweet stamp of approval on the step I had taken in order to get to know him better.
>
> Before this time the Lord had on some occasions visited me with mighty anointings of the Spirit, but this was something different; this was just sweet communion with my blessed Lord.[2]

Prayer is a relationship whereby God interacts with us at the deepest level of human communication. We must never forget that while prayer takes place between two persons, it is not an exchange between equals. We are creatures of dust. God is our Creator. There is an infinite gap between who we are and who God is. The way we pray reveals whether we really understand this truth. When Job pled his innocence to God and began to question why God had allowed calamity to befall him, God answered him out of a whirlwind and out of a storm (Job 38:1; 40:6). By the time God had finished speaking to Job, all Job could say was, "I have heard of You by the hearing of the ear; but now my eye sees You; therefore I retract, and I repent in dust and ashes" (Job 42:5–6). Job was not a spiritual slouch. He was a righteous man. He was a man of integrity. Yet when he lined himself up against God, all he could do was humble himself in the presence of perfect holiness.

We must be careful not to apply a "charter of rights" mentality to our relationship with God and assume we have the right to relate to God as we choose. This assumption says if we are angry, we have a right to vent that anger toward God. If we don't feel like obeying, we are within our rights to justify our resistance. We should take our feelings to God and surrender them to him. But in times of our greatest struggles, we need to hear from God more than ever. When we are frustrated, we can spend our entire prayer time venting our anger and questions without ever bothering to wait for God's answer. The writer of Ecclesiastes said, "Do not be hasty in word or impulsive in thought to bring up a matter in the presence of God. For God is in heaven and you are on the earth; therefore let your words be few" (Eccles. 5:2).

What Happens When We Pray?

Do you ever try to change God in some way when you pray? You may suspect God does not care about your suffering loved one the way he should. You may worry that God will neglect to bless you and those you love unless you regularly remind him.

Sometimes our prayers imply God must be preoccupied with other things and we must gain his attention so our needs are not overlooked. In our praying we may inadvertently seek to change God's priorities and concerns to what we think they should be. We are disoriented to what prayer really is. Prayer is not designed as a means for us to change God. It is a time for God to change us.

Prayer is a transforming activity. Moses' face glowed, physically reflecting the wonder of his encounter with God (Exod. 34:30; 2 Cor. 3:7). Jesus' prayer time on the Mount of Transfiguration was so glorious, he was transfigured before his disciples. His face shone like the sun, and his garments glowed like a brilliant light (Matt. 17:2). Paul said, "We all with unveiled faces, are reflecting the glory of the Lord and are being transformed into the same image from glory to glory" (2 Cor. 3:18 HCSB).

The key to God transforming us is not found in what we say as we pray but in what we hear. As God speaks to us, we cannot remain unchanged. Once Isaiah saw God in his brilliance upon his throne, the young prophet was never the same again (Isa. 6). Until then Isaiah had every reason to take pride in himself; he was a brilliant young scribe with connections to the royal family. After being in God's presence, his thoughts were of his own sinfulness and absolute unworthiness. Saul of Tarsus topped the Jewish "Who's Who" list of religious leaders until he met the risen Christ. That encounter changed his name, his perspective, his career, and his entire life (Acts 9:1–9). Near the end of his life, Paul was still trying to comprehend all he had heard Christ say to him that day on the road to Damascus (Acts 26:4–19).

Scripture tells us God never changes (Mal. 3:6). It is futile for us to seek to change him. If we are frustrated with God because he doesn't answer our prayers as we think he should, this is a sure sign something needs to change in us. When our hearts are aligned with God's heart, we will discover the prayers rising up within us are the desires God is pleased to bless.

Hudson Taylor, the great prayer warrior for China, observed: "Sometimes it may be that while we are complaining of the hardness of the hearts of those we are seeking to benefit, the hardness of our own hearts, and our feeble apprehension of the solemn reality of eternal things, may be the true cause of our want of success."[3]

As Randy discovered during his futile recruiting trip, God's agenda sometimes involves breaking our own will before we are ready to make a difference in the world around us.

What Do God's Answers Look Like?

Over and over the Gospels record Jesus' disappointment at peoples' lack of faith (Luke 9:41). Even when God answered their prayers, they missed what he was seeking to communicate (Mark 6:52). Do you recall the incident where the Jerusalem church was praying for Peter while he was in prison awaiting execution? The newly escaped Peter arrived at the door of the house where the church had gathered to pray. As he stood there knocking, eagerly anticipating the reunion with his friends, they argued with the servant that it couldn't possibly be Peter! (Acts 12:15). Poor Peter. After all he'd been through, now he was forced to stand outside the locked door while those inside debated whether God had answered their prayers! When they finally let him in and saw him in the flesh, "they were astounded" (Acts 12:16 HCSB). Learning to recognize God's answer to our prayers is critical because answered prayer is one of the powerful ways God speaks to us.

The truth is, God always responds to our prayers. The way he does so reveals as much about us as it does about God. We can become frustrated when we pray for one thing and receive another. But we are wise to look beyond God's answer to see his message behind it.

When God's Answer Is Yes

Scripture holds incredible promises for those who pray:

"Call to Me, and I will answer you, and I will tell you great and many things, which you do not know" (Jer. 33:3).

"And everything, whatever you ask in prayer, believing, you will receive" (Matt. 21:22 HCSB)

"Keep asking, and it will be given to you. Keep searching, and you will find. Keep knocking, and the door will be opened to you" (Luke 11:9 HCSB).

"If you abide in Me, and My words abide in you, ask whatever you wish, and it will be done for you" (John 15:7).

"I assure you: Anything you ask the Father in My name, He will give you" (John 16:23 HCSB).

"We have confidence before God, and can receive whatever we ask from Him because we keep His commands and do what is pleasing in His sight" (1 John 3:21–22 HCSB).

Walking so closely with Christ that the desires of your heart are the things God longs to do is an exhilarating experience. When you allow the Holy Spirit to guide you in your praying, you will find yourself seeking answers God is delighted to give (Rom. 8:26–27). When you pray in the name of or according to the character of Jesus, you ask for things that are on God's heart and consistent with his nature. To ask something "in Jesus' name" is not simply to tack on that phrase at the end of a prayer. It is asking God to accomplish his heart's desire.

Yes

Hudson Taylor was on a ship heading for China for his first tour of missionary duty when the ship sailed directly into a perilous situation. A strong current was carrying the vessel toward dangerous reefs. The crew gave a valiant effort, but they could not change the direction of the doomed ship. With no wind there was no way to steer the ship away from the deadly rocks. Finally the captain declared: "We have done everything that can be done. We can only wait the result."[4]

There were four Christians aboard the ship. Hudson Taylor suggested that each of them retire to his cabin to pray. Taylor later explained: "I had a good but very brief season in prayer, and then felt so satisfied that our request was granted that I could not continue asking, and very soon went up again on deck."[5]

Taylor instructed an officer to lower the main sails as a wind was most assuredly coming. Soon a wind did arise, and the crew was able to steer the ship to safety. Hudson Taylor knew God's voice well enough that he understood when God had said yes. He knew it was unnecessary to continue asking for something God had already agreed to give. It is important for us to know when God has said yes, so we can adjust our focus from asking to awaiting God's answer and responding to that answer.

When God's Answer Is No

Like it or not, sometimes God's answer to our prayers is no. What do we do then? Do we keep pleading and begging for him to change his mind? Some people would say that's exactly what we should do. They cite the example of the persistent widow who nagged the unrighteous judge until he finally relented and gave her what she wanted (Luke 18:1–5). However, the point in that story is not that we should pester God until he succumbs to our tenacity. The point is if even hard-hearted people will eventually give to those in need, how much more will a perfect heavenly Father take care of those he loves? There is a difference between persisting in faith as God leads us and continuing to cajole him when we know his answer is no. Our personal view is myopic; we don't always know the ramifications of what we are asking. We must be careful not to confuse persevering prayer with pestering prayer. Because we often pray without seeking God's will, we pray in ignorance or shortsightedness. In such cases God's answer will be no because he loves us, not because he doesn't.

Accepting No for an Answer

God responds to us from the perspective of eternity. We only see the events of today. When King Hezekiah became mortally ill, he wept before God in prayer and pleaded with the Lord to spare his life (Isa. 38:1–8). God prolonged the good king's life for fifteen years. Yet during Hezekiah's extended reign, two events occurred that brought enormous hardship on his people.

First, in a foolish and prideful moment, Hezekiah disclosed the royal treasury to messengers from Babylon (Isa. 39:1–8). These Babylonian spies reported their findings to their king and one day the Babylonian armies arrived to brutally relieve Jerusalem of its wealth.

A second, even more onerous, event was the birth of Hezekiah's son, Manasseh. Manasseh was arguably the most evil king ever to rule Judah. He was so wicked even the subsequent leadership of the godly King Josiah was unable to overcome the insidious idolatry and immorality that permeated Judah during Manasseh's tenure. Did God know this would happen if he prolonged Hezekiah's life?

Certainly. This instance would forever stand as a bleak testimony to the folly of seeking our will over God's.

Do you ever become angry when God does not give you what you want? Even Jesus knew what it was like to ask the Father for something and to be told no.

Jesus in the Garden

As Jesus approached the day of crucifixion, he spent precious moments in the garden of Gethsemane with his Father. In the anguish and dread of what lay ahead, Jesus prayed, "My Father! If it is possible, let this cup pass from me." Yet his Father did not give him what he asked (Matt. 26:39 HCSB). Why? Because there was no other way to save humanity. The Father had to say no, and Jesus knew it. Even as he asked, Jesus expressed his acceptance of the answer he knew must follow. He prayed, "Yet not as I will, but as you will." If you ever wonder why God would say no to you, revisit Jesus in the garden on that hallowed night. If you ever wonder what your response should be, even before you receive an answer, look at Christ's example. The greatest mark of maturity in faith is the ability and willingness to reverently accept God's answer, no matter what it is.

James, Peter, and Answered Prayer

We read in Acts that King Herod viciously persecuted the early church. He arrested James, the brother of John, and had him executed (Acts 12:1–2). When Herod saw how much this pleased the Jews, he arrested Peter with the same evil intent. The church in Jerusalem prayed fervently for Peter's release, and God answered their prayers and miraculously saved Peter from certain death (Acts 12:6–17).

We can assume the church's prayers for James were whole-hearted. Yet God's answer in this case was no. Later Peter would face his own execution while the disciple John would be spared. Did God love some disciples more than others? Was God being unfair? Whereas the disciples asked such questions of Jesus (John 21:20–23), the Bible does not record the early church asking these kinds of questions. It seems they had come to understand that God was perfectly loving and eternally wise. They trusted sovereign God to do what was best.

D. L. Moody: Sometimes Yes and Sometimes No

When his mission school reached dire financial straits, D. L. Moody called on his friend Cyrus H. McCormick, a wealthy philanthropist, to seek financial help. McCormick knew Moody's heart and his desire to spread the gospel. He often had given generously to Moody in the past. So, when Moody asked for $1,000, McCormick went upstairs to write a check. As soon as McCormick disappeared upstairs, Moody chastised himself. He really needed $2,000 for the mission but had been timid to ask for such a sum. Moody prayed that somehow the Holy Spirit would move in McCormick's heart to give twice the amount that had been requested.

With McCormick's envelope in hand, Moody raced to his friend, W. T. Harsha, told him the story and asked him to open the envelope. Inside was a check from McCormick for $2,000. God had been pleased to say yes to Moody's prayer.

Later, Moody remarked: "God gave me the money that day because I needed it. And he has always given me money when I needed it. But often I have asked him when I thought I needed it, and he has said, 'No, Moody, you just shin along the best way you can. It'll do you good to be hard up awhile.'"[6]

Yes, but Not Yet

At times we pray and God, says "Yes, but in my timing." When God promised Abraham a son, God's word was true but it would take twenty-five years before it came to pass. God promised young David he would be king of Israel but not until he had first suffered several years in exile. Many days David prayed for an end to his suffering and deprivation. But God was preparing David's character for the assignment ahead of him. Hannah prayed for some time before God gave her a son (1 Sam. 1:5–11). She waited many years for a child, but that child became one of the greatest, most godly men in Israel's history.

The timing of God's answer is crucial. We mistakenly assume the moment God reveals his will everything must happen immediately. Sometimes God gives us a glimpse of what he plans to do in the future. It is critical, however, that we trust him to carry out his plans in the right timing. The worst thing to do is to take matters into our own hands. Many Christians have suffered great disappointment because they sought to rush God's timing. Sarah knew God had promised her and Abraham a son. When the child was not forthcoming, she suggested Hagar as a surrogate mother, and Abraham agreed. As soon as Ishmael was born, Sarah's mistake was obvious. Sarah's and Hagar's descendents continue to suffer at each other's hands to this day (Gen. 16).

God acts in the fullness of time (Gal. 4:4). God never acts prematurely, and he is never late. God's timing never leaves things unfinished, and it always produces the maximum effect. Don't become discouraged, assuming God has said no to your prayers if the answer is not immediately forthcoming. Trust that his ways are best and adjust your life to his schedule.

Jesus was keenly aware his actions needed to be on his heavenly Father's timetable (John 2:4; 7:6, 30). Jairus was a synagogue official whose precious twelve-year-old daughter was terminally ill. He sent an urgent request to Jesus, and Jesus immediately began making his way toward Jairus's home.

Along the way the crowds pressed in on Jesus. Amid the throng was a woman who had been hemorrhaging for twelve years. She boldly forced her way to Jesus' side and, in the anonymity of the crowd, reached out to touch him.

Immediately the power of Jesus healed the desperate woman. What happened next is characteristic of Jesus. He stopped. "Who touched Me?" he asked (Luke 8:45 HCSB). To his task-oriented disciples, this was a naïve question. The crowds literally mobbed Jesus. It could have been any of hundreds of people who were jostling all around him.

Furthermore, what did it matter? A prestigious official's daughter was gravely ill, and time was of the essence. To delay for even a moment could be fatal for the young girl. Yet Jesus took time to identify the woman and to give her the opportunity to bring glory to God.

At first glance it may seem that Jesus was oblivious to the urgency of the moment while the disciples grasped the importance of the situation. Clearly this was not the time to allow an unknown woman to give a testimony while a prominent citizen was left wringing his hands desperately awaiting the arrival of the great healer. Jesus was fully aware of all the dynamics of the day. He saw that the Father wanted to heal this woman. Moreover, she would bring glory to God as would the imminent miracle in Jairus's home. Because of God's perfect timing, the crowds saw Jesus' power to heal, and now would witness his power over death. The progressive way in which Jesus revealed who he was is masterful.

When we pray and God's answer is "not yet," we must understand that God has his reasons for waiting. Waiting is one of the hardest things we do! Yet maybe we need to grow in our faith first. Or maybe God is preparing us for an even greater work he wants to do in us in the future.

What If There Is Silence?

Why are we sometimes met with silence when we pray? According to the Bible, if we allow sin to remain in our lives, God will not respond to our prayers. The psalmist said, "If I regard wickedness in my heart, the Lord will not hear" (Ps. 66:18). The prophet Isaiah concurred: "Behold, the LORD's hand is not so short that it cannot save; nor is His ear so dull that it cannot hear. But your iniquities have made a separation between you and your God, and your sins have hidden His face from you so that He does not hear" (Isa. 59:1–2).

Clearly God maintains the right to withhold answers to our prayers. It is an affront for us to sin against him, then brazenly expect him to respond unreservedly to our prayers. He gives us fair warning: "So when you spread out your hands in prayer, I will hide My eyes from you, yes, even though you multiply prayers, I will not listen. Your hands are covered with blood" (Isa. 1:15). God's silence sends a strong message: we should examine our lives to ensure no sin is provoking him to remain silent.

The Bible singles out a particular sin that impedes our prayer life. That is the sin of broken relationships. God obviously places relationships at a high priority, for Jesus said: "Therefore if you are presenting your offering at the altar, and there remember that your brother has something against you, leave your offering there before the altar and go; first be reconciled to your brother, and then come and present your offering" (Matt. 5:23–24). Likewise Peter stressed the importance of harmony within the sacred marriage relationship: "You husbands in the same way, live with your wives in an understanding way; and show her honor as a fellow heir of the grace of life, so that your prayers will not be hindered" (1 Pet. 3:7 NASB).

Jesus talked often about relationships. He also spoke at length about forgiveness. He taught his disciples to pray: "And forgive us our debts, as we also have forgiven our debtors" (Matt. 6:12 HCSB). Jesus said our standard of forgiveness will be the standard by which God measures us. At the close of the Lord's Prayer, Jesus explained: "For if you forgive people their wrongdoing, your heavenly Father will also forgive you as well. But if you don't forgive people, then your heavenly Father will not forgive your wrongdoing" (Matt. 6:14–15). When there is silence from heaven when we pray, we should carefully examine our relationships.

A third factor we should consider when our prayers are not answered is our faith, or lack thereof. Why ask God for something we don't really believe he will give? Jesus warned his followers not to pray like the hypocrites, who loved to pray long, elaborate prayers in public meetings. They may have impressed their listeners, but they did not believe their own words (Matt. 6:5–6). Jesus did not tolerate unbelief among his disciples (Matt. 14:31; Mark 4:40; Luke 9:41). On the other hand, Jesus repeatedly commended those who prayed in faith. He would say, "As you have believed, let it be done for you" (Matt. 8:13; 9:22, 29; Luke 7:50).

How Should We Pray?

Prayer is God's sacred gift to his children. In order for God to grant us access to his presence, a sacrifice had to be made. In Old Testament times, people sacrificed animals on the altar to atone for their sin so they could enter God's presence. The New Testament tells us the Son of God died an excruciating death so we might have access to the Father (Heb. 10:19–22). God went to immeasurable lengths to provide access to his presence. For us to respond by living prayerless lives is a travesty!

Prayer is a privilege, yet we can treat it as our gift to God. What is spiritual arrogance to the extreme? It is dutifully rushing in and out of the presence of holy God, while carving out plenty of time for anything else that amuses or entertains us. The Christian life is not motivated by guilt. Guilt was defeated on the cross. If we simply discipline ourselves to spend time with God but our hearts are elsewhere, we are missing the point.

If we want the favor of an audience with God, our Creator, we must understand something: God relates to us on his terms, not ours. Moreover, God expects us to ready ourselves before entering his throne room. He commands us to make sure our hearts are right before him and before others. To enter God's presence and allow ourselves to be rushed and distracted is an affront to almighty God. God expects us to remain in his presence long enough for him to reveal what is on his mind. God has profound things to say to us, and it is to our detriment if we limit him to ten minutes per day in which to say them.

When the Israelites met God at Mount Sinai, they had to take three days to prepare themselves for the encounter (Exod. 19). Before the priests could enter the tabernacle to offer sacrifices to God, they first had to carry out an elaborate ritual. A person could not simply barge into the holy of holies. A common person could enter only so far into the tabernacle and that only after properly preparing himself. Priests had to undergo specific cleansing rituals to make sure they were clean before entering into God's presence. Numerous rules and restrictions were followed to make sure that God's holiness was not offended in any way. To treat God's standards carelessly could mean death (Lev. 16:1). To a pious Jew a cavalier stroll into the presence of God was unthinkable!

Praise God that, through Christ, we have unimpeded access to God's presence! However, this truth does not mean God is any less holy now. Do you want a prayer time where you sense the profound reality of God's presence? Do you want to hear God reveal to you the awesome things on his heart? Then you must conduct yourself in a manner befitting an audience with your Creator. Stumbling into God's presence, your mind swirling with concerns about your business will not suffice. Spiritual concentration requires time and preparation. Moses was instructed to remove his sandals as he stood on holy ground in God's presence. We too must understand whom we are meeting and reverently prepare ourselves to enter his presence.

The psalmist wrote:
Who may ascend into the hill of the LORD?
And who may stand in His holy place?
He who has clean hands and a pure heart,
Who has not lifted up his soul to falsehood
And has not sworn deceitfully.
He shall receive a blessing from the LORD
And righteousness from the God of his salvation"

(Ps. 24:3–5).

Paying Attention
(a personal example from Henry)

When you pray, pay close attention to what happens next. I knew a Christian woman who expressed concern that despite her prayers, "nothing seems to be happening in my life!" I pointed out that from my vantage point as her pastor, all kinds of things were occurring. Her unbelieving husband had once declared he would never enter a church. Now he was accompanying her weekly, hearing the gospel and becoming friends with some of the Christian men. I observed she had been noticeably growing as a Christian. She was involved in ministry both at the church and in her neighborhood. To her surprise this dear woman came to realize that God had been responding in marvelous ways to her sincere prayers. She had simply not stopped long enough to notice.

We must learn to make the connection between our prayers and what happens next. For example, when we pray for God's provision, do we make the connection between our prayers and the blessings that follow, whatever form they take? When we pray for our unbelieving coworker, do we recognize what is happening when one Monday morning she asks us why we go to church? Spiritual concentration means looking for the relationship between our prayers and the ensuing events. Those who pay attention will discover God is far more involved in their daily lives than they ever imagined.

How Should We Pray for Others?

Intercession originates from God's heart. God is always at work redeeming people from their sin. He knows far better than we do who needs prayer and why. We may offer prayers on behalf of those for whom we are concerned, but true intercession always originates from God speaking to us.

When God was planning to punish the cities of Sodom and Gomorrah, he chose to reveal his intentions to Abraham (Gen. 18:16–21). Abraham could never have imagined the enormous devastation that was looming over the twin cities had God not disclosed it to him. Rather than accepting the dreadful fate as irrevocable, Abraham immediately began interceding on behalf of the sinful people (Gen. 18:22–33). Despite the peoples' depravity, Abraham almost single-handedly saved them from destruction through his intercession.

When God revealed to Moses his intentions to judge the children of Israel for their idolatry, Moses immediately began interceding. He even offered to have his own name stricken from the book of life if it would save his people (Exod. 32:9–14, 30–32).

Jesus is our divine intercessor. As Jesus observed the Father at work in a person's life, he too got involved in that individual's life. Praying to the heavenly Father, Jesus said: "Righteous Father! The world has not known You. However, I have known You, and these have known that You sent me. I made Your name known to them and will make it known, so that the love with which You have loved Me may be in them, and that I may be in them" (John 17:25–26 HCSB).

That is the pattern for our intercession today. Jesus reveals the Father's work to us by his Spirit. As we are alerted to God's activity in a person's life, we respond by praying for that person. For example, God may give us a burden for a particular coworker. When God sensitizes us to his work in that person's life, we need to pray for him. As we observe what God is doing, God will invite us to join him. We respond by praying and ministering as God leads. Ultimately when our colleague responds to Christ, we can both celebrate God's work in our lives.

Interceding for China

While Hudson Taylor was a young man, God laid a concern on his heart for the spiritual condition of China. Taylor became consumed with thoughts of evangelizing the millions of people in the world's most populous nation. Taylor went to China as a missionary and made heroic efforts to spread the gospel. Upon his return to England, however, God revealed not only his love for the people of China but also his plan for bringing them the gospel.

Taylor later observed: "I had a growing conviction that God would have me seek from him the needed workers and go forth with them. . . . I knew God was speaking. . . . Meanwhile a million a month were dying in that land, dying without God. This burned into my very soul. For two or three months the conflict was intense. I scarcely slept night or day more than an hour at a time."[7]

The thought of recruiting missionaries to evangelize every province in China, with no resources to pay them, staggered Taylor in its immensity. Yet God had given Taylor an assignment, and he could not escape what God was asking him to do. Finally, as Taylor prayed he adjusted his life to God's will. Taylor concluded:

> There the Lord conquered my unbelief, and I surrendered myself to God for his service. . . Need I say that at once peace flowed into my burdened heart? . . . Then and there I asked Him for twenty-four fellow-workers, two for each of the eleven provinces, which were without a missionary and two for Mongolia; and writing the petition on the margin of the Bible I had with me, I turned homeward with a heart enjoying rest such as it had been a stranger to for months, and with an assurance that the Lord would bless His own work and that I should share in the blessing.[8]

God not only answered Taylor's prayers, but he ultimately sent him far more missionaries and opened up many more mission fields than the humble missionary could have imagined. As Taylor adjusted his life, in both prayer and action, to God's will, the Lord included him in one of the greatest missionary endeavors in history.

Oswald Chambers said, "Prayer is not a preparation for work, it is the work. Prayer is not a preparation for the battle, it is the battle."[9] The tragedy regarding intercession is that God often looks in vain for those willing to enter the deep levels of prayer required in interceding for others. One of the most pitiful passages in Scripture is found in Ezekiel 22 where it says no one would intercede for God's people. The prophet recorded God's response: "'I searched for a man among them who would build up the wall and stand in the gap before Me for the land, that I would not destroy it; but I found no one. Thus I have poured out My indignation on them; I have consumed them with the fire of My wrath; their way I have brought upon their heads,' declares the Lord GOD" (Ezek. 22:30–31).

Few are willing to pay the price to intercede at the deepest spiritual levels. When Wilbur Chapman, renowned Christian author and evangelist, was preparing to conduct a series of meetings in England, he had an encounter with a true intercessor, "Praying Hyde." It has been said of Hyde that he "mastered the language of heaven."[10] Here is Chapman's description of meeting Hyde:

> At one of our missions in England . . . the audience was extremely small. Results seemed impossible, but I received a letter . . . saying that an American missionary known as "Praying Hyde" would be in the place to pray God's blessings upon our work. Almost instantly the tide turned. The hall was packed and my first invitation meant fifty men for Jesus Christ. As we were leaving, I said, "Mr. Hyde, I want you to pray for me." He came to my room, turned the key in the door, dropped on his knees, waited five minutes without a single syllable coming from his lips. I could hear my own heart thumping and beating. I felt the hot tears running down my face. I knew I was with God. Then with upturned face, down which tears streamed, he said, "Oh, God!" Then for five minutes at least he was still again, and when he knew that he was talking to God, his arm went around my shoulder, and there came up from the depths of his heart such petitions for men as I have never heard before, and I arose from my knees to know what real prayer was.[11]

Intercessors seek the heart and mind of God. Intercessors do not set the agenda for their praying. God does. Without first hearing God speak, you cannot intercede.

What Is God's Pattern for Prayer?

God is consistent in the way he speaks to us in prayer:

1. God takes the initiative to cause us to want to pray. We do not naturally seek God (Rom. 3:10–12). The fact that we desire to pray is evidence of God's work in us. When we pray it is because God has summoned us into his presence.

2. The Spirit of God reveals the will of God through the Word of God. The Holy Spirit takes the words and truths of Scripture and impresses them on our minds. As we pray, he will bring specific Scriptures to our mind.

3. The Holy Spirit helps us pray in agreement with what God is saying (Rom. 8:26). Our natural tendency is to meet God's Word with unbelief. The Holy Spirit works to align our heart and mind to accept all God is saying.

4. When God gives us direction in prayer, he will confirm that word to us through the Bible, circumstances, and other believers.

5. We adjust our lives to what God says. Once God speaks to us, we cannot remain the same. God's word always requires adjustments on our part. It is impossible to obey God without making adjustments.

6. We obey God. All of God's speaking to us means little unless we do what he tells us.

7. God works in and through us to accomplish his revealed purposes.

8. We experience God through our obedience as the Holy Spirit revealed we would. Experiencing God comes out of an obedient response to God's Word to us.

Conclusion

Too often Christians assume prayer is primarily about us telling God what we think he should do. In reality, prayer is primarily about what God has to say to us. If we will spend more time in God's presence and ask him to reveal his will to us through prayer, we are sure to be overwhelmed by what God has to say!

Questions for Reflection

1. What was the last thing you know God said to you as you prayed?

2. Do you reverently prepare yourself before entering into God's presence in prayer? What adjustments in your preparation do you sense God would have you make?

3. Do you allow ample time in prayer for God to speak to you?

4. How much of your prayer time is taken up with your speaking and how much is devoted to God speaking? Who has been setting the agenda for your prayers?

5. Is there sin in your life that is affecting how God is responding to your prayers? A broken relationship? Unbelief?

6. Has God said yes to you lately? Why do you think he said yes?

7. Has God said no to you lately? How did you accept his answer?

8. Are you awaiting an answer from God? What are you doing to prepare for God's answer when it comes?

9. For whom are you currently interceding? Is your life truly available to God when he looks for intercessors?

CIRCUMSTANCES: A TIME FOR GOD TO SPEAK
CHAPTER SEVEN

L ife happens whether you're ready for it or not! To many people life is merely a series of random experiences—some good, some not so good. In Jesus' day there was a philosophy known as Stoicism. Stoics were people who saw no meaning or purpose in life. All people could do, they claimed, was to accept their fate with grim determination and a stiff upper lip.

God created the universe. He is a God of order, not chaos. He does things intentionally, not randomly. He has a purpose for what he does and for what he allows. God does nothing by accident. At any time God may use an event in your life to reveal something about himself and his will.

God Interprets Our Circumstances

God Spoke through a Tornado
(a personal example from Henry)

A middle-aged couple approached me at a conference with concern written across their faces. They were at a crossroad in their life. They explained that several years earlier they had both clearly sensed God leading them to sell their home and to spend the remainder of their careers as international missionaries. However, they had just built their dream retirement home, and they candidly confessed to me they had been unwilling to sell it. They had tried to serve God in their local church, but they carried the nagging sense that their attachment to their home was preventing them from fully obeying God. Then that spring, a violent tornado passed by their town; their house was on the outskirts. The tornado tore through their house, completely obliterating it, then veered back into the countryside. Their home was the only building in town that was destroyed.

Still shaken from the recent events, they asked, "What should we do?" I told them only God could explain their circumstances to them. However, if they sensed God had allowed their house to be taken from them for a reason, they needed to carefully respond to what God was telling them. The next night I saw them come before the entire congregation to yield their lives to serve God as missionaries, anywhere he might send them.

Circumstances can take many forms. They might be a job offer, a marriage proposal, a promotion, a natural disaster, a sudden death, a car accident, an unexpected gift, a surprise phone call, a letter of encouragement, an illness, a miraculous recovery, an unusual conversation, a failure, or a success. The key is not the occurrence itself but the presence of the Holy Spirit as he communicates through life events. This does not mean we should seek a hidden meaning behind every traffic jam or thunderstorm. It does mean we should be sensitive to what God might be saying during the course of events in our day.

For the purposes of this book, we use the term *circumstances* in a limited sense. We are referring to a special type of occurrence that is set apart because God chooses to speak through it. The event itself is not the important thing. It is God's choice to speak in the event that makes it unique.

Circumstances are events that God uses to speak about himself and his will.

We face circumstances in life every day. Unless we see God's activity in the midst of them, we will be unaware of their spiritual significance. They will simply be events in a long succession of confusing occurrences. A miracle could take place, and we would miss it. But if we are sensitive to God's voice, these same events can hold enormous significance for us. Hudson Taylor described God as "the One Great Circumstance."[1]

The Bible reveals numerous instances when God spoke through circumstances, both ordinary and miraculous, to communicate with people.

Zaccheus in a Tree

Jesus was keenly sensitive to his Father's activity all around him. As Jesus made his way down the bustling, crowded streets of Jericho, he noticed the despised tax collector, Zaccheus, in a tree (Luke 19:1–10). To the people lining the streets, it was simply another example of a despicable man doing an embarrassing thing. Jesus, however, saw what they missed. To the shock and dismay of the religious elite, Jesus left the multitude and went to have lunch with this social outcast. How did Jesus know that event was not merely a random coincidence but the work of his Father? Jesus used another occasion to explain how he knew.

A Lame Man

As Jesus entered Jerusalem to attend a religious feast, he came upon a pool by the Sheep Gate called Bethesda. Tradition said an angel would periodically come and stir the waters of the pool. Whoever entered the whirlpool first would be cured of his or her ailment. Naturally, a large crowd remained constantly near the pool, desperately hoping to be healed. A man who had been lame for thirty-eight years was vainly waiting in the courtyard.

When Jesus saw him, he went directly to him and healed him. Scripture doesn't indicate that Jesus healed anyone else on that occasion, only that solitary man. Jesus was on his way to attend a feast, not to heal anyone. However, when he noticed the lame man, he immediately recognized his heavenly Father at work.

When asked why he ministered to that particular man, Jesus gave this explanation: "I assure you: The Son is not able to do anything on His own, but only what He sees the Father doing. For whatever the Father does, these things the Son also does in the same way. For the Father

loves the Son and shows him everything He is doing'"
(John 5:19–20 HCSB). Jesus did not set the agenda for his
life. Rather, he continually watched to see what his Father
was doing. In the midst of an ordinary circumstance such
as walking through a crowded courtyard, Jesus had seen
his Father at work in someone's life. Jesus immediately
recognized and accepted the Father's invitation to join him
in his work (John 6:44–45, 65).

Miraculous Signs

Jesus' first recorded miracle in the Bible was to turn
water into wine at a wedding feast in Cana (John 2:11).
We're told he did this to display his power so his disciples
would believe in him. While others marveled at the good
wine being served, Jesus wanted his disciples to see he was
the supernatural Son of God. John's Gospel says Jesus performed many signs "so that you may believe Jesus is the
Messiah, the Son of God, and by believing you may have
life in His name" (John 20:31 HCSB).

Everything Jesus did had significance for those who
could recognize God's activity. Scripture indicates that
after Jesus performed a miracle some people were "astonished at the greatness of God" (Luke 9:43 HCSB).
Nevertheless, while some quickly discerned the significance of Jesus' actions, others in the same crowds failed to
understand the reality of what Jesus did. Jesus said those
whose hearts are hardened toward God will not accept a
word from him even if it is presented by someone who was
raised from the dead (Luke 16:31).

Raising Lazarus

When Jesus raised Lazarus to life, the miracle was so
spectacular many people believed in Jesus. However, some
witnessed the same miracle and were motivated instead to
betray Jesus (John 11:47–48). How could people witness
such an event yet miss God's message? It was a matter of
spiritual perception. Even the most dramatic circumstances will have no meaning for you unless you are sensitized to hear what God says.

We have witnessed this irony repeatedly played out in churches all over the world. We have seen churches suddenly experience spiritual renewal. Spontaneously, church members became revitalized in their faith, and many new converts were added to the fellowship. People began confessing their sins. Lives were transformed. Amazingly, this fresh visitation of the Holy Spirit caused some church members to become disgruntled. They didn't approve of all the changes taking place, so they left the church! Incredibly, while the church was spiritually lifeless, these people were content to remain; but when God began to work, they suddenly felt uncomfortable. Some people can be so disoriented to God that when he begins to work around them, they actually become annoyed at the interruption! Jonathan Edwards experienced a mighty revival in his church during the First Great Awakening. Nonetheless, some church members were so spiritually blind they ultimately fired their famous pastor!

Church Planting Critics
(a personal example from Henry)

While we were starting mission churches across western Canada during the seventies and eighties, we were met with a mixed response from other churches. When people witnessed our congregation starting several new missions with our limited resources, they usually reacted in one of two ways. Some saw what God was doing through us and were encouraged to believe God could do great things through their church as well. Others observed the same events and criticized our foolishness for attempting to do so many things. They would question our motives and suggest we were presumptuous for assuming God would provide for all the mission pastors we were calling.

How could people view the same events so differently? Some recognized God working through circumstances. Others only saw the circumstances. Naturally, if people only saw what we were doing, it did seem preposterous. However, those who recognized God's activity were encouraged as they sought God's will for their church. The key to understanding the circumstances of your life is hearing from God, not scrutinizing the circumstances.

God Guides
Through Open and Closed Doors

Anyone who travels in Christian circles is likely to hear the phrase, "God opened a door for me to. . . ." It's true. God does open doors of opportunity as he guides people. However, this matter of open and closed doors must be approached with caution because it is easily misunderstood. Many Christians base their decision-making on the "open door policy." If the door of opportunity opens, they take that as God's invitation to enter. For example, if someone is offered a promotion or a new job that includes a pay increase, they immediately assume God must be in it.

The problem with open doors is the emphasis is erroneously placed on the door rather than on God. Some people enter open doors under the mistaken assumption that God only allows good opportunities to come their way. Therefore, any good opportunity that comes along must be from God. Looking for open doors can appear easier than developing a relationship with God. Various opportunities, including questionable business opportunities and marriage proposals, can be treated as open doors. As you might imagine, this can often lead to disastrous results!

If decision-making were based entirely on open doors, people would not need a relationship with God; they could merely become "door watchers." Moses saw an open door to deliver a Hebrew being oppressed by an Egyptian. He went through it, and it cost him forty years wandering in the wilderness (Exod. 2:11–15). King Saul seized an opportunity to offer an unauthorized sacrifice to God, and it cost him his kingdom (1 Sam. 13:8–9). King David stumbled through an open door to an improper relationship with Bathsheba, and his house was filled with violence and heartache for the rest of his life (2 Sam. 11). Conversely, David twice had the opportunity to murder

King Saul. Doing so would have removed his greatest enemy and opened the door for his rightful place as king. Yet both times David wisely recognized the opportunity before him was not from God (1 Sam. 24, 26). Simply entering an open door without checking to see if God opened it can bring catastrophic consequences.

Just as an open door is not in itself a sign of God's will, neither is a closed door a sign that something is against God's will. The Bible gives several examples of God opening doors that were dead-bolted shut. The children of Israel found the doors of Jericho shut tightly before them, but God brought the doors (and the walls) down with devastating power (Josh. 6:20). Peter found the doors to his prison cell sealed tightly, but the angel of the Lord brought him through those doors effortlessly (Acts 12:6–11). The risen Christ described himself as: "The One who has the key of David, who opens and no one will close, and closes and no one opens" (Rev. 3:7–8 HCSB). There is no door the risen Christ cannot open if he chooses to lead you through it. But when Christ closes a door, no amount of effort will ever cause it to open.

At times you may sense God saying you are to go in a particular direction in your life, but the "door" appears closed. It might be that someone is actively opposing you or seeking to prevent you from doing what God told you to do. The truth is no one can prevent you from obeying God's will. When God tells you to proceed, no power on earth can thwart God's intentions. The world may tell you the door is closed, but you never know that for sure until God says so. While it may appear a door of opportunity for a job or place of service has been closed to you, God promises that no one can close the door of access to his presence. As long as your access to God is intact, every resource of God remains available to you.

There are innumerable historical examples of doors that were seemingly closed but were instead opportunities for God to do a greater work. The young D. L. Moody was so uneducated and had such poor grammar, the members of his church requested he not speak publicly. While no one in his church could have imagined him ever becoming a public speaker, God intended to make Moody one of the greatest preachers of his era. When Billy Graham was a young college student, his college president told him he was a failure who would never amount to anything. Coming from such a prominent leader, it appeared that Graham's ministry potential was limited. Yet what mattered was not what other people thought but what God planned.

An Author in Jail

John Bunyan was a popular preacher in Bedford, England, in 1660. Because he was a separatist preacher, he was imprisoned for not following the laws of the official Church of England. Bunyan could have renounced his faith and been released from jail to join his wife and four children. But he declared that he would rather stay in prison until moss grew on his eyelids than to disobey what God told him to do!

The door to his Christian service appeared closed by the English authorities. Bunyan languished in jail from 1660 to 1672. While confined to his cell, he wrote an allegorical story as a means of encouragement to fellow believers. It is known as *The Pilgrim's Progress*. Perhaps no Christian book in history has been read more widely or encouraged more people in their faith than that book. The civil authorities, declaring the dissident preacher could not minister any more, confined him behind locked doors. God purposed to use Bunyan to write a Christian classic that millions would cherish for centuries to come. Furthermore, God used the English authorities to provide his meals and a quiet, isolated room in which to write! Even when people try to close the door on a Christian's life, they may be inadvertently opening the door God intends his child to enter.

Praying Hyde

While John Hyde was traveling from village to village in India, he came upon a particular village where many of the men had accepted Christ as their Savior. But for some reason the women had resisted the gospel message. The first morning Hyde awoke with a terrible headache. So severe was his pain that he could not walk about the village to share the gospel. Nevertheless, after considering his situation, Hyde decided that even intense pain was not reason enough to stay in his room. He had to tell people about Jesus. So he had the pallet upon which he was lying carried over to the shade of a tree so he could speak with passersby about Christ.

When the women of the village noticed the traveling teacher lying in pain beneath the tree, they went by, one by one, to express their concern. On each occasion Hyde shared his faith in Christ, and many women were converted. After several of them expressed a desire to be baptized, Hyde observed: "I now see the reason for the severe headache this morning. Without it I would not have been enabled to win those women."[2] A door that appeared disappointingly closed had in fact been God's divinely ordained means of bringing people to faith in Christ. When God allows one door to close, it may be because he is preparing to open a more effective door of service to you somewhere else.

One Closed Door
Led to Many Open Doors
(a personal example from Henry)

Marilynn and I both grew up with a strong commitment to missions. After serving in two churches in California, we both began to sense a stirring in our hearts that God was preparing to move us to another country. We applied to our denomination's international missions agency and were preparing to serve in a country in Africa. Suddenly, our oldest son Richard experienced some fainting spells. We took him to the doctor who ran him through a battery of medical tests, but they did not determine the cause of the blackouts. The mission agency approved us as missionaries but counseled us to delay until the doctors could determine what was wrong with Richard. The door to Africa was closed to us.

Shortly after that, a small church in Canada contacted me and asked if I would consider coming to be their pastor. God began to stir up many things in my heart. I grew up in Canada and had often prayed that a spiritual awakening would sweep across my land. Canada desperately needs new churches across the country. The Spirit confirmed to us through Scripture, prayer, and the counsel of other believers that God was leading us not to Africa but to my native land. We accepted the call to that small church and moved our family to Saskatoon, Saskatchewan.

Many people didn't understand what we were doing. It didn't make sense to some that we would leave a thriving church in the Los Angeles area to move to the bitterly cold environs of the Canadian prairies. The church we were going to had less than a dozen active members. One well-meaning pastor traveled more than one hundred miles to warn me face-to-face that if I went to Canada, I would never be heard from again!

As soon as we arrived in Canada, we began to see why God had led us there. A carload of men traveled ninety miles to meet us the day we arrived in Saskatoon. They asked if we would start a church in their northern city of Prince Albert. We did. In the subsequent years we saw several dozen churches planted across Western Canada. Interestingly, the doctors in Canada determined there was nothing wrong with Richard's health. They immediately discontinued the powerful medicines that were prescribed for him in California. He never had another fainting spell. Because human and financial resources were so scarce for the mission work we were doing, we constantly had to rely on God to provide for our needs. God answered our prayers of faith in numerous ways. We came to experience God in a rich and unique way we had never known before.

Because of the special experiences we enjoyed as we walked with God in Canada, I was eventually asked to write a book about what I had learned. It was called *Experiencing God*. Only a small number of copies were originally printed and little marketing was done. No one, least of all me, anticipated the enormous response it would receive. Presently it has sold millions of copies and has been translated into forty-five languages. I can't begin to describe all the doors of opportunity that have subsequently opened for me to serve God. I'll just tell you about one.

Several years after I wrote *Experiencing God*, the newly elected president of our denomination's international missions agency spoke with me. He told me his life had been deeply impacted when he read *Experiencing God*. He believed our denomination's international mission efforts should be conducted in accordance with the truths taught in my book. He asked if I would be willing to travel to every region in which our denomination had missionaries to teach them the truths I had learned.

When I told him I had once applied to be a missionary, he made an interesting observation. He said he doubted I would ever have developed the insights into walking with God that I had were it not for the years I spent serving God in Canada. Then it dawned on me. By closing the door to missionary service in one country, God was not being arbitrary or unkind to Marilynn and me. Rather, he was planning to work through our lives in a way that was exceedingly, abundantly beyond anything we could have ever imagined! At the writing of this book, Marilynn and I have traveled to eighty-three countries and have tried to encourage many wonderful missionaries. I have learned to trust that when my Lord closes a door in my life it is because he loves me too much to give me less than his best.

Paul's Open and Closed Doors

The apostle Paul was an ambitious missionary. Paul knew he had been assigned to carry the gospel message to the Gentiles, and he knew the key to his mission was in evangelizing the major population centers. On his second missionary journey he set out to build upon his earlier successful missionary endeavors. It seemed logical to evangelize Asia. However, every time Paul sought to enter that region, God closed the door. Read Luke's account:

> They went through the region of Phrygia and
> Galatia and were prevented by the Holy Spirit from

speaking the message in the province of Asia. When they came to Mysia, they tried to go into Bithynia, but the Spirit of Jesus did not allow them. So, bypassing Mysia, they came down to Troas. During the night a vision appeared to Paul: a Macedonian man was standing and pleading with him, "Cross over to Macedonia and help us!" After he had seen the vision, we immediately made efforts to set out for Macedonia, concluding that God had called us to evangelize them (Acts 16:6–10 HCSB).

The key for Paul was not what he wanted to do for God, or what made sense to him, or even where the greatest need was. The key was going where God wanted him to go. The most important thing for Paul was clearly determining God's will for his life. In Paul's case God closed one door and redirected him through another.

Pros and Cons and Open Doors

Some Christian leaders promote a dangerous teaching that encourages decision-making by merely listing pros and cons. When deciding which job offer to accept, for example, they would say you need to make a list. On one side of the page, list the pros. On the other side list the cons. If the pro side is significantly longer than the con side, you should accept the job. If the con side is longer, don't accept. Although they would encourage you to pray before you begin this process, it essentially boils down to which side has the longest list.

How does this differ from the way unbelievers make decisions—except for the perfunctory prayer? This process seemingly frees Christians from having to hear God's voice before making a decision. The key is not to make decisions that seem the most reasonable to you but to determine which ones align with God's will. Sometimes the two are compatible, but often they are not. What Paul wanted to do made perfect sense. He was seeking to serve the Lord by spreading the gospel throughout Asia (Acts 16:6–7).

Could anything be wrong with that? Yes. God wanted Paul to evangelize Europe. Scripture indicates the Holy Spirit kept saying no to Paul when he sought to enter Asia.

We're not told exactly how, but we know God firmly closed the door to Asia for Paul. Paul got the message. Then he gave Paul a vision to travel to Philippi (Acts 16:9). If Paul had not been sensitive to God's voice, he would have done the logical thing but missed God's will.

God Is Above Our Circumstances

Circumstances can be confusing! Events can regularly occur in your life that seem to thwart God's plans for you. In those times only God can give you the proper interpretation of what is happening. Sometimes that interpretation comes years after the event.

It's Not Over until It's Over

Joseph received a vision from God that one day he would be a great ruler. Yet every circumstance in his life seemed to mock that dream. His own brothers resented him so fiercely they sold him into slavery. When he tried to act honorably for his master Potiphar, his reward was false accusations and a jail term. When he interpreted the dreams of his fellow prisoners, his payback was to be abandoned in jail and forgotten.

With such an array of dismal circumstances, he could have easily concluded the vision God gave him for his life was just a cruel farce. Nevertheless, Joseph did not become bitter over his circumstances. Rather, he sought God's perspective on the difficult events of his life and remained confident God was in control. In time Joseph saw and understood every circumstance of his life from the perspective of God's perfect will (Gen. 50:20).

Paul's Sufferings

The apostle Paul also experienced circumstances that might have confused and discouraged him. Consider some of Paul's tribulations:

> With far more labors, many more imprisonments, far worse beatings, near death many times. Five times I received from the Jews forty lashes minus one. Three times I was beaten with rods. Once I was stoned. Three times I was shipwrecked. I have spent

a night and a day in the depths of the sea. On frequent journeys, I faced dangers from rivers, dangers from robbers, dangers from my own people, dangers from the Gentiles, dangers in the city, dangers in the open country, dangers on the sea, and dangers among false brothers; labor and hardship, many sleepless nights, hunger and thirst, often without food, cold, and lacking clothing. Not to mention other things, there is the daily pressure on me: my care for all the churches (2 Cor. 11:23–28 HCSB).

Talk about trying times! Without the Holy Spirit's help in clarifying these dreadful experiences, Paul might have easily come to some wrong conclusions. Yet God spoke to Paul and helped him understand why he was allowing such hardships. Paul explained: "But he said to me, 'My grace is sufficient for you, for power is perfected in weakness.' Therefore, I will most gladly boast all the more about my weaknesses, so that Christ's power may reside in me. So because of Christ, I am pleased in weaknesses, in insults, in catastrophes, in persecutions, and in pressures. For when I am weak, then am I strong" (2 Cor. 12:9–10 HCSB).

What an exemplary approach to tribulation! Only God could help Paul not only endure such suffering but actually celebrate what God had done in his life! That's the difference God makes when he interprets our circumstances for us.

Focus on Christ

The key to understanding our circumstances is to focus on Christ rather than on our circumstances. At times we can become so obsessed with what we are experiencing that we fail to allow Christ to give us his perspective on our situation. For example, if we have a family member who becomes gravely ill, we may be tempted to dwell on the fact God has allowed a special person in our lives to suffer. We can grow angry with God for sanctioning what appears to be meaningless pain for someone we love. The more we focus on the suffering, the more indignant we can become at God.

When we do this we are allowing our circumstances to inform us about God. That is backwards. We ought always to allow God to inform us about our circumstances. When we encounter trying and confusing times, our first response should be to turn our focus from the circumstance to God. This can be difficult to do, but as we meditate on God's sovereignty, his unfailing love as demonstrated on the cross, and his infinite wisdom, we will be prepared to hear what he has to say about our present condition.

The apostle Paul said, "What then are we to say to these things? If God is for us, who is against us? He did not even spare His own Son, but offered Him up for us all; how will He not also with Him grant us everything?" (Rom. 8:31–32 HCSB). If you want to determine whether God loves you, don't look at your current situation; look to the cross. "But God proves His own love for us in that while we were still sinners Christ died for us!" (Rom. 5:8). If God would go to such incredible lengths to forgive you and save you, what would he not do for you?

When we are in the midst of bewildering circumstances, that is not the time to make conclusions about what God is like. We should have already reached our conclusions before we entered the difficult experience. We ought always to assume that God loves us and is in control of our world. Based on those truths we can approach him with confidence and wait patiently for him to reveal why he is allowing us to experience our present circumstances. Often through the crises of our lives God communicates most powerfully to us. We generally learn far more about what lies within our hearts when we experience hardship than when we are receiving a blessing. We also tend to rely more on God's grace when we are enduring trials than when we are enjoying comfort. Would God allow us to undergo crises if it meant he could teach us more about himself and the changes we needed to make in our lives? Most certainly. Robert Murray M'Cheyne understood this and wrote in his journal: "If nothing else will do to sever me from my sin, Lord, send me such sore and trying calamities as shall awaken me from earthly slumbers. It must always be best to be alive to Thee, whatever be the quickening instrument."[3]

God's Presence Brought Peace

Hudson Taylor and his fellow missionaries faced innumerable dangers as they served in China during periods of war. Often they were unsure how they could endure the persecution from those hostile to Christianity. Nevertheless, after experiencing some grievous trials, Taylor concluded: "What circumstances could have rendered the word of God more sweet, the presence of God more real, the help of God more precious?"[4]

Speaking of the trials he faced, Taylor confessed: "My faith was not untried; it often, often failed, and I was so sorry and ashamed of the failure to trust such a Father. But Oh! I was learning to know him. I would not even then have missed the trial."[5]

Taylor discovered that often in life's trials God's voice is most clear and most precious. Taylor learned far more about God through his difficulties than he did through times of prosperity. When his beloved wife became ill, God spoke to Taylor to give him hope in the midst of her suffering. "The precious words were brought with power to my soul, 'Call unto me in the day of trouble. I will deliver thee, and thou shalt glorify me.' I was at once enabled to plead them in faith, and the result was deep, deep, unmistakable peace and joy. All consciousness of distress was gone."[6] Once Taylor received a word from God, he experienced peace, for he was reminded that God loved him and was sovereign over every circumstance.

Truth

Jesus taught his disciples that they didn't know the truth of a situation until they heard from God. When his disciples saw a huge crowd gathering around Jesus as evening approached, they urged him, "Send the crowd away, so they can go into the surrounding villages and countryside to find food and lodging, because we are in a deserted place here" (Luke 9:12 HCSB). This was conventional wisdom at its best. Normally if a crowd of that magnitude had gathered late in the day, a logical concern would be to disperse them in time for everyone to find shelter before dark. However, because Jesus was present, the reasoning that made sense to the Twelve was not necessarily the automatic response.

Rather than using common sense, Jesus gave the extraordinary command, "You give them something to eat" (Luke 9:13 HCSB). The order would have been ludicrous had it come from anyone else but Jesus. The disciples saw the situation and its logistical nightmare. Jesus saw the opportunity to perform a miracle that would cause thousands of people to glorify God. The disciples did not understand the truth of their circumstances until they heard from Jesus.

After Jesus fed the five thousand, the disciples entered a boat and set out for the other side of the Sea of Galilee. In the early morning the disciples encountered dangerously strong winds. When Jesus approached the struggling seamen on the water, the disciples saw him and assumed he was a ghost! The disciples were more afraid of their surprise visitor than they were of the storm. They were responding exactly as people might be expected to react.

Four of them were experienced fishermen. They knew the sea. If they were concerned, it was reasonable for everyone else to be afraid too. Furthermore, none of them was accustomed to seeing people walk on water in good weather or bad. The only assumption was that it must be a ghost.

If it were not for a word from Jesus, the disciples would have remained in their fear and confusion. But Jesus said, "Have courage! It is I. Don't be afraid" (Mark 6:50 HCSB). A word from Jesus changed everything. Even in the midst of incredibly frightening and confusing circumstances, Jesus' words put everything into perspective. Now the disciples knew they were safe. Rather than fearing for their lives, they marveled at the power and authority of their Lord. You, too, will not know the truth of your situation until you hear from God.

God Spoke in a Tragedy

George W. Truett, pastor of First Baptist Church, Dallas, was one of America's finest preachers during the early twentieth century. However, a crisis early in his life almost ended his ministry. The Dallas police chief, J. C. Arnold, was a member of Truett's church. He and Truett were good friends. One day Arnold invited Truett and a mutual friend to go quail hunting. While Truett was shifting his gun from one arm to the other, it accidentally fired and struck Arnold in the leg. Arnold assured Truett the wound was not serious, as did the doctors and nurses once they arrived at the hospital. Nevertheless, Arnold died from complications of his wound.

Truett was devastated. He told his wife he could never stand before a congregation to preach again. He concluded he would have to leave the ministry. For the rest of that week Truett prayed and read Scripture, desperately seeking comfort and understanding for his heartbreaking circumstances.

Saturday evening, he could be heard praying, "My times are in thy hands," over and over again. Finally, he fell asleep for the first time since the accident. That night he had a dream where Jesus came to him and said, "Be not afraid. You are my man from now on."[7]

Truett awoke and told his wife what had happened. Returning to sleep, Truett had the same dream a second time and then a third. Truett went on to preach that Sunday, but those who heard him said his preaching was changed. His biographer notes: "But his voice! I shall never forget his voice that morning, as we heard for the first time the note of sadness and pathos which now we know so well. . . . His vast capacity for helping people in trouble, as well as his power in the pulpit, is born of the tragedy which remade him." A devastating circumstance seemed as if it would destroy him, but a word from Jesus changed everything. Jesus turned a tragedy in a young preacher's life into an event through which God would fashion one of his greatest servants of that era. That is the difference a word from God makes.

Conclusion

Circumstances provide God with an opportunity to speak powerfully to us. However, unless we have prepared our hearts, we can miss what God is saying (Col. 3:1–2). Circumstances, apart from the work of the Holy Spirit to interpret them for us, are merely events. The events of our lives have little meaning unless the Holy Spirit communicates to us through them. To seek to understand the circumstances of our lives apart from God is foolhardy. Only he has eternal perspective. Only he knows what lies in the hearts of people. Only he knows what he intends to do next. Therefore, we must continually lift up the circumstances of our lives to God and allow him to reveal his will to us through them.

Guidelines for Understanding Your Circumstances

1. Settle in your mind that God forever demonstrated his love for you on the cross. That love will never change. Regularly revisit this truth.

2. Do not try to understand God based on your circumstances. Go to God and ask him to help you see your situation from his perspective.

3. Wait on the Holy Spirit. He will take the word of God and help you understand your circumstances. Learn patience! Patience means trusting God (James 1:2–4). God's timing is always best.

4. Adjust your life to God and to what you see him doing in your circumstances. Let God work in you thoroughly, so he can work through you effectively and completely.

5. If there is no clear instruction, wait and do the last thing you know God told you to do. Waiting is not inactivity but continuing until God speaks.

Questions for Further Reflection

1. Are you in the midst of difficult circumstances? What has God been teaching you through your situation?

2. How do you choose which doors of opportunity to enter? Have you entered doors you should not have? Have you assumed a door was closed before you sought a clear word from God?

3. Have you allowed your circumstances to affect your view of God? Or, have you trusted God with your circumstances?

4. Are you alert to God to recognize his voice in the midst of your circumstances?

GOD SPEAKS TO PEOPLE THROUGH PEOPLE

CHAPTER 8

Before Randy Bond joined Richard at the seminary in Canada, he was director of recruiting for one of the largest seminaries in the United States. He was enjoying his job, and God was blessing his work. At the beginning of 1999, Randy and his wife prayed about what God might have in store for them in the new year. Randy's wife caught him by surprise when she said she sensed God would move them to a new place of ministry that year. It didn't seem likely—he was in the middle of completing a master's degree at the seminary for which he worked. Besides, he was enjoying his most successful year in his job. They were happy and settled where they were. Why would they move?

A few weeks later Randy received a call from a friend. The caller said, "Randy, I know you already have a great ministry. But I was talking to the academic dean for the Canadian Southern Baptist Seminary and he said they needed someone to do recruiting for them. I felt God leading me to give him your name." Randy discovered the Canadian seminary was only an hour away from a conference he planned to attend two weeks later. In fact, the conference attendees were scheduled to take a tour of the seminary one afternoon during a break in their meetings.

Randy received an E-mail from Dr. Falkner, the Canadian seminary's academic dean. Falkner told him the school had been praying for someone to assist them, and Randy sounded like the kind of person they needed. "However, " Falkner added, "I need to tell you we have no funds to pay you if you come. You would have to raise your own support." Falkner noted that the seminary president, Dr. Richard Blackaby, would be in touch soon.

Shortly afterwards, a letter arrived in the mail. It was from a woman who had experienced many hardships in her life. Randy and his wife had been sending her some money to help her get back on her feet. Inside the envelope was a check. She indicated God had told her Randy and his family would need financial assistance in the coming days and she wanted to do what she could to help them.

By now his interest was definitely piqued. Richard did contact Randy shortly afterward. He told Randy he would be out of town for a few days, but if Randy were interested, they would set up a meeting when he returned to the office.

Randy also had a trip to make. He was scheduled to recruit at a statewide annual conference of college students in Louisiana. As Randy was setting up his booth at the conference center, he asked who the speaker was to be for the meetings. "Richard Blackaby," he was informed.

Now God had Randy's full attention! Richard and Randy met and talked about the enormous spiritual need in Canada and of the Canadian vision to plant one thousand new churches over the next two decades. Recruiting new students was a top priority due to the desperate need for pastors and church planters.

Randy knew in his spirit this was what God had been preparing him to do. Randy and his family moved to the seminary that summer. He finished his master's degree at the Canadian seminary, and he currently serves as its vice president for enlistment and development.

Randy would have been content to remain where he was, enjoying the rewards of his labor. Then, a succession of conversations, letters, E-mails, and phone calls changed everything. Through what others said, Randy clearly discerned the voice of God. How did he know these were not just personal opinions he was hearing? How did he know it was God? Randy's future depended on a correct response to what he was hearing. Randy was able to connect the various messages he received from people all over North America to determine what God was saying to him. Through prayer God confirmed to Randy that he was indeed calling him to Canada. Could Randy have remained where he was? He could have, but he would tell you that would have been a terrible mistake.

God Speaks through Believers

The Bible is filled with accounts of God using people to convey his message. That was the role of the prophets. If people ignored a prophet's message, they did so at their own peril (2 Chron. 36:15–16). However, when people responded to God's word, it always came to pass just as the prophet had said.

Young Samuel relayed God's message of impending judgment on Eli's family. Judgment occurred just as God said (1 Sam. 3:10–18). Samuel later delivered God's displeasure to King Saul (1 Sam. 13:13–14; 15:23). The prophet Nathan informed King David of the irrevocable consequences for his adultery with Bathsheba (2 Sam. 12:7–15). Throughout the Bible the record shows God repeatedly using people to relay both his pleasure and his dissatisfaction to people. The New Testament is the account of God imparting the good news of the gospel through his disciples.

Since the Holy Spirit dwells within every believer, it is particularly important that we pay attention to what our fellow Christians say. Jesus said, "I assure you: The one who receives whomever I send receives Me, and the one who receives Me receives him who sent Me" (John 13:20 HCSB). The apostle Paul observed, "Therefore, we are ambassadors for Christ; certain that God is appealing through us, we plead on Christ's behalf, 'Be reconciled to God'" (2 Cor. 5:20). People do not have to be Christians for a long time before God will speak through them. There are no educational, age, or gender prerequisites to be a spokesperson for God. Christ can use any person he chooses to be his messenger.

A time came when Charles Spurgeon, the famous London pastor, became extremely worn out and discouraged. He felt like a waiter for a wedding feast at which he longed to be a guest. He traveled to a small village and decided not to preach again until he resolved his feelings of self-pity. That Sunday he attended a small Methodist chapel. As the local pastor preached, Spurgeon was deeply moved, and God spoke powerfully to him through the sermon. At the close of the service, Spurgeon approached the pastor and sincerely thanked him for the helpful message. The pastor was pleased and asked for his visitor's name. When Spurgeon told him, the pastor turned red faced and stammered that the message he had preached was one of Spurgeon's own published sermons. Spurgeon acknowledged that to be true but confessed that as he had enjoyed the message that morning he made a delightful discovery: his sermons were as much for him as they were for his hearers. God had renewed the weary preacher's fervor by using his own words spoken through a fellow believer.[1]

God created us for relationships. From the beginning God declared: "It is not good for the man to be alone" (Gen. 2:18). God designed people for interdependence and community. Sin is self-serving by nature. Once sin entered Adam and Eve's family, it was not long before history's first murder tore a family asunder (Gen. 4:8). Relationships of interdependence within the Christian community serve to mutually benefit believers as we build one another up and hold one another accountable to obey God.

God called James Stewart to be a catalyst for revival across Europe. Although God used him in mighty ways in his travels to various European cities, a time came when Stewart was somewhat confused about his next assignment. He had been preaching in Oslo, Norway, and was uncertain where he should go next.

God seemed to be telling him to travel north to the city of Trondheim, a fourteen-hour journey by train, yet Stewart had doubts. He had depleted his funds, and he was unsure of the response he might find in that part of the country. Then a woman stopped by to see him. She had heard his testimony in her church the previous day. "God has revealed to me that He is going to do a mighty work in Norway," she told him. "Don't get discouraged and go away; He will do it."[2]

That word from a fellow believer resonated in Stewart's heart as truth, and he determined to set out for Trondheim the next morning. As Stewart arrived at the train station the next day, he realized he did not have enough money for a ticket. Sensing it was God's will for him to go, he trusted the Lord to provide for his needs, even as he approached the ticket counter.

Suddenly the same woman appeared: "Brother Stewart, God sent me down to pay your railway ticket to Trondheim, and when I realized what a long journey you have before you, I thought I had better bring a lunch for you to eat on the train!" This encouragement from a fellow believer enabled Stewart to continue his ministry throughout regions of Europe where the gospel was greatly needed.

God Speaks through the Church

Since Christ's ascension, the church has been God's strategy for uniting people. As Christians commit themselves to their fellow believers, God speaks through the church to benefit every member. Estranged from the church, Christians will not hear all God has to say to them. The early church realized the importance of meeting regularly together. God speaks through the church in numerous ways, so it is important to understand the way God has designed the church to function. The following are several points to consider regarding Christ's work in and through the church.

Christ Sets the Agenda
(a personal example from Henry)

While I was speaking in a church in the Northwest, I mentioned a commitment I had made to pray for the Armenian people. After the service an Armenian woman came to me and tearfully told me about her family's move to America. She felt hopeless for the people in her homeland. During the next service I mentioned the woman and asked, "Why do you suppose God placed her in your church? Is God saying something about reaching Armenians through your church?"

The pastor asked people from other countries to come to the platform. Soon the front of the auditorium was flooded with people from all over the world. He said, "God is speaking to us. Let's pray and ask him how we should respond." Some of the dear refugees prayed with great emotion for their people facing persecution.

Finally an older man stood and prayed, "Oh Lord, forgive us! We didn't know you sent these people to our church so you could minister to the nations of the world through us. We repent of our hardness of heart. Please Lord, if you will, use our church!"

We all wept with joy. God was speaking! His people were hearing, and they were ready to obey him. Until then the church had not made the connection between those God was adding to their fellowship and his assignment for their church. From that day God began using that church in significant ways for the furthering of his kingdom around the world.

Every church has the capacity to hear specifically from God just like the one mentioned above. Christ has a purpose for every body of believers. In order to fulfill God's plans for them, every local church must recognize an important truth about who is in charge. It's not the pastor. It's not the board of elders or the deacons. It's not a bishop or even the pope. Christ alone is the head of the church, and he sets the agenda for the body.

When Jesus walked in the flesh, God walked among us. To see Jesus was to see God. To hear Jesus speak was to hear God's voice. Jesus sought to be entirely obedient to his Father's will, and he succeeded through to his crucifixion. After Jesus ascended to heaven and was no longer present in a physical body, the Father chose to continue expressing his presence through the collective body of believers. Just as Jesus carried out the Father's will on earth, now the church is designed to carry out God's eternal purposes on earth with Christ as its head (Col. 1:18).

As head of the church, Christ intentionally guides it to carry out his Father's purposes on earth. This means Christ has an assignment for you and for your church. You are not free to run your life or your church any way you choose. At any moment under any situation, Christ has the right to exercise his lordship over you and your church. Jesus said: "I have called you friends, because I have made known to you everything I have heard from My Father" (John 15:15 HCSB).

Throughout the Book of Acts, we see a process of the risen Christ sharing his Father's plan through the working of the Holy Spirit in the church. For example, it was the Father's desire that the Gentiles as well as the Jews hear the gospel. Therefore, Christ mobilized the church to carry out the Father's will (Acts 1:8). The risen Christ encountered Saul of Tarsus and told him how he would be his ambassador to the Gentiles (Acts 9:5–6, 15–16). Likewise, Christ sent an angel to enlighten Peter about the Father's redemptive plan for the Gentiles (Acts 10–11). The Holy Spirit guided the church at Antioch to send Paul and Barnabas on their first missionary journey to the Gentiles. Gradually, through Christ's leadership, the church grew to understand its part in God's mission to the entire world (Acts 13:2–4).

It is crucial for every Christian who wants to hear God speak to be part of a church body. The local church was God's idea. That's the way God chooses to work. God the Father will speak through his Son Jesus to the church. Some people want to be Lone Ranger Christians, so they don't commit themselves to a local fellowship. They choose not to become closely connected with a body of believers. Rather, they treat the churches in their area as a spiritual smorgasbord from which they select only those services that strike their fancy. The testimony of the New Testament summarily rejects this self-centered Christianity. The New Testament understanding of a Christian is one who is intimately connected with and committed to a community of fellow believers. In fact, the Bible reveals that Christ is the one who matches individual Christians to their church according to what the Father wants to do through both the believer and the church body.

Christ Speaks through the Members

Paul talked a great deal about the way the church body is to function: "But now God has placed the parts, each one of them, in the body just as He wanted" (1 Cor. 12:18 HCSB). Paul explained: "For as the body is one and has many parts, and all the parts of that body, though many, are one body, so also is Christ. For we were all baptized by one Spirit into one body, whether Jews or Greeks, whether slaves or free, and we were all made to drink of one Spirit. So the body is not one part but many" (1 Cor. 12:12–14 HCSB).

The Father had a specific will for his Son; he also has a distinct purpose for each church. Every local church is to be a center for God's activity. The Book of Revelation shows Christ relating to each local church individually. While every church is commanded to carry out the Great Commission, specific assignments for local fellowships will be unique. Christ may assign one church the responsibility of evangelizing the local university campus. Another church might be led to reach out to the inmates of a nearby prison. A third body may experience a particular burden for ministering to homeless people. As each church undertakes its assignment, the Holy Spirit adds the members it needs to carry out Christ's work. Hopefully you are presently in your church because you followed the Holy Spirit's leading to join there. If so, you must understand that you are not at your church by accident. Christ knew your church needed you in order to accomplish its mission.

Each person is unique, so there are obviously many types of church members. Every person has some special way to contribute to the body. Paul observed: "If the whole body were an eye, where would the hearing be? If the whole were an ear, where would be the sense of smell? . . . And if they were all the same part, where would the body be? Now there are many parts, yet one body" (1 Cor. 12:17, 19–20).

Likewise a healthy church has many members. Each perceives the world in a slightly different way. Some are "feelers." They are equipped with great compassion. When the church encounters a situation where it is tempted to overlook a needy person, the feelers sensitize the church body to act with empathy. Most churches have some who are particularly strong in their faith. When God leads the church to take on a God-sized assignment, some members may become fearful, but God will use the faithful ones to help strengthen the less resolute. Without all the members allowing God to use their strengths and sensitivities, the body would miss out on much it could experience and accomplish.

It is important for Christians to understand why Christ placed them in their church. If members choose not to function the way God designed, fellow members may go wanting in important areas of their Christian life. Paul said:

> And He personally gave some to be apostles, some prophets, some evangelists, some pastors and teachers, for the training of the saints in the work of ministry, to build up the body of Christ, until we all reach unity in the faith and in the knowledge of God's Son, growing into a mature man with a stature measured by Christ's fullness. . . . Let us grow in every way into Him who is the Head, Christ. From Him the whole body, fitted and knit together by every supporting ligament, promotes the growth of the body for building up itself in love by the proper working of each individual part (Eph. 4:11–13, 15–16 HCSB).

When believers function in the church body the way God calls them to, the entire church body is strengthened, and God's purposes for that body are accomplished.

God Spoke through and to the Members
(a personal example from Richard)

While I was a pastor, I learned to take seriously each member God added to our church body. In order to understand God's assignment for our church, I needed to pay attention to every person God placed in our fellowship.

Brian had been a member of our church for many years. He had a passion for Christian camps, but neither our church nor our association of churches had a camping program. As Brian shared his burden with the church, he was pleased to discover others who also sensed God was speaking about such a ministry.

Brian, along with others from our church and our sister churches, organized our association's first children's camp. It was a tremendous success! Those who volunteered to serve as counselors, cooks, and nurses came back exuberant about the way God had worked in their midst.

Some time later God brought another Brian to our church. His passion, of all things, was barefoot waterskiing! I thought to myself, *Only God can take a passion like that and use it for his kingdom!* But God did.

Brian discovered that our children's camp was held at the same lake where he had a cabin. During camp week he brought his ski boat and some friends to the camp and they gave a barefoot water-ski demonstration. Then he gave waterskiing lessons to the kids. It was the highlight of the week!

While Brian was teaching the kids how to ski, he discovered something about himself; he was good at working with kids! When Brian returned home, he volunteered to become a children's Sunday school teacher. He became popular with the kids and was used by God to bless our church.

We've seen this dynamic occurring over and over. As God speaks to one member of the body and that person responds in obedience, this provides the opportunity for others to become involved in what God is doing. Like a pebble tossed into a pond, every member's obedience makes the circle of Christ's influence bigger and bigger. Only God knows the number of lives that were ultimately affected because a couple of men responded obediently to his voice. But then, that was his plan all along.

There is a two-sided dimension to the way God speaks within the church. God will not only speak through you to communicate his message to your church. He will also speak to you through your fellow church members. When you are actively involved in a church body, all the members have an opportunity to observe God's activity in your life. When you are drawn in a particular direction, others can help you discern whether God is leading.

We have seen this dynamic occur often where God spoke through the body to help individual members recognize their need to adjust their lives to God's Word. A man involved in a sinful relationship offered to teach a Bible study. A wise deacon helped him see the need, first, for him to personally apply truths of Scripture he already knew.

A young lady was in love with a non-Christian and claimed God was leading her to marry him. A mature Christian woman came alongside her and helped her realize the voice she was hearing was not God at all. It was her own desires, which went contrary to God's Word. A loving church family must care enough about its members to challenge their conclusions that God is telling them something when it is clear they are mistaken. Sometimes those in your church will observe your life and see God at work in ways you have not even recognized yourself. The following example illustrates what we mean.

God Spoke through Others

George Truett was a bright, talented young man who planned to become a lawyer. He was active in his church and served as its Sunday school superintendent. One Saturday evening Truett arrived at the church to attend a service. At the close of the sermon, an elderly deacon arose and made a motion that the church leaders convene a presbytery to ordain Truett to the gospel ministry. The motion was promptly seconded. Truett jumped to his feet, protesting that he intended to become a lawyer. Tears flowed down people's faces as, one by one, they shared their deep conviction that God had called Truett to the gospel ministry. Truett urged them to delay their action for at least six months. They replied they could not delay for six hours; to do so would be to disobey what God was telling them to do.

Truett later expressed frustration to his mother, who replied: "Son, these are praying people. These are God's people. And you saw how they felt. They felt that they couldn't, even in the face of your plea, your protest, your exhortation to delay. It was a whole church in solemn conference assembled."[3]

The people in Truett's church had observed his life, and they recognized the Holy Spirit's anointing on him. Ultimately Truett recognized it too, and he entered the gospel ministry. He shepherded one of the largest churches of his day, and he emerged as a masterful preacher. Could Christ have bypassed the church body and gone directly to Truett with the call? Yes. But he chose to work through the body to call out one of his servants. Never underestimate the power of God to speak to you through your church.

Christ dwells within each believer. As you relate to Christians, you relate to Christ. This has profound implications for when you seek counsel from others. The writer of Proverbs understood the wisdom of godly counsel:

"Where there is no guidance the people fall,

But in abundance of counselors there is victory" (Prov. 11:14).

"Without consultation, plans are frustrated,

But with many counselors they succeed" (Prov. 15:22).

When you want to confirm God's will, you are wise to seek counsel from others, for God may choose to speak through them. This is especially important when you have to make a big decision. You can't afford to be haphazard in such commitments. At times you can struggle to be objective as you seek God's will. For example, you may contemplate a career change or whether you should marry a certain person. It's hard to be objective when you're immersed in the emotions of the decision. That's where godly counselors can help. Church is a great place to find them. In your church you will most likely have people of all ages and walks of life. You will have access to the wisdom of people who have walked with God for many years. Each person will bring a unique perspective to your situation. It is a dangerous practice to make important decisions without seeking others' counsel. Through the church God has placed much wisdom and experience at your disposal. It would be foolish to disregard the resources God provides within your church family.

When believers relate to one another, more is happening than you may think. The Spirit knows what you need to hear. He may lead someone to say the exact words at the right moment so you get the message. Even casual statements by those around you can be the Holy Spirit's method of dramatically speaking to you.

Christ Speaks to Foster Interdependence

Christ could tell his people everything they need to know through direct revelation. However, he often chooses to speak through other believers. In this way Christians learn to depend on one another. When God spoke to young Samuel, the boy did not recognize God's voice (1 Sam. 3:1–10). The older priest Eli helped Samuel know how to respond to God. Eli was certainly not perfect. In fact, he would soon face God's judgment. Still he had something to offer the emerging spiritual leader.

When the risen Christ encountered Saul of Tarsus on the road to Damascus, Christ could have revealed his will directly to Saul. He certainly had Saul's attention! Instead Christ commissioned Ananias to visit Saul and give him a message (Acts 9:10–19).

Why did God choose this method of instructing his new convert? Perhaps God was already teaching Saul about the need to depend on fellow believers. It was a lesson Saul certainly needed to learn. God chose to send Peter to answer the prayers of the righteous centurion Cornelius (Acts 10). The Holy Spirit continually connects believers so they hear God speaking together and not just in isolation. In Ira Sankey's case, the Lord informed him in a rather surprising way of a career change he was to make.

I Have Been Looking for You!

D. L. Moody was emerging as a compelling preacher of God's Word, but he needed an associate who could help by leading worship for his meetings. While attending an international YMCA conference in Indianapolis, he heard the twenty-nine-year-old Ira Sankey leading the hymn, "There Is a Fountain."

Moody went to introduce himself to Sankey and peppered him with questions: "Where are you from? Are you married? What is your business?"

When Sankey answered, "New Castle, Pennsylvania. I am married, two children. In government service, Revenue."

Moody replied: "You will have to give that up." Sankey was dumbstruck. "What for?" he asked.

"To come to Chicago to help me in my work," replied Moody.

Sankey explained that he could not possibly leave his career and his home, but Moody persisted: "You must. I have been looking for you for the last eight years."[4]

The Spirit of God spoke so powerfully through Moody that Sankey was willing to adjust his life to a clear word from God. Sankey did join Moody, and together they forged one of the greatest evangelistic teams the world has ever known.

Christ Speaks to Strengthen the Body

God Spoke through a Member
(a personal example from Richard)

When I was a college student, our church was without a pastor for a time. My father had been the pastor for twelve years, but God had recently called him to a new assignment. Dad taught our church to rejoice every time the Holy Spirit added a new member to our body. We understood that Christ was the one who brought each new person. Therefore, our custom whenever someone joined the church was for members to welcome the new person receiving-line style at the close of the service.

I remember one particular Sunday when a fellow member, Connie (now my sister-in-law) noticed something that deeply troubled her. That morning, at the close of the service, a shy young girl named Jenny shared the exciting news that she had accepted Christ. She was ready to be baptized and to join the body. Jenny was about ten years old. She wasn't likely to dive right into teaching Sunday school or chairing a committee. Yet, according to the Bible, she was vitally important to the body.

Only God knew the potential in this brave little girl's life. To Connie's dismay, however, only a handful of people lined up to greet Jenny. It had not been long since Connie herself had become a Christian and shared her decision with the church. She recalled the joy she had felt as virtually the entire church membership stood in line to welcome her.

All afternoon Connie was heartbroken over the church's seeming indifference to Jenny's decision. Finally, Connie called the interim pastor and asked if he would address the problem from the pulpit. He wisely counseled that, since the Spirit had laid this burden on Connie's heart, she should be the one to express it to the rest of the body.

During that evening's service Connie shared her burden. The Spirit affirmed her message in the hearts of those present. We were deeply convicted to realize we'd been insensitive to God's activity in our midst.

Connie was not a preacher. She was not a Bible teacher or a worship leader, but that day she was a prophet. Through her sensitivity to the Holy Spirit's prompting, our entire church was led to reexamine our priorities. From that point on, when God added a new member, our church acknowledged God's gift by warmly welcoming the one God had sent us.

When God speaks to one member of a church body, it is critical for that person to respond to what God tells him. God's Word usually has an exponential effect on others as individuals share with their church what God told them. When someone is actively involved in a local church, he enjoys the benefit of hearing what God is saying, not only to him personally but also to the entire church body.

Today's society places premium importance on individuality. The Bible emphasizes community. The Scriptures generally address the corporate body of believers, not individuals. God speaks to promote the common good among the church body. Over and over there are injunctions in Scripture to "build up" the body. Paul taught: "A manifestation of the Spirit is given to each person to produce what is beneficial" (1 Cor. 12:7).

He exhorted the Christians at Corinth, "Seek to excel in building up the church" (1 Cor. 14:12 HCSB).

Paul continually urged Christians to help one another. The Holy Spirit's role is to create unity in the church body. After the early church received the Holy Spirit, a tremendous sense of community was evident. The members in Jerusalem were "together and had everything in common" (Acts 2:44 HCSB), and "the multitude of those who believed was of one heart and soul, and no one said that any of his possessions were his own, but instead they held everything in common" (Acts 4:32 HCSB). The majority of prayers cited in the Bible are offered on behalf of believers. The common theme of unity runs throughout the New Testament. With this truth in mind, consider two points of caution regarding the way God speaks to the church.

First, any purported "word from the Lord" that causes division in the church should be suspect. At times people will say things like, "Well I know this is going to cause some of you to become upset but . . ." or, "I know this is controversial but . . . ." Then they will launch into a tirade about what the church is doing incorrectly or about the "unspiritual" behavior of certain church members. Before long the entire church body is in an uproar. This is not to say a church never deals with difficult and even divisive issues. However, when Christ communicates with his church, he speaks words of truth that ultimately unify the church rather than tear it apart. If someone in the church consistently brings up issues that divide the church, that person is probably not hearing from God.

Second, the church is not intended to spawn individual ministries. At times people claim the Lord has directed them to a specific ministry. They may inform the church of their plans and ask for prayers and financial support, but they do not want to be accountable to the body. The church is not the place for solo spirituality.

God's desire is to build up his body. Christ equips the members of the body so when they function in the place Christ assigned them the whole body is strengthened. The entire body has the ministry.

Len Koster Equipped Others
(a personal example from Henry)

While I was a pastor in Saskatoon, Saskatchewan, our church sensed God telling us to plant churches in the numerous towns and villages across our province. While our church was still small, we called Len Koster to serve as our minister of missions.

Len undertook the work with a great spirit and plenty of gusto. He traveled up and down the prairie highways sharing the gospel in the communities as he came across them. Along the way he discovered people in several towns who were interested in starting churches.

Len was always delighted to see God at work, and he never turned down an invitation to get involved. He was a giant of a man and an extremely hard worker. He had a burning desire in his heart to share the gospel in every community. Yet he had to remember his task was not to do the mission work of our church but to equip our church to be on mission. So Len would regularly share with the church what God was doing across our province.

Whenever Len shared his heart for missions, other church members wanted to become involved. Scores of young people, some university students, and some career persons volunteered their services. They would drive as far as one hundred miles on Sunday mornings to teach Sunday school and to help lead worship. Many experienced the call to full-time Christian ministry themselves. Len could not possibly have met the needs of the mission churches on his own. As he shared with the body what he sensed God was doing, this was Christ's invitation to the rest of the body to make the necessary adjustments and join God in his divine work.

Christ Speaks to Conform Us to His Image

Romans 8:29 says, "For those He foreknew he also pre-destined to be conformed to the image of His Son" (HCSB). The purpose for Paul's teaching and preaching was to "present everyone mature in Christ" (Col. 1:28). Never dismiss God's ability to use a fellow believer to make you more like Christ. God can use the words of a teenager, the prayer of a senior citizen, or the candid remark of a child to convict you of the need to make changes in your life.

More often than not the life-altering message will come from a completely unexpected source. When Richard was in university, he knew God was calling him to be a pastor. Therefore, he followed the obvious path for preparing himself for the ministry. He took courses that would prepare him for seminary. He accepted opportunities to preach at nearby mission churches. He served in leadership positions in his student organization. But God chose a special messenger to deliver a critical message to him.

Mrs. Clark
(a personal example from Richard)

One Sunday when I was a college student, I took a seat in the church auditorium as usual before the service. I glanced around at those in attendance. I noticed people of all ages. Some were my friends. Some were visitors.

Then I spotted Marion Clark. I had known her for many years. That spring, after almost fifty years of marriage, she had lost her beloved husband Arthur to cancer. As I continued to peruse the congregation, the Holy Spirit kept drawing my attention back to Mrs. Clark. She was a tiny, elderly woman.

The thought suddenly entered my mind, *Now that Mr. Clark is gone, who will mow her grass and care for her lawn?* I quickly thought, *I don't know. I'm sure someone will take care of her. Perhaps the deacons will do something.* The Holy Spirit gave me such a deep concern in my heart for Mrs. Clark that I finally left my seat and went to talk with her. I mentioned my musings about how she would care for her yard that summer. A look of anxiety immediately flooded her face.

Mrs. Clark was a dignified, gracious woman from England. Her greatest fear was that she would become a burden to her church. Her yard had been sorely neglected since Arthur's illness, but rather than telling anyone, she had been praying earnestly that God would help her know what to do. Suddenly this gangly college student found himself at her side offering to help!

When I arrived at her house later that week, I was dismayed to see the sorry condition of her yard. Arthur had kept it as neat as a pin until his illness. Poor Marion! How it must have bothered her to see her property fall into such a dismal condition. It took me most of the day to get her yard back in shape.

As I prepared to leave, she approached me with some money to pay me for my work. If there was ever a time God clearly spoke to me it was then, when he warned me not to take any money from this dear woman! She received little from her husband's estate, and she lived on a modest income. However, to my great delight, the following Sunday she brought me a huge basket of her baking! The church foyer was filled with the delicious aroma. My roommates and I ate like kings all week!

As the weeks went by, I continued to care for her lawn and we developed a wonderful friendship—an elderly widow and a young college student. And she continued to bake for me!

God used Mrs. Clark to teach me much about prayer, faith, and joy in suffering! My walk with God was immeasurably enriched as a result of my friendship with that godly woman. I learned more about Christlikeness from Mrs. Clark than any class or book could have taught me.

God Speaks: Some Cautions

We have discussed many ways God speaks through other people and the life-changing significance of what he says through fellow believers. There are a few points of caution, however, on this subject. First, the nature of interdependence that allows Christians to build one another up also provides the forum for us to hinder one another's walk with Christ. When we share a false or self-serving word with another Christian or when we hold back what God wants to say through us, we are harming those in the church whom we are called to help. The following are four dangers to watch out for as you relate to your Christian brothers and sisters.

God's Voice: Stymied by Sin

The Bible says when one member of the body suffers, the entire body suffers (1 Cor. 12:26). When people become disgruntled and decide to withdraw from the body, they are hurting themselves as well as the rest of the body. If an arm decided to detach itself from the body in protest against a perceived slight, the body might survive, but it would suffer. Tragically, there are disabled church bodies everywhere. They struggle to achieve all Christ assigned for them because so many of their members are no longer serving where Christ placed them.

Achan's Sin

Sin in the body has a devastating ripple effect. The children of Israel learned this hard lesson when they attempted to conquer the small city of Ai. They had already defeated the major fortified city of Jericho; subjugating the inconsequential town of Ai was sure to be a cakewalk.

To their horror and dismay, they were the ones who were soundly defeated! Whereas God had explicitly told them how to defeat the major city of Jericho, he had said nothing about their impending defeat by the citizens of Ai. When the humbled Hebrews sought God's explanation, he gave it to them.

Achan had sinned against God's explicit command. As a result, God allowed his countrymen to be defeated. This was a tangible lesson that one person's sin can affect everyone around him. So it is within the fellowship of believers. The sin of parents hinders their children's ability to hear from God. When church leaders bicker among themselves, the entire congregation suffers. Sin isolates people and fosters self-centeredness. Sin prevents people from hearing from God. The people in Amos's day were so sinful the Bible reports a "famine" of God's Word (Amos 8:11).

The real tragedy when parents sin is that it robs their children of God's purposes.

Unforgiven
(a personal example from Richard)

While I was attending seminary, my church did a door-to-door survey of its neighborhood. I was assigned to visit the houses that backed up to the church property.

At that time our church was thriving. We had gone to three services in the morning and an overflow evening service. Many people in the church were hearing God speak to them about his will for their lives and his will for the church. There was much excitement and anticipation about what God was doing.

I will never forget my visit to one particular house. An aging woman greeted me at the door. When I told her I was from the church located behind her house, she promptly informed me she was a member of my church! A little embarrassed, I apologized for not recognizing her. Then she filled me in.

Almost twenty years earlier, she, her husband, and their two daughters were active members in the church. Then one day a man in the church joked with her husband. Although the man had not meant to, he had deeply offended her husband. Their feelings hurt, she and her husband stopped attending the church. When their girls' Sunday school teachers visited to ask the girls to return to Sunday school, the parents had refused to allow them. Their hurt festered, and they decided not to attend any church.

When I asked how her family was doing, the woman's face fell. They had suffered great emotional trauma. Her marriage had floundered, and eventually the couple had divorced. Her older daughter was serving time in the state prison. Her younger daughter was in a drug rehabilitation center. Grim-faced, the woman told me she preferred watching religious programming on television to attending church and interacting with its people.

I will never forget the impression that made on me as I walked away. I wondered what might have been had this family chosen to model forgiveness for their daughters rather than bitterness. How might the church have helped them in their marriage and with their girls? But when they disconnected themselves from the church body, they lost access to all the ways God could have spoken to them through his people.

When members become angry and unforgiving toward one another, this impairs the ability of the church body to hear from God. Disharmony can creep into a body almost imperceptibly. The church of Galatia experienced such a subtle division between Jewish and Gentile Christians that even Peter and Barnabas were unaware of its danger (Gal. 2:11–16). Paul, sensitized by the Holy Spirit, publicly rebuked Peter and other church leaders for allowing division to occur within the church body. Paul understood a divided church hinders everyone in it from hearing clearly from God.

If Christians presently in a broken relationship did what they know God wants them to do in seeking reconciliation, a mighty revival would certainly result! There is much the Holy Spirit wants to say to the church, but broken relationships and disunity prevent people from hearing.

Another danger exists that is not as obvious as broken relationships, and that is the danger of limited relationships.

God's Voice: Limited to One

The concept of one-on-one discipleship has been the victim of a subtle, unhealthy shift in emphasis. The church is a corporate enterprise. It does not foster individualism. Yet many churches promote the practice of mentoring, or one-on-one discipleship. The idea is that each new Christian should find a mentor with whom to meet regularly for purposes of discipleship. Some mentors have castigated broader discipleship programs within the church, claiming their one-on-one approach was more effective.

Certainly seeking the guidance and wisdom of more mature believers is a good idea, but the pattern of one-on-one discipleship is generally not found in the New Testament. The New Testament portrays the church teaching and encouraging corporately within the body. People often cite Paul's discipleship of Timothy as an example of mentoring, but it appears Paul's training of Timothy was done "in the presence of many witnesses" (2 Tim. 2:2 HCSB). Moreover, Timothy was taught by his mother and grandmother. The value of discipleship in a group context is that it protects you from the biases and limitations of the one discipling you. In some cases, overly possessive mentors actually isolate their disciple from others so they exert a singular influence on the new believer. Some disciples tend to look to their mentor for direction rather than turning to God. In a larger setting you gain the insights of fellow believers from all stages and walks of life. Studying the Bible with several other believers adds a rich diversity to your Christian experience. In biblical times, elder Christians taught and encouraged the younger ones. The Lord's Supper was practiced corporately. Baptisms were public events. The members of the church body did not break off into isolated pairs; they were of one heart and mind, and they grew into Christian maturity together.

As pastors, both of us found there were some people who wanted us to spend inordinate amounts of time with them individually helping them to grow in their faith. While we valued these people as individuals, a pastor cannot bring a church member into the fullness of Christ on his own. Even the most energetic and talented pastors have limitations. As a matter of policy, we would not continue to counsel people who were unwilling to participate in the life of the church. We encouraged them to be involved in the church as much as possible. We urged them to attend the worship services so they could hear God speak to them through the body. We invited them to join a church Bible study so they could grow along with fellow believers as they studied God's Word together. We prompted them to join in the many corporate prayer times available through the church.

Only the church body as a whole is equipped to help people experience the fullness of the Christian experience. Pastors who try to single-handedly disciple individual church members are doing those members a disservice by robbing them of greater church involvement in their lives. The disadvantage is two-sided, for a pastor who is tied up with one or two "high maintenance" Christians is not free to minister to the entire flock as he has been called to do.

Charles Spurgeon relates a humorous, yet poignant account that relates to this situation: A visitor arrived at his home without an appointment and insisted Spurgeon meet with him. When Spurgeon declined, the insistent visitor refused to leave and sent word that "one of the Master's servants wishes to see him on the Master's business." Spurgeon sent back the reply that he was sorry but that at the moment he was engaged with the Master himself and therefore could not stop at that time to visit with the Master's servant.[5]

We have observed the growing popularity of another form of one-on-one discipleship; that is Christian counseling. It is good to seek counsel when it is needed, but this, too, is an area that must be approached with caution. This is not to say there is no place for Christian counseling as a part of a believer's spiritual journey. However, the world's way is long-term, one-on-one counseling where a person's primary or sole guidance is from their counselor. God's way to bring people to spiritual health is the church body. The former should never substitute for the latter. Paul said when one member of the body hurts, all the parts suffer (1 Cor. 12:26). God uses many members of the body when he brings someone to spiritual health.

God's Voice: Unique for Everyone

Oswald Chambers noted, "There was never a second Moses. God does not repeat his servants."[6] One of the many advantages of interdependence within the church is the collective diversity of the Christian experience. By that we mean each member can benefit from the rich experience and wisdom of other believers.

John Newton, the eighteenth-century slave trader famous for the hymn "Amazing Grace," cautioned against assuming everyone should share the same spiritual pilgrimage. He used the majestic analogy of ships entering a harbor.

Have you ever stood on a point where you could see a number of sailing ships heading in to port? Sometimes standing on a dock at a marina you will get this same impression. All the boats coming in have a number of things in common—a compass to steer by, the port in view, and general rules of navigation that are the same for all the pilots.

They also differ. No two of them would meet the same proportion of wind and weather at the same moment. Others would have a favorable wind one minute and, just as they think they are almost home, the wind will shift. Some are really threatened by wind and wave, and just as they are about to go on the rocks, they escape and get home safely. Some meet their greatest difficulties at first. They put out in a storm and are often beaten back. Finally, things calm down, and they go and come without further mishap. They return to port with a rich cargo. Some are hounded by enemy ships and must fight their way through. Still others have a routine voyage with nothing unexpected occurring.

Our lives as believers are just like that. Forgive my simile here. It's just that I have had a long time to think about such things. All true believers walk by the same rule and pay attention to the same things. The Word of God is their compass. The Lord Jesus is both their polar star and their sun of righteousness. Their hearts and faces are all set heavenward. They are one in Body. One Holy Spirit lives in them. Yet their experiences, based on these same principles, are far from identical.

The Lord knows the situation, the temperament, and the talents of each one, as well as the particular services or trials He has appointed for him. Some pass through life more smoothly than others, but everyone is tried at times. But the One "who walketh upon the wings of the wind" (Ps. 104:3) and measures "the waters in the hollow of his hand" (Isa.40:12) will not allow anyone in His charge to perish in the storms, although some might at one time or another be ready to give up hope.

We must not make the experiences of others a rule binding us, nor make our experiences a rule for others. My own history has been extraordinary. I do not think I have met a single person who has a testimony like mine. Very few have been retrieved from as wicked a state as I have lived in. Those that have been have come through deep conviction, and the Lord has given them peace and a future more zealous, bright, and inspiring than is commonly the case.[7]

Newton alerted Christians to the danger in assuming every word God gives them is intended for the entire body. For example, a man might be convicted of his lack of compassion for inmates in a local prison. He might be so grieved at his former callousness that he begins ministering to the prisoners at every opportunity. This could be exactly what the Holy Spirit is leading him to do. However, if he presents his conviction to the church as a directive for everyone, he might discover that others are not prompted to join him. Some may already be serving the Lord in other ways. People may be equally burdened for orphans or the homeless or refugees. When this man's fellow church members do not wholly respond with the same zeal he has for prison ministry, he should recognize that this is a personal word for him and not get frustrated with the body, chastising them for their disobedience to God's directive.

One final word of caution. If we are not careful, our carelessness with "a word from God" can actually harm those we care about most.

God's Voice: Altered by Well-meaning Friends

A foolish prophet. The Bible tells an intriguing story about the danger of allowing yourself to be sidetracked from heeding God's Word. God sent the prophet

Shemaiah to Bethel with a message for the wicked King Jeroboam (1 Kings 13:1–6). The prophet chastised Jeroboam for endorsing idol worship. Furthermore, he declared the pagan altar would be destroyed and the wicked priests slain. King Jeroboam tried to arrest Shemaiah, but God intervened, leaving the king with a withered hand.

King Jeroboam realized God was with the prophet, so he begged for his mercy and invited him to his palace. Shemaiah refused, saying God had explicitly warned him not to stop to eat with anyone but to return immediately to his own house. So Shemaiah set out for home. But along the way he encountered an older prophet who invited him to come with him to his home. Shemaiah reiterated God's instructions that he should not stop at anyone's home to eat or drink.

To this the older prophet declared: "I also am a prophet like you, and an angel spoke to me by the word of the LORD saying, 'Bring him back with you to your house, that he may eat bread and drink water'" (1 Kings 13:18). The Bible tells us the older prophet was lying. But Shemaiah fell for it. "So he went back with him, and ate bread in his house and drank water" (1 Kings 13:18–19). Shemaiah knew he could not trust the evil King Jeroboam, but he let his guard down with someone he considered a friend. Shemaiah had known what it was like to receive a true word from God. He had seen the consequences for those who rejected God's word, yet he allowed a false word to distract him from what he knew God told him to do. His mistake cost him his life (1 Kings 13:24).

There are times when your most dangerous counsel will come from those who care about you the most. Just as Peter misguidedly tried to prevent his friend Jesus from going to the cross, so your friends and family may try to dissuade you from following God's will. Why? Because they don't want you to get hurt. Concern, even when voiced by those who love you, can be the subtle instrument of Satan (Matt. 16:23).

When the apostle Paul was in Caesarea, the prophet Agabus foretold that Paul's enemies would bind him and deliver him to the Gentiles if he went to Jerusalem (Acts 21:10–11). The word of the respected Agabus was immediately recognized as coming from the Lord. However, Paul's friends, including Luke, begged Paul not to go to Jerusalem.

Can you imagine their arguments? "Paul, look at the great ministry you have! Don't let the Jewish leaders bring that to a premature end! Think of all the churches you still want to start! You haven't been to Spain yet like you want to. Think of what could happen to all the churches you have started if you aren't available to protect them from false prophets!"

There would have been plenty of fodder for persuading him to stay away from Jerusalem. Whatever their entreaties Paul remained resolved to obey God's leading and to go to Jerusalem. Luke concluded: "Since he could not be persuaded, we stopped talking and simply said, 'The Lord's will be done!'" (Acts 21:14). Paul knew God's will for him, and no one could dissuade him from following it—not even his best friends.

Tragically, often those who care about you the most will be the greatest hindrance to your following God's will. Your family and friends don't want to watch you make sacrifices. They don't want you to suffer. We have known many young couples who clearly felt God leading them to the mission field. However, their parents did everything they could to discourage them because they did not want their grandchildren to be far from them. Sadly, those who loved them the most were the ones robbing them of God's purpose for them. How wonderful it is when those who love you are your greatest encouragers for following God's will!

Encouraged at the stake. In fifteenth-century England those who were considered heretics were often burned at the stake. William Tyndale and his friend John Frith were considered horrendous heretics by the English authorities. They were hunted down because they sought to do such fanatical things as making Bibles available to people in their own language!

A large ransom was placed on Tyndale's head. Frith, who risked his life to support Tyndale's work, was eventually captured by the authorities. He was ordered to recant or face burning at the stake. The government placed enormous pressure on Frith to renounce that which he believed God had told him to do. They offered him a number of enticements, even providing a means of escape if he would simply retract his position on certain theological issues.

Frith faced the agonizing reality of parting from his beloved wife and children. As Frith struggled with whether to remain true to God's Word, Tyndale sent him a message from his wife that read, "Sir, your wife is well content with the will of God, and would not, for her sake, have the glory of God hindered."[8] Frith remained steadfast, and his martyrdom become one of the seeds of the spiritual renewal that eventually swept across England.

When you know God's will for you, you must not let anyone distract you by claiming they have a different word from God. Measure their words against what you know God has said, and hold on tenaciously to what you know to be God's will. By the same token, be watchful that you don't attempt to sway someone you love from obeying God's voice, just because you don't like what God told them to do.

Conclusion

A corporate dimension to Christianity is often misunderstood. God established the church, and facets of the Christian life can be fully experienced only in the midst of God's people. Believers who choose to set themselves apart from an interdependent relationship with other believers will not be in a position to hear all God has to say. Likewise, by isolating themselves they will be holding back a blessing from other believers. It is essential that Christians find the place in the church body that Christ has assigned for them so they and those around them can hear and respond to God's voice.

Questions for Reflection

1. Are you presently involved in a church body to the degree Christ wants you to be? Who decided on the level and the areas of your involvement, you or Christ?

2. Why do you think Christ led you to the church he did? What do you think Christ wants to do through your life in your church that will build up the body?

3. Are you in a close enough relationship with fellow believers that they feel free to share concerns they have with you?

4. What is the Holy Spirit presently trying to say to you through fellow believers?

5. How is the Holy Spirit presently using fellow believers to help you to become more like Christ?

6. Is there any sin in your life right now that might be adversely affecting you and others?

7. Is anyone trying to persuade you to adjust what you know God has said to you? How are you responding?

LIES AND HALF-TRUTHS

CHAPTER 9

During Charles Spurgeon's ministry, he was checking the sound system in the large Crystal Palace auditorium before a service. Spurgeon tested the microphone by quoting the verse, "Behold the lamb of God that taketh away the sin of the world!" A workman heard Spurgeon's words and was so profoundly impacted by the statement that he went home under deep conviction and was ultimately converted.[1]

As we seek to follow God's will, we want to know God is speaking before we act. God's voice can take many forms, so we want to be open to hearing from him in any way he chooses to speak. At the same time we want to be absolutely sure whose voice we hear. Could it be God? Is it Satan trying to deceive us? Are we simply hearing what we want to hear? Is someone trying to manipulate us?

The good news is that those who belong to Christ can discern his voice. Jesus said: "I am the good shepherd. I know My own sheep, and they know Me . . . My sheep hear My voice, I know them, and they follow Me" (John 10:14, 27 HCSB). Over and over as people have asked us for help in clarifying God's will, a little probing has revealed the same truth: they already knew what God was telling them. People will say, "I guess I already knew what God was saying: I just needed to have it confirmed." Or they will admit they didn't like what they were hearing, and they hoped for a different interpretation!

Distinguishing between God's Voice and Satan's Voice

We are surprised to meet so many Christians who worry that Satan is trying to mislead them under the guise of giving a word from God. Numerous people have asked, "How can I be sure I am hearing from God and not Satan?" The Bible sheds plenty of light on this question. Paul observed: "For our battle is not against flesh and blood, but against the rulers, against the authorities, against the world powers of this darkness, against the spiritual forces of evil in the heavens" (Eph. 6:12 HCSB).

Satan is a master at deception, but the better you know God's voice, the more obvious Satan's counterfeit words will be. The Bible tells us that God allowed Satan and his forces to tempt people. Satan was in the Garden of Eden to tempt Adam and Eve (Gen. 3). Satan met Jesus in the wilderness and made three unsuccessful attempts to snare him (Matt. 4; Luke 4). Jesus was able to sidestep the traps because he knew his Father's voice so intimately. Paul advised Christians to "put on the full armor of God so that you can stand against the tactics of the devil" (Eph. 6:11 HCSB).

Jesus warned against the many antichrists who will seek to deceive people (1 John 2:18). Christians are admonished to "test the spirits" to determine whether they are from God (1 John 4:1). In these passages as well as several others, Christians are well warned about Satan's schemes. Let's review several facts about Satan, lest we attribute undue power to him. First and most important, Satan is completely under Christ's subjection (Eph. 1:20–23). He has been mortally wounded, though he continues to wage war until his final demise (Col. 2:15). He has limited powers. In fact, as Job's life showed, Satan cannot act against a Christian unless God allows it (Job 1:12; 2:6; Luke 22:31–32). The Bible never refers to Satan as omnipresent the way God is. Satan is restricted to one place at one time, as are all of God's creatures. Satan's minions, however, continue to fight a losing battle. Nowhere does the Bible indicate that Satan can read our thoughts. Ultimately, the Bible tells us, God will destroy Satan in the final judgment (Rom. 16:20; Rev. 20:7). Until then, he is recognizable in several ways. The following are six ways to distinguish between God's voice and Satan's lies.

1. Satan Lies—Christ Does Not.

God says one thing; Satan says another. We have to decide who is telling the truth (John 8:44; 14:6). God told Adam and Eve not to eat the forbidden fruit or they would die (Gen. 2:16–17). That's pretty straightforward. But Satan brazenly assured Adam and Eve, "You surely will not die!" (Gen. 3:4). Satan will lead you to question God's Word. We have all seen the tragic results when people listened to Satan and his demons rather than the voice of the Holy Spirit. Satan not only lies outright; he is also the master of half-truths and escape clauses. For example, Christians know their marriage vows are sacred, but they can become convinced their circumstances are "special." A deceived Christian would be the first to say, "I don't believe in divorce," but they would hastily add, "My situation is unique." When you hear someone say, "Yes, I'm married, but it's not a healthy marriage, so God released me to have a relationship with someone who would love me," you have just heard from Satan. God could not have made himself more clear, "You shall not commit adultery" (Exod. 20:14).

Satan's biggest lie is that sin is not destructive. Not true. Sin always destroys. The extent of the damage varies, but the result of sin is always pain. The moment you are tempted to do something against your better judgment, take heed. Don't be deceived that you are somehow exempt from the inevitable consequences of sin. If the voice you obey is not from God, you and those around you will suffer the consequences.

Paradoxically, one of the times Satan's voice is heard the loudest is during periods of spiritual revival. When revival takes place, large numbers of people are moved to repentance. That's a time to be on guard as much as ever for Satan's interference. He cannot fight against the Holy Spirit, so he tries to mislead God's people by producing "counterfeit revival." Throughout history God's obvious opponents have not quenched the Holy Spirit's work as much as his supposed supporters have. During the First Great Awakening, America was blessed with some great Christian leaders. God worked powerfully through men such as Jonathan Edwards and George Whitefield to turn the nation back to Christ. Others rose up as Christian leaders but ultimately promoted questionable doctrines and unbiblical theology. Caught up in the emotional fervor of revival, they and those who followed them failed to ground their teachings in God's Word. One scholar noted: "Without question, the rise of the fanatical element coincided with the decline of the spiritual power of the Awakening. Those who spoke most loudly of being led by the Spirit were the very persons responsible for quenching the Spirit's work."[2]

Henry Alline, an itinerant preacher in the Canadian Maritimes, observed during his travels: "But O how common it is in a time of revival, for many to be deceived, and to take up with something short of Christ. . . . But O how apt are young Christians to be led stray, being so fond of every thing that appears like the power of God, that they receive almost any thing that has a zeal, not considering, that when God is at work, that then is the time for the devil to counterfeit."[3] Christians must carefully evaluate the relevance of their feelings as a part of their Christian experience. Emotions are not bad; they can be valid expressions of praise and worship. However, when emotions begin to cloud those things we know to be true, this can be the open door for the voice of a cunning deceiver. It's imperative that Christians test the word of every Christian leader against the Bible. Times of spiritual revival and awakening demand even more diligence in this regard. When you seek God with all your heart, the Spirit of truth will guide you into all truth (John 16:13).

2. Satan Offers Shortcuts.

Sometimes Satan will tempt you to stop short of fully obeying God. He'll seek to convince you God will still be pleased with your halfhearted obedience. This is not a new tactic. This was his *modus operandi* in the wilderness with Jesus. Here's one of many examples found in the Bible: God told King Saul to destroy the Amalekites. Saul obeyed, almost. He was persuaded to spare the king's life and to save the finest livestock. Incredibly, Saul expected

God's praise for his partial obedience! (1 Sam. 15:13–15). Instead, God took his crown and his life in judgment. God is no more pleased with us when we try to pass off the desire to obey as obedience. Any temptation to take short-cuts in following God's word, or to bypass his directions, has *Satan* written all over it.

3. Satan Justifies Sin—God Calls for Repentance.

Pay attention to what happens after you sin. Satan will encourage you to justify your actions. He'll tell you your sin was not so bad. After all, you were tired and under a lot of pressure. You became angry, but you couldn't help the way you felt. You lost your temper, but you're a passionate person by nature. That's the way God made you. On the other hand, God will identify sin as sin. Satan's lenient and generous attitude may appear more attractive, but accepting his excuses will dull your senses to the reality of your sin. You'll be much more likely to repeat it, in an even bigger way next time. And, of course, included in Satan's gift pack is the inevitable heartbreak and destruction your sin will cause.

There is something positive you can do after you sin, but justifying yourself is not it. Repentance is. When you find yourself making excuses for your behavior or your attitudes, understand that such thoughts do not come from holy, righteous God. God abhors sin. He always leads you to repent (Amos 5:15; Rom. 12:9). Satan thrives on sin. The last thing he wants to see is your repentance.

4. Satan Divides—God Unites.

Once Satan tempted people to sin, it wasn't long until the first family feud occurred, culminating in the first murder. Satan is masterful in stirring up enmity. When you contemplate saying or doing something you know will be divisive, understand that your impulse is probably not coming from God. God is not the author of disorder (1 Cor. 14:33). God draws people together (James 3:13–18). We sometimes hear people boast about their hurtful behavior: "I know I am outspoken and step on toes, but that's just the way I am!" Such people have never seriously considered the source of their offensive and divisive comments. If they did, they might be shocked to discover they were actually Satan's mouthpieces.

5. Satan Fosters Pride—God Brings Humility.

Satan's downfall was pride. Now he seeks to bring others down with him. Satan will tempt you to do and say things that make you look good. The Holy Spirit will lead you to bring glory to God. Satan will encourage you to exalt yourself and to bolster your self-esteem at the expense of truth and humility. The Holy Spirit will encourage you to deny yourself.

When you have offended someone, Satan will fan the flames of pride in you so you are unwilling to humble yourself for reconciliation. Pride will defend what you did and deflect the blame. A word from the Holy Spirit, however, will always lead you to humility and restoration (Mic. 6:8).

Pride in Manchuria. In 1908 Jonathan Goforth, a Canadian Presbyterian missionary to China, arrived in Manchuria to preach. Goforth spoke clearly and powerfully, calling for repentance from all manner of sin. The people began confessing their sins and the crowds grew. Then Goforth recognized that ironically, the more others were turned from their sin by his words, the closer he was to sinning. He confessed: "On the fourth morning an unusually large congregation had assembled. The people seemed tense, expectant. During the singing of the hymn immediately preceding my address an inner voice whispered to me: 'The success of these meetings is phenomenal. It will make you widely known, not only in China but throughout the world.' The human in me responded, and I experienced a momentary glow of satisfaction. Then immediately I saw that it was the evil one, at work in his most insidious form, suggesting that I should divide the glory with the Lord Jesus Christ. Fighting the temptation down, I replied: 'Satan, know once and for all that I am willing to become as the most insignificant atom floating through space, so long as my Master may be glorified as he ought.' Just then the hymn ended and I rose to speak."[4] Goforth knew God's view of pride. He easily identified his attitude as coming from Satan. The Holy Spirit used Goforth's message powerfully that day to bring many people to a point of repentance.

6. Satan Excuses the Means.

Satan wants to lure you into using questionable methods to accomplish God's will. That was the crux of Satan's temptations for Jesus: accomplish a good goal using bad methods. Satan offered him a way other than the cross. Jesus saw through Satan's deception immediately. Often people don't. In their zeal to serve God and advance his kingdom, many people have succumbed to the temptation to sidestep God's ways. Ultimately, they bring shame on themselves and dishonor to God's name. You can avoid this pitfall. You know it is God when you are led to use a means and to achieve an end that both bring glory to God.

Summary

- Satan lies. Christ does not.
- Satan offers shortcuts.
- Satan justifies sin. God calls for repentance.
- Satan divides. God unites.
- Satan fosters pride. God brings humility
- Satan excuses the means.

Distinguishing between God's Will and Your Will

Both of us have heard many sincere Christians say, "With all my heart I want to do God's will. How can I be sure the direction I'm leaning is not just my own dreams and desires?" It can be easy to want something so much we begin to feel God is telling us we should have it! When believers long for something, we can struggle to know whether our feelings are from God. As we will see, the two are not always mutually exclusive, but we must also realize that our own human desires can rob us of God's better purposes. Thankfully, there are ways to discern the difference. Some red flags are the same ones that warn you of Satan's temptations. We will touch on those briefly as they apply here. When you want to know if your will lines up with God's purposes, ask yourself these questions:

Will My Decision Honor God?

Let's say you are in dire financial straits. The burden of debt is becoming unbearable. You have a few options. They include: (1) declaring bankruptcy, (2) quitting your job for one that pays better but will tempt you to compromise your values, (3) withholding your tithe from your church as well as reneging on some of the outstanding debts you carry, (4) downsizing your home and selling off assets. The choice you make will reveal whose voice you are following. This book is not about money management, but God's Word does have much to say about financial and personal integrity. Whatever you decide to do must honor God's standard of holiness and not simply help you escape the consequences of previous bad choices.

What does it look like when people compromise God's standards to get what they want? Organizations have distorted the truth in order to raise money for a good cause. Ministerial students have cheated on ethics exams. We know of one seminary student who stole library books so he could preach better sermons! You may want something so much you justify your sin to pursue it. However, God cares about how something is done as well as the end results. God does not need you to compromise your integrity to accomplish his work. He will not ask you to bring him glory through sinful or questionable means. When you begin considering such actions, realize that the voice you are hearing is not God's. Rather, it may be coming from your own heart (Jer. 17:9).

Am I Looking for an Excuse to Quit?

People are notorious for breaking commitments and not finishing what they start. Christ is the Alpha and the Omega, the beginning and the end. What Christ begins in us, he always works through to the finish (Phil. 1:6). Just because the going is tough, God is not necessarily leading you to quit. In the garden of Gethsemane before his crucifixion, Jesus faced the consummate test of obedience. How he must have recoiled at the horrendous thought of the cross! Nevertheless Jesus knew he had been sent to earth to die. Even as he prayed, "Father, if You are willing, take this cup away from Me," he knew his Father would complete the redemptive work he had begun (Luke 22:42 HCSB).

When God told Abraham and Sarah he would give them a son, it seemed impossible. Eventually, Abraham sought a "fresh word" from God. He suggested perhaps he should adopt Eliezer, one of his slave children, and make him his heir (Gen. 15:2–4). This was a common practice in Abraham's day. When God rejected that proposal, Abraham tried another plan, making Ishmael his heir (Gen. 17:18). In each case Abraham tried to fast-track God's promise to its conclusion. It was not necessary, and God was not honored. God always completes what he starts, in his timing.

At times people tell us they sense God leading them to drop out of school or to renege on an obligation. They'll explain, "That's what God wanted me to do then, but now I sense a freedom to stop and do something else." Translation: "This is tougher than I thought, and I am bailing out!" We have seen people in their final semester of school receive a job offer and announce they did not "feel led" to finish their final few courses and graduate. You will not find an instance in Scripture where God failed to complete what he started. God ultimately accomplishes his purposes in the lives of his people (Isa. 55:10–11). If you sense God is telling you to abandon a commitment before its fulfillment, you can know one of two things: You didn't hear from God in the first place, or you are not hearing from him now. Either way, its time to take your cue from God. God never leaves loose ends. God never loses his resolve. God never stops short.

What Does the Bible Say?

Do you want to know if the voice you hear is God's or your own? Psalm 119:105 calls God's words "a lamp to my feet and a light to my path" (HCSB). The Bible takes the guesswork out of our decision-making. Go to the Scriptures often; they are amazingly candid and specific.

For example, you borrow something from a friend but don't get around to returning it. Time elapses, and you begin to feel guilty. You console yourself with the fact that everyone forgets to repay borrowed items. In fact, you are doing without all kinds of things others have borrowed from you. However, when you consider Psalm 37:21, "The wicked borrows and does not pay back" (HCSB), you are left with no doubt about what you should do.

We have had people try to convince us God gave them the love they feel for another person's spouse. Richard once drove four hundred miles to urge a friend to stop his affair and return to his wife and four children. Incredibly, no matter how many Scriptures he shared, the man maintained that his love for his mistress was "from God." Ultimately two families, several friendships, and an entire church were decimated by this "God-given" love. No wonder the Bible talks so often about the foolishness of men!

If I Want It, Can It Be God's Will?

Often Christians worry that if something makes them happy, it can't be from God. There is a real danger in projecting your desires on to God and using your happiness as a gauge for God's will. But the danger goes both ways. You should never discount what God says because it would bring you joy! Jesus said: "If you remain in Me and My words remain in you, ask whatever you want and it will be done for you . . . I have spoken these things to you so that My joy may be in you and your joy may be complete" (John 15:7, 11 HCSB). The more your heart is like Christ's, the more you will want the things he wants. Things that please Christ will please you. Joy is one of the fruits of the Spirit (Gal. 5:22). Helping others come to know Christ will bring you joy. Encouraging others will bring you joy. Serving others will bring you joy.

We have never understood people who think the Christian life should be devoid of joy and laughter. Some bad-mood believers are convinced that if something brings a smile it cannot be from God. They tend to view a dour disposition as a sign of deep spirituality. They are sadly mistaken! If anyone has reason to celebrate life, it is a

Christian. Don't automatically assume that because you like what you are hearing it must not be from God. Nothing can bring you more joy than hearing from God! Jim Elliot concluded: "In my own experience I have found that the most extravagant dreams of boyhood have not surpassed the great experience of being in the will of God, and I believe that nothing could be better."[5]

Distinguishing between True and False Prophets

What should you do when someone claims to receive a word from God that is binding on you? For example, a church member rises in a church meeting and announces that God told her that your church is to conduct a ministry to the local prison. Another member declares the Spirit revealed to him through Scripture that the church should only sing hymns and not choruses. A member of the nominating committee approaches you and tells you she's been praying about who should teach the five-and-six-year-old Sunday school class, and guess what? God gave her your name! The pastor declares that when he spent the week in prayer in a cabin on a mountaintop, God clearly revealed to him in a dream that your church was to build a brand-new, much larger church facility. Your husband informs you God has called him to take you and the children to the mission field. Your Bible study teacher says God has told her to discard the church's regular curriculum to lead an intensive study on the Book of Revelation. A man informs your church he has been called to a particular ministry, so God wants him to quit his job and allow your church to support him financially. How do you respond when this happens? We've had people tell us, "Well what can I do? They say they heard from God!" Maybe, but these instances could also be nothing short of spiritual bullying.

The Bible is clear that we are not to blindly accept what others claim is a word from God. In Paul's day the people who lived in Berea were considered to be "open-minded" because they were open to hearing a word from

God through the lips of the apostle Paul. However, we are also told "they welcomed the message with eagerness and examined the Scriptures daily to see if these things were so" (Acts 17:11 HCSB). The Bereans were eager to have received a word from God, and they were open to hearing it through other believers, but they tested every word against the Scripture's teachings.

When Peter witnessed the Holy Spirit coming upon the Gentiles in the house of Cornelius, Peter informed the Christians at Jerusalem. It may seem incredible to us, but when Peter told the church what had happened, they took issue with him. This was Peter! One of the inner circle of Jesus' disciples! Nevertheless, Peter's experience did not match what they understood to be the way of God. However, after talking with Peter and recalling Jesus' words, the Jerusalem Christians affirmed that Peter had indeed shared a word from God, and they adjusted their lives to that word (Acts 11).

The apostle John warned the early church against people who would come to them and falsely proclaim a word from God. John cautioned: "Dear friends, do not believe every spirit, but test the spirits to determine if they are from God, because many false prophets have gone out into the world" (1 John 4:1 HCSB). Unfortunately, there have always been those who erroneously claimed to receive a word from God. When Ahab, king of Israel, was seeking direction from God concerning whether he should go into battle against Ramoth-Gilead, he inquired of the professional prophets. Their leader, Zedekiah, spoke on behalf of all the prophets but one. He took horns of iron and declared that the Israelite army would gore the enemy until they were defeated (2 Chron. 18:9–11 HCSB). However, the prophet Micaiah delivered a starkly different message. His prophecy was that if they went into battle, King Ahab would be slain (2 Chron. 18:12–22). Obviously God would not give two contradictory messages. One of them had to be incorrect. In this case Zedekiah was wrong, and King Ahab lost his life just as Micaiah said he would.

During Jeremiah's time God told him to foretell the Babylonian destruction of Jerusalem. However, the prophet Hananiah declared on behalf of all the prophets:

Thus says the LORD of hosts, the God of Israel, "I have broken the yoke of the king of Babylon. Within two years I am going to bring back to this place all the vessels of the LORD's house, which Nebuchadnezzar king of Babylon took away from this place and carried to Babylon. I am also going to bring back to this place Jeconiah the son of Jehoiakim, king of Judah, and all the exiles of Judah who went to Babylon," declares the LORD, "for I will break the yoke of the king of Babylon" (Jer. 28:2–4).

Once again God's people received conflicting messages. How were they to know what to believe? Once again, the majority was wrong. The lone prophet was correct, and Babylon did destroy Jerusalem just as Jeremiah foretold.

Bible Interpretation and Jesus' Second Coming

Some people claim to have unusual insight into Scripture. In 1831, William Miller presented his views on why he believed Jesus would return to earth in 1843. Miller, a self-taught Bible student, had focused on Daniel 8:14, which states that after twenty-three hundred days the sanctuary would be cleansed. Miller determined the starting date for this prophecy was the year 457 B.C. Using one day in the passage to equal one year in time, Miller concluded that Jesus would return some time between March 21, 1843, and March 21, 1844. Miller wrote numerous articles and made compelling presentations all over the United States. He elaborate charts and graphs filled with scriptural and historical references. Many people were persuaded that Miller was correct. As the predicted dates approached, many people quit their jobs and suspended their secular commitments to prepare for Christ's return. After the dates came and went, some followers set new dates. Eventually some leaders from the movement reinterpreted the Scriptures to mean Christ would enter his temple in heaven at that time rather than return to earth.

Miller is only one of an endless stream of false prophets history has witnessed. In 1988, a would-be prophet wrote a pamphlet with eighty-eight reasons why Jesus would come in 1988. The author used every manner of Scriptures to prove his point. Incredibly, many who read the pamphlet believed it was true. When Jesus didn't come back in 1988, there was one more religious book on the bargain tables at bookstores.

Distinguishing between God's Voice and the World's Voice

What is the difference between the world's voice and God's voice? The more you get to know God's ways, the more evident the disparity will be. We're talking about two completely different things. The examples are endless, but here are a few to consider.

The World Steers You to Your Strengths; God Works through Your Weaknesses

Secular thought says to protect your interests. Jesus says try to save your life and you'll lose it. Human reasoning instructs you to know your limitations and live within them. God says he will do the impossible through you. The world says work to your strengths. God says he works best in your weakness. The world speaks to affirm your actions. God speaks to change your life. The world lives for personal excitement but finds emptiness. Ironically there is no more exciting or fulfilling life than one lived God's way.

The World Says Claim Your Rights; God Says Take Up Your Cross

Called to Sacrifice
(a personal example from Henry)

I had the privilege of preaching at a gathering of Christians in Taiwan. As I spoke, the Spirit of God descended upon the people in the room, and there was a great sense of brokenness before God. While I was still speaking, people spontaneously began to come forward to pray at the front of the auditorium. I noticed one young man sobbing. After he had been praying awhile, I knelt beside him. I said, "My brother, you seem to be under great distress. I sense God has spoken to you. What did he say?"

His face still wet with tears, he said, "God did speak to me. He told me I should go to China and tell people about Jesus."

I replied, "Do you understand that doing so could cost you your life?"

The young man replied, "Yes sir. That is the issue I just settled with God."

The world will tell you to pursue your own interests and pleasures and save your life from any distress. Christ will tell you to deny yourself, take up your cross, and follow him (Matt. 16:24–25).

The World Measures Success Differently than God

People today feel enormous pressure to be "successful." This push for eminence is reaching down to younger and younger ages. Parents are frantically trying to get their children in the right niche—be it a sport or a musical discipline—at a young enough age so they can succeed. Richard's son Daniel wanted to take up hockey at age twelve but was warned he was too old to become very good at it. (Fortunately he didn't listen, and he thoroughly enjoyed playing the game.) Likewise when Richard's daughter Carrie began figure skating at ten, she was encouraged to take extra lessons to "catch up" to the other future Olympians who had been on skates since potty training! In both cases the driving force behind the advice was not enjoyment of the sport but becoming better than anyone else. Ironically, both Daniel and Carrie proved their advisors wrong and enjoyed not only genuine pleasure in their sports but also substantial success. The world claims you must come in first to be successful; Jesus directly contradicted such nonsense. In fact, Jesus turned the world's values upside down.

There is no area of life where the world's views affect Christians any more than in the area of money. We need money to live. Churches need money to function. Organizations, even Christian ones, require money to operate. The important thing, as Jesus said, is that you cannot serve two masters. Christians must be careful that their desire to be good money managers does not overrule their responsibility to heed God's voice. At times what appears to be most prudent might not be God-directed. We have known people who said, "I know God is calling me to take that ministry position, but I won't as long as it involves a reduction in pay." Or, "I know God is telling me to contribute funds to that church project, but I can't afford to!" Sooner or later everyone must decide whether the world or God determines how they manage their money.

Warned by the Spirit
(a personal example from Richard)

One of the greatest challenges for the seminary I lead is to increase its endowment funds. Endowment funds are investments whose interest earned is used to finance an institution. When I came to the seminary, the school had a meager endowment fund. I began looking for ways to add to the principal as well as to increase the annual rate of earnings. I discovered a number of financial institutions eager to take our money with the promise they could substantially increase our earnings. One particularly intriguing institution approached me about investing our money with them. The people involved were trusted in the religious community. The rates of return the organization had enjoyed were remarkable. Many people I respected had used their services and gave glowing reports. It looked like a solid, smart financial venture.

Nonetheless, as I prayed for wisdom, I sensed a discomfort in my spirit. Despite the attractiveness of the opportunity, the Holy Spirit would not give me peace about investing our funds with that institution. Even as others I knew were investing their retirement funds with the company, our school ultimately chose to decline. A few years later, I understood why. It was revealed that the company was involved in many questionable investment and accounting practices. Numerous lawsuits were launched. Company assets were insufficient to return the funds people had invested. Many people lost their life savings, receiving only pennies on the dollar. Investing our endowment funds with that organization could have destroyed our fledgling school. Only God's intervention prevented that from happening. I was reminded once again of how critical it is that I walk closely with the Spirit.

In today's world, money is the ultimate gauge in determining success. Even Christian radio stations will shamelessly advertise and promote schemes to accumulate wealth for the sake of enjoying "the good life." We have repeatedly witnessed the life-transforming effect a word from God can have. A financial advisor resigned a job that would have made him wealthy to help plant a new church. A skilled surgeon left a secure medical practice in the United States to serve the poor on the mission field. A wealthy businessman maintained a modest lifestyle so he could give more money to mission causes. A gifted musician chose to sing in less lucrative venues to support Christian causes rather than marketing herself to achieve national fame. We have met many wonderful Christians who heard God speak to them and who were profoundly impacted to renounce worldly success in favor of kingdom success.

The World Operates on Common Sense— God Uses Divine Wisdom

When someone tells you to use common sense, he is saying do what appears logical. This can be a good rule to follow. "A penny saved is a penny earned" and "a stitch in time saves nine" are helpful adages. However, the Bible warns that what seems like wisdom to the world can be foolishness to God (1 Cor. 1:18–25; Col. 2:8). At times God will lead you to do things that seem downright illogical.

For example, if a powerful army besieged your city, would you choose to attack them with your choir in the lead? That's precisely what God told King Jehoshaphat to do, and he was victorious (2 Chron. 20:20–23). If you were seeking to overcome a formidable enemy, would you command your soldiers to march around the city seven times and then shout? That's what God told Joshua to do, and it brought down the walls of Jericho (Josh. 6:15–16). If you were ministering to a crowd of five thousand men and their families, would you try to feed them with five small fish and two loaves of bread? That would not have appeared logical. But that's what Jesus did, and there were leftovers (Mark 6:33–44).

One reason some Christians don't experience God working powerfully through their lives is because they succumb to the allure of worldly thinking. They rule out any word from God that does not make sense to them. If you refuse to accept every word from God that does not match your human reasoning, then you will miss a great deal of what he says!

The World Offers Management— Christ Is the Good Shepherd

When Jesus described us as sheep, it was not the most complimentary metaphor he could have chosen. Sheep often find themselves in trouble. They cannot be left unattended. They wander obliviously into danger. They tend to follow other sheep even when the "leaders" are going the wrong way. Because sheep have a tendency to get lost, they need someone to guide them. Frankly, they're just not that smart.

Jesus cautioned about several types of people who will take advantage of us if we let them. First there are *strangers* (John 10:5). You can easily identify strangers by their language. It is foreign. It doesn't sound like Christ. If you know Jesus, you will not be swayed by the unfamiliar voice of a stranger.

Next Jesus mentioned the *hired hand* (John 10:12–13). The hired hand will care for the sheep to a point and for a price. But the moment he sees a wolf coming, he'll run for safety, leaving the sheep to their fate. After all, it's just a job. Talk shows abound with red-faced, fallen evangelists who promoted their "ministry" rather than their Lord. Discerning Christians will be cautious about listening to anyone who speaks out of self-interest.

Jesus identified a third type of person as a *thief* (John 10:8, 10). Thieves use deception to take advantage of us. They gain our trust, then use us for their own benefit. Many cult leaders have enticed people with their smooth, winsome words, ultimately robbing their victims of everything, including their lives. Recently a documentary aired on television about Charles Manson, notorious leader of the Helter Skelter murder spree in the 1960s. Amazingly, Manson convinced a group of young adults to commit a series of brutal murders. With chilling coldness he refused to take responsibility for his actions, repeatedly claiming, "I didn't force anyone to listen to me." When his former cult members, now middle aged, were interviewed they concurred that it was their foolish choice to follow him. They were still in prison paying the price. Be careful to examine the track record of those clamoring for you to follow them. If they are thieves, you will know it by the trail of incriminating evidence.

Jesus identified the good shepherd as the only one who loves the sheep and willingly lays down his life for them. Sheep know when they are in the shepherd's care. They feel secure with him. He is gentle with them, and he leads them to green pastures and still waters (Ps. 23). As the sheep spend time with the good shepherd, they become fondly familiar with his voice. The good shepherd does not have to raise his voice to be heard by his sheep. Sheep aren't the brightest species in the animal kingdom, but when they are smart enough to respond to the good shepherd's voice, they are always led to safety, rest, and nourishment.

The World Divides—God Unites

We are aware of a church that fired its pastor and became bitterly divided, all because a child from an ethnic minority was allowed to attend its Vacation Bible School!

Such foolishness does not come from God. The world promotes division and prejudice. There will be no segregation in heaven! Nor will there be politics. Some churches are run by a handful of people who control all the important decisions and jealously guard their positions of influence.

Power struggles do not originate from God. They represent world values. Pursuing position is not something you do in the church or in the kingdom of God. It is something the world does. Worldly thinking tempts you to use people for your own purposes. Christ advocates submission to others out of love (Eph. 5:21; Phil. 2:3–4). The world equates submission with weakness. The world values excellence. God values obedience. Worldly values easily creep into our thinking, and before we know it, we are attributing worldly thinking to God. It is critical that we base our actions not on worldly values but on truths we have learned from God.

Using the Correct Frequency

Discerning God's voice can be likened to tuning a radio. If your radio is set to the wrong frequency, you will not pick up the right station. The problem is not with the radio station. It has been broadcasting to your location all along. However, you were not tuned in to its signals. That's how it is with many Christians. They are on the world's wavelength so they miss God's voice. God is at work around them, but they are busy listening to other voices. To hear God speak, Christians must decide whether to focus on messages sent by the world or the true word spoken by God.

Distinguishing between Good and Best

Often the hardest enemy to identify is the one within your own ranks. That's how spies operate. They blend in. There is a danger to Christians that is hard to identify because it imitates God's will. It is in choosing good rather than God's best. One definition of *sin* is "missing the mark." Sin is missing out on what God intended. Often Christians can miss the mark because we are distracted by good things.

This dilemma of good versus best is particularly acute for multitalented people. People with multiple skills and gifts often struggle to know what God wants them to do. They face so many good options they have to be careful not to get sidetracked from God's best. Just because an opportunity presents itself does not mean it is God's will. Many sincere but overcommitted Christians have burned out in their attempts to fill their lives with good things. God will not burn you out. That's why it is essential for you to distinguish between good activities and God's will.

We knew a college student—we'll call him Dan—who was an unusually gifted young man. He was a talented athlete who enjoyed a natural aptitude for many different sports. He was a skilled musician, sought after by respected bands and orchestras. He also had a brilliant mind and was strongly encouraged to do doctoral work in preparation for an academic career. As Dan proceeded through university, God spoke to him about his future. One Sunday he announced that God had called him to be a pastor. He was to attend seminary in preparation for a lifetime of Christian service. The following summer Dan volunteered at a small mission church and thoroughly enjoyed the experience. He returned to university in the fall and reiterated to his home church that over the summer God had confirmed his call to the ministry.

That year was filled with good opportunities for Dan. An elite musical group invited him to join them. Dan felt so honored to be invited that he decided to give them a year or two in order to enhance his musical abilities, in case he could later use them in the Lord's service. Then a friend presented the opportunity to purchase a small business. The potential was there to make a large profit in a short amount of time. Dan reasoned that this way he could finance his way through seminary as he prepared for ministry. Dan also had the opportunity to pursue many of his hobbies, some of which earned him a great deal of money. And so the years passed by. Dan knew what God's best was for him, but he wanted to juggle the numerous good opportunities that arose along the way while he prepared to do God's will.

One day he was called to do a special job. A tragic accident occurred and Dan lost his life. He never made it to seminary. He never entered the ministry. He never experienced the many things God intended for him. Good had robbed him of best. It even cost him his life.

Some basic guidelines can help you determine whether you are responding to a good opportunity or to God's will.

First, listen to the Holy Spirit. The Holy Spirit will confirm in your spirit whether an invitation is from God. When someone invites you to participate in a home Bible study on Tuesday evenings, the Spirit within you will confirm the invitation as God's will or whether it is actually a distraction from what God wants you to do. The key is to recognize when the Spirit is speaking. And that brings us back to the recurring theme of this book: the closer you are to God, the more easily you'll recognize his voice. If you accept every good invitation that comes your way, you may ultimately become overwhelmed and find yourself functioning on guilt rather than on the Holy Spirit's leading.

Second, seek peace. Do you know how inner peace feels? You will feel tremendous peace when you are in God's will and great unrest when you are not. Even as you do many good things, you can experience weariness and dissatisfaction in your soul with all you have to do. If you are doing things because you feel guilty or because no one else is doing them, you can develop a deep sense of resentment, even while you undertake your good activities. Not so when you follow God's lead. Christ's yoke is easy and his burden is light (Matt. 11:28–30). Have you ever suffered through a Bible study where the teacher had neither the desire nor the aptitude for teaching but only taught because, like eating oatmeal, "it's the right thing to do"? What torture! No doubt God has a much more joyful task in the church for such people if only they would ask. One way to distinguish a word from God is whether the Holy Spirit gives you (and others!) a sense of peace about what you are doing (John 14:27).

Third, timing is important. There are some good things God does want you to do but not now. Some people tend to race ahead with whatever they think God might want them to do. They eventually fail because they jumped the gun. Ironically, one of the places this guideline is heeded the least is in seminaries. We knew many students who were frustrated with preparing for ministry when they already had a burning desire to be doing ministry. Some enthusiasts looked for every opportunity to preach or teach or undertake mission projects. Being involved in ministry is a good thing for those training for their calling, but these zealots went overboard and sacrificed their schooling. They would often do poorly in their classes because they had no time to study. Some even dropped out of school because they had no time to attend classes while attending to their various ministries. Unfortunately, many of these students ultimately discovered they were ill prepared for the long haul of ministry. They mistakenly assumed that if God called them to something in the future, they must immediately begin doing it today.

If you are currently in a transitional stage of life, such as in school, don't fall for the lie that you must always be simultaneously performing the exact role for which you are training. Trust in God's timing, and don't worry about what your resume says. It is far better to do things God's way so your family and your walk with God are healthy and strong when the time comes to do what God has been leading you to do.

Fourth, take your time. Rarely do you have to make decisions immediately. If you are being pressured to say yes on the spot, decline the invitation. Just as it is unwise to spontaneously purchase major items from telemarketers or door-to-door salesmen, it is foolish to routinely agree to new commitments on the spur of the moment. Take time to pray through each decision. Seek the counsel of your family and friends. Often your friends know you well enough to recognize whether an opportunity fits with what God has been doing in your life. Allow God to speak to you through his Word to confirm whether the new direction you are considering is from him. This may take time, but it will involve far less effort than later having to disentangle yourself from commitments you foolishly made without seeking God's guidance.

Missing God's Voice

So far we have talked about how to distinguish between God's voice and competing voices such as Satan's lies, your own desires, false prophets, the world's ways, and good opportunities. Each of these has the power to distract us from God's voice. What happens then? The Bible speaks at length about the peril of missing God's voice.

There are consequences to not recognizing when God is speaking. At times those consequences can be enormous. The Bible issues grave warnings to those who miss hearing and responding to God's voice. Consider a few of them:

"The Lord, the God of their fathers, sent word to them again and again by His messengers, because He had compassion on His people and on His dwelling place; but they continually mocked the messengers of God, despised His words and scoffed at His prophets, until the wrath of the Lord arose against His people, until there was no remedy" (2 Chron. 36:15–16).

"Why was there no man when I came?

When I called, why was there none to answer?" (Isa. 50:2).

I will destine you for the sword,
And all of you shall bow down to the slaughter.
Because I called, but you did not answer;
I spoke, but you did not hear.
And you did evil in My sight
and chose that in which I did not delight" (Isa. 65:12).

So I will choose their punishments,
and will bring on them what they dread.
Because I called, but no one answered;
I spoke, but they did not listen.
And they did evil in My sight,
And chose that in which I did not delight" (Isa. 66:4).

"And I spoke to you, rising up early and speaking, but you did not hear, and I called you but you did not answer" (Jer. 7:13).

"Not everyone who says to Me, 'Lord, Lord!' will enter the kingdom of heaven, but the one who does the will of My Father in heaven. On that day many will say to me, 'Lord, Lord, didn't we prophesy in Your name, drive out demons in Your name and do many miracles in Your name?' Then I will announce to them, 'I never knew you! Depart from Me, you lawbreakers!'" (Matt. 7:21–23 HCSB).

Perhaps the single greatest reason people miss God's voice is their lack of faith. If you don't believe God speaks to people today, it is doubtful you will hear him. If you refuse to believe what God has already told you, you are unlikely to hear what he says next. The writer of Hebrews drew this lesson from the children of Israel's plight as they wandered in the wilderness for forty years.

> While it is said, "Today if you hear His voice, do not harden your hearts, as when they provoked Me." For who provoked Him when they had heard? Indeed, did not all those who came out of Egypt led by Moses? And with whom was He angry for forty years? Was it not with those who sinned, whose bodies fell in the wilderness? And to whom did He swear that they would not enter his rest, but to those who were disobedient? So we see that they were not able to enter because of unbelief. Therefore, let us fear if, while a promise remains of entering His rest, any one of you would seem to have come short of it. For indeed we have had good news preached to us, just as they also; but the word they heard did not profit them, because it was not united by faith in those who heard" (Heb. 3:15–4:2).

Impatience also can prevent people from hearing God's voice. Some people rush into God's presence and expect him to hand off a divine word to them like a baton in a relay race as they continue to charge out into their busy day. God does not speak to us on our terms. He speaks to us as he pleases. As the aforementioned Scriptures tell us, he expects us to stop and listen in order to hear him. We would have more time to listen to God if we spent less time listening to other voices. The opinions of others, fads, speculation, and even gossip prove to be tantalizing distractions from what God wants us to hear (1 Tim. 4:7; 2 Tim. 2:16). If we spend more time reading newspapers and magazines and watching television than we spend reading our Bibles and praying, it should not surprise us that our thinking mirrors the world's thinking (Josh. 1:8; Ps. 143:5). Sadly, even many "Christian" books written to promote a Christian lifestyle are often filled with the latest wisdom of the world, yet there is not a single reference to Scripture.

When you seek a word from God, it must be with an attitude that is primed to obey. God's opinion is not just one of your options. God is not interested in debating with you about your best course of action. He already knows what that is. If you only respond to God on your terms and in your timing, then you are not prepared to hear from him.

Sometimes the cost of ignoring God's voice extends to those around you. If you are not in the habit of regularly communing with God, when you need to hear God's voice, you will be disoriented to it. If you never take time to read your Bible or to pray, you will be caught off guard when your children need your help in an important life decision. Such unfamiliarity can have tragic consequences. As Jim Elliot observed, "He will not reveal his will by fires or earthquakes but by that quiet dwelling in his presence which sons soon learn to interpret in their lives."[6]

The Bible explicitly encourages us to surround ourselves with godly counselors, yet many people are still determined to go solo and seek God's will without ever consulting others (Prov. 11:14; 15:22). These loners struggle to hear God's voice because they cut themselves off from God's people, through whom he often chooses to speak. God has provided the perfect forum for Christians to interact, the local church. Those people truly wanting to hear from God will make use of this provision and put themselves in various settings such as in Bible studies and accountability groups where they can experience God speaking to them through fellow believers.

Some people miss God's voice because they lack a healthy fear of God. They don't revere God as his Word says they should. Proverbs 1:7 admonishes, "The fear of the *Lord* is the beginning of knowledge." While you would not necessarily expect non-Christians to fear God, the astounding fact is that Christians seem to have no more fear of God than their unbelieving friends. Those who do not fear God tend to treat his word casually and carelessly (Jer. 5:22–25). Such people are more likely to argue with God when he says something they don't like. They are more likely to make excuses for not responding to what God said. On the other hand, the person who reveres God understands that "it is a terrifying thing to fall into the hands of the living God!" (Heb. 10:31 HCSB).

Conclusion

The world is abuzz with voices all clamoring for your response. This is a dangerous environment for someone who is incapable of distinguishing between God's voice and the competing voices of self, Satan, and the world. Learning to unmistakably recognize God's voice is too critical a matter to neglect. Take time to evaluate how well you recognize when God is speaking. Settle it once and for all that above everything else you will come to know clearly when God is speaking to you. Are there voices you have been listening to that you know are questionable? Are you uneasy about a message you are presently receiving? Check it out! Don't be hasty to move forward until you are satisfied you are responding to God. Spend time with God. Learn to recognize his voice. It will be the most important thing you do.

Questions for Reflection

1. Are you confident you will recognize God's voice when he speaks to you?

2. What do you think God wants you to do so you can better recognize his voice when he speaks?

3. What other "voices" are presently clamoring for you to listen to them?

4. Has your life been diverted from God's best to merely good things?

5. Are you taking time to properly evaluate the messages you are receiving?

6. Do you regularly seek counsel from others about what you sense may be God's will for you?

7. Do you habitually test what you hear against the plumb line of God's Word?

A HISTORICAL VIEW
CHAPTER 10

God's Word is progressive; he builds on it by confirming today what he said yesterday. Scripture continually reminds us to regard carefully what God said in the past. The reason the Israelites fell so deeply into sin once they entered the promised land was because they forgot what God had done before: "All that generation also were gathered to their fathers; and there arose another generation after them who did not know the LORD, nor yet the work which He had done for Israel" (Judg. 2:10). Many centuries later the prophet Jeremiah exhorted, "Stand by the ways and see and ask for the ancient paths, where the good way is, and walk in it; and you will find rest for your souls" (Jer. 6:16).

God does not contradict himself. Nor does he make things up as he goes. He knows where he is going; in fact he's already there! Whatever God is doing today will be based on what he did yesterday. History is important. Whether it's the spiritual background of your family, your church, your organization, or your life personally, it's essential to know what God did in the past. This will help you determine if the word you receive today matches or contradicts God's activity to this point.

King David walked closely with God. His heart was like God's heart. God expressed his deep pleasure with David by promising: "But My lovingkindness shall not depart from him, as I took it away from Saul, whom I removed from before you. Your house and your kingdom shall endure before Me forever, your throne shall be established forever" (2 Sam. 7:15–16). Clearly David's descendents were to reap a blessing due to David's faithfulness. But in the very next generation there was trouble—

David's son Solomon did not walk with God as his father had done (1 Kings 11:4–8). God condemned Solomon's sin and determined to punish him. "Nevertheless," God said, "I will not do it in your days for the sake of your father David, but I will tear it out of the hand of your son. However, I will not tear away all the kingdom, but I will give one tribe to your son for the sake of My servant David and for the sake of Jerusalem which I have chosen" (1 Kings 11:12–13; 34–36). Solomon received an undeserved blessing because of his father, David. But Rehoboam lost most of his kingdom because of the sin of his father, Solomon. It is important to know what God said to the generation before yours! It is also important to understand what God promises you about your descendants. God may be setting some things in motion in your life that will reach completion later. Permit us to illustrate with a personal testimony from our family.

Our Family Tree

In our family there have been Christian ministers for centuries. In our family tree we discovered a Richard Blackerby who was a chaplain in England in the 1500s. During the days of Charles Spurgeon, a number of Blackabys were enrolled in Spurgeon's pastoral college. Henry once spoke at a church in Wales where four other Blackaby ministers had preached over the years. Henry's father was a lay church planter, and his wife's parents, Melvin and Carrie Wells, were missionaries in Zambia, Africa. We believe God made some promises to our ancestors from which the current generation is still reaping the spiritual benefits.

Every family has a history. As you study God's activity in your family's previous generations, you will better understand his work in your family now. Perhaps God is blessing your generation because of the faithfulness of your grandparents. Or, your current generation may be experiencing the inherited consequences of the sins of your ancestors.

An Example from the Past
(a personal example from Henry)

My father, Gerald Richard Blackaby, was a devout Christian as a young man. At a critical juncture in his life, he told his pastor he sensed God calling him into full-time Christian ministry. Tragically, his pastor scoffed at the notion and said he was far too talented to waste his life on the ministry! Rather, his minister encouraged him to enter the business world. Right or wrong, my sincere father yielded to the counsel of his pastor. Ultimately he became a bank manager for the Bank of Montreal in Canada. I don't know all God said to my dad as he sought to live his life in a way that would honor God. Whatever it was God promised my father, it is clear God gave him an inescapable passion for sharing the gospel and for building up the church.

Dad was constantly leading clients to the Lord. I remember him often bringing strangers home with him and saying, "I'd like to introduce you to a new believer in Jesus Christ. My friend here just prayed with me this afternoon to receive Christ!"

When my father was transferred to a branch in Prince Rupert, British Columbia, he began a small church that originally consisted solely of our little family. Dad served as the first pastor until someone could come full-time. Our family went to the same lake for a month of vacation each summer. During those weeks my father would lead a Bible study for the people in the area. To this day I run into people who tell me they became Christians as a result of those Bible studies.

It was a proud moment in my father's life when I was called into the Christian ministry. Although he was extremely ill, he journeyed to be with me when I was ordained and to attend my graduation from seminary. Dad was equally proud of my brother William. Just as my father had been, my brother Will was an active layman, committed to serving faithfully in his church. He ministered to thousands of families and young people as a youth sponsor and as a school guidance counselor.

My father always wanted a grandson. He was from the English tradition that there should be male heirs to carry on the family name. His name was incredibly important to him. He once gave me a poem about his name. He said he couldn't pass on much to his children in terms of wealth and possessions, but he had spent a lifetime investing in his godly name. Now he was passing it on to his children. He hoped we would continue to give integrity to the name of Blackaby as he had tried to do.

Richard was my father's first grandchild. We named him Gerald Richard, after my father. Dad died six months after Richard's birth. He never saw any of the other nine grandchildren that were to make up the next generation of Blackabys. As for me, Dad only knew I was the new pastor of a small church in a difficult suburb of San Francisco. I often wish my father could have seen how God chose to bless my life, leading me to serve as a pastor for thirty years, then allowing me to write books such as *Experiencing God*. I wish my father could have known my four sons and my daughter. All four of my sons are in full-time Christian service today, and my daughter is a career missionary in Europe.

My brother William had four children. His two sons, Rob and Pete, graduated from seminary and are both in full-time pastoral ministry. William's older daughter, Shirley, is married to a fine layman and she serves as the worship leader in her church. His younger daughter, Ruth, spent two years helping plant churches in Montreal. She is currently in seminary.

Now we are the grandfathers, and dad's great-grandchildren are approaching adulthood! Every one of them is actively involved in church, as much as their age permits. The teenagers serve on worship teams and go on mission trips. They all love the Lord and want to honor him with their lives.

If only dad could see us now! But I suspect in some ways maybe he did see. I have a feeling God said some things to my father and made some promises to him that God has faithfully carried out long after my father went to be with him. Many of the blessings my family and I have enjoyed can be explained in no other way except that God must be honoring the faithfulness of my mother and father. Surely this is why God ordained that the various generations of family members should talk with one another and rehearse what God has done in their midst (Deut. 6:4–9). I can imagine Isaac raising his children, Esau and Jacob, and having grandpa Abraham tell them the stories of how God walked with him and Sarah for so many years. As each new generation is informed of what God taught and promised their parents, they begin to know what they should expect.

It is good to know your family heritage. If you are the first generation to walk with God, then you are beginning a new heritage. Be sure you rehearse with your family what God has done in your life. A tradition that has developed in our family is for Henry to pass down his worn-out Bibles to his children. He's hard on Bibles! His kids discover all sorts of notes in the margins of his Bibles including dates when God spoke and what God said. Needless to say, these are treasures!

It is also good to study the history of God's activity in the church where you are a member. It may be the saints of previous generations faithfully walked with God in such a way that God continues to bless your church as a result. At times it is difficult to explain the vibrancy of some churches except that God is somehow pleased to bless them. Other churches seem to be constantly under a cloud. How do you study God's previous activity in your church? You search for prayers and commitments the people made to God. You seek to discover what the people sensed God saying to them. You talk with longtime godly members and ask them to tell you the story of your church. You take seriously what God has said to others in the body.

Christian organizations have a spiritual history, and so do nations. What was on the hearts of those people who started the organizations? For what purpose did the founding members believe God was leading them to establish the city or the nation? Why did they believe God led them to do what they did?

The writer of Hebrews devoted much space in his letter to a glorious accounting of the great saints of the faith. Notice how that chapter ends:

> And what more can I say? Time is too short for me to tell about Gideon, Barak, Samson, Jephtah, of David and Samuel and the prophets, who by faith conquered kingdoms, administered justice, obtained promises, shut the mouths of lions, quenched the raging fire, escaped the edge of the sword, gained strength after being weak, became mighty in battle, and put foreign armies to flight. Women received their dead raised to life again. Some men were tortured, not accepting release, so that they might gain a better resurrection, and others experienced mockings and scourgings, as well as bonds and imprisonment. They were stoned, they were sawed in two, they died by the sword, they wandered about in sheepskins, in goatskins, destitute, afflicted, and mistreated (Heb. 11:32–37 HCSB).

Each of these people had an amazing walk with God. They knew God so intimately they were willing to suffer anything for him. Significantly, the next chapter in Hebrews appeals to current Christians and begins, "Therefore, since we also have such a large cloud of witnesses surrounding us" (Heb. 12:1 HCSB). In other words, the generations are connected. Their faith affects our faith. What God said to them has ramifications for us.

God's Promise
(a personal testimony by Henry)

While I was the pastor of a fine church in the greater Los Angeles area, God clearly and unmistakably instructed me to return to my native country of Canada. I went to a small church in the prairie city of Saskatoon and asked the Lord what he wanted to do through me there. God linked my life with Jack Conner, who became the first mission pastor from our church. I remember going into a remote area in northern Canada and praying with Jack about God's will for reaching Canada. God revealed to us that he wanted to start a thousand churches through our little group of churches. At the time the number seemed absurd. We had fewer than sixty small churches with few resources. It was truly a heavenly vision!

At that time Jack and I did all we knew to do. We sensed if Canada were to be evangelized, we would need to reach university students who could devote their lives as Christian leaders to their nation. We established a small Bible college, the Canadian Baptist Theological College. The first semester we had two full-time students! Over the next ten years more than four hundred students took classes in our makeshift school. We also started more than three dozen mission churches, one five hundred miles away. Still, it seemed so little in light of what God had told us he wanted to do. When God called Jack and me to other assignments in Canada, the new leadership disbanded the school, and much of the mission work was shut down. I wondered why this was happening. We had sensed so clearly that God wanted to do so much through our churches and our school.

Time has a wonderful way of making things clear! In 1985, the Canadian churches established a national convention. The first thing the convention did was to begin a full-fledged seminary to train the Canadian church leaders of the future. To my great delight, in 1993, the seminary called my oldest son Richard to serve as its president. As I preached at his installation service, God reminded me of what he had told me two decades earlier. His Word was still true, and he was continuing to work out his purposes through my children.

The national convention called a new national leader in 1998—Gerry Taillon. I had baptized Gerry. He had been a student at the little college where Jack and I shared the vision of starting a thousand churches. Gerry called a meeting of all the leaders of the convention, now consisting of 140 churches. As leaders prayed, they sensed God telling them he wanted them to plant a thousand new churches over the next twenty years. When I heard that, I was joyfully reminded that God's Word never returns to him empty (Isa. 55:10–11).

Jack and I had not orchestrated our plans on anyone. Rather, God—who had placed a thousand churches on our hearts—was now laying that same burden on the hearts of the next generation of leaders. It is imperative that organizations and churches carefully review what God has said to earlier generations. God is consistent in what he says. What he does in this generation will be built on what he promised the previous generation.

Responding to Job Opportunities

Both of us have had churches approach us, asking us to be their pastor. These churches have been wonderful places of ministry and would have provided tremendous opportunities for serving the Lord. However, we knew they did not match what God had already told us we were to do. We sensed these churches believed we were the kind of person they were looking for in a pastor, but we were not the specific person God had for them. As we walked daily with our Lord, the Holy Spirit regularly affirmed that we were right where he wanted us to be. As the Spirit guided us, we sensed God giving us many new opportunities to serve him where we were. Under such conditions, when invitations came along, we did not need weeks to pray and fast over how to respond. Though there are many marvelous places to serve the Lord, they are not the place God has called us to serve him. To accept one of these offers would mean leaving unfinished much of what God had told us he wanted to do where we are. God doesn't leave loose ends when he guides people.

God Provides Spiritual Markers

A spiritual marker is an event in your life that God has interpreted for you. Whenever God allows an event to take place in your life, whether a failure or a success, allow God to interpret the event for you. You need to do something to remember and rehearse what God taught you through that circumstance. To fail to process an event in your life is to waste a precious opportunity. The Bible records that men and women took care to establish a remembrance when they had an encounter with God.

Often this involved building a stone altar. This took time and effort, but stone altars were relatively permanent. Some of the patriarchs could trace their pilgrimage with God through a series of altars they built during their lives.

After Noah survived the great flood, the first thing he did was build an altar (Gen. 9:20). On several occasions when Abraham had an encounter with God, he built an altar to remember the experience (Gen. 12:8; 13:4; 22:9). For example, when God provided a ram to take Isaac's place as a sacrifice, Abraham built an altar and named it, "Jehovah-Jireh," which means "the LORD will provide" (Gen. 22:14). Abraham had personally experienced God's provision. Now he had a permanent reminder that God provides for his every need. While Isaac was at Beersheba, God appeared to him with a promise: "I am the God of your father Abraham; do not fear, for I am with you. I will bless you, and multiply your descendents, for the sake of My servant Abraham" (Gen. 26:24). Isaac built an altar and sought the Lord at that place. God appeared to Jacob at Bethel. Then God instructed him to build an altar to remind him of the promise God had made to him (Gen. 28:10–22; 35:1–7).

After God helped the Israelites defeat the Amalekites, Moses built an altar and named it, "The Lord is My banner" to remind them that it was God who went out to battle on their behalf (Exod. 17:15). When God miraculously parted the waters of the Jordan River so the Israelites could enter the promised land, God instructed Joshua to construct a monument of stones to remind the following generations what God had done for them (Josh. 4:1–7).

People have a troubling tendency to quickly forget even the greatest works of God. Therefore, God placed prominent reminders of his activity where the people could not fail to see them. When an angel came to Gideon and told him he was to deliver his people from the oppression of the Midianites, Gideon responded by building an altar. He called it "the Lord is peace" (Judg. 6:24). When God gave the Israelites a victory over the Philistines, Samuel erected a stone and called it "Ebenezer," meaning "The Stone of Help," to remind the people of God's powerful deliverance

(1 Sam. 7:12). When God punished the nation of Israel for King David's sin, David erected an altar to the Lord that brought God's wrath to an end (2 Sam. 24:18–25).

A clear biblical pattern can be seen wherein God instructed people to commemorate their encounters with him in a tangible way. At times they would erect an altar. Sometimes they would hold a special feast, such as the Passover, to remind them of God's miraculous deliverance. Physical markers such as circumcision were intended to remind the people of God's promise to them. At other times the people would be exhorted to remember what God had done through stories told to successive generations. When times grew difficult or confusing, the Israelites could rehearse all God had done and said to them thus far. This gave them a clear sense of purpose and direction for the present.

After Christ came, people no longer built physical altars when they encountered God, but they constructed spiritual markers all the same. If you asked Peter why he was devoting himself to the cause of Christ, he would have had numerous spiritual markers to review. He most certainly would have recalled the day Jesus passed by his fishing boat and said, "Come follow me." Peter might recall the day Jesus renamed him Peter and tell you the significance of the name change. He would probably mention the day he walked on water, albeit briefly, and how Jesus saved him when his faith wavered. Peter's recollections might include the night he saw Jesus transfigured on the mountain and the time Jesus humbled himself and washed Peter's feet. Peter might also recount his troubling time when he failed Jesus and how Jesus forgave him. If Peter ever wanted to remember how he got where he was, all he had to do was review the great moments he had experienced with Christ when his Lord guided him and taught him about himself.

Choosing between Good and Best

When you come to a crossroads and need to decide which path to take, your problem is not always choosing between good and bad options. Often the choice is between good and best. In such times a "good" opportunity may not take you in the same direction God has been leading you thus far. This is where spiritual markers can help. God does not lead you partially down one path, then have you change directions several times. You may not always be sure where God will lead you in the future, but as you reexamine the path you have already traveled, you can detect a purposefulness about the way God has guided you. That's why it is important to mark down every time you know God has spoken to you. Then the next time you sense God guiding you in a decision, you can measure what you are hearing against his last word to you. God will not contradict himself. He will not lead you to do something that cancels what he asked you to do previously. God's revelations to you will always build on what he already told you.

Understanding this truth is critical as you make important life decisions. For example, God may have given you a strong passion for missions when you were young. Perhaps you were fascinated by international missions as a child and loved to hear visiting missionaries tell their stories in your church. Then at youth camp God spoke powerfully to you about his call on your life. At camp you dedicated your life to serving God on the mission field. Next God led you to choose a college where you could prepare yourself to be a missionary. You may have gone on several mission trips with your college group, and each time God increased your passion to be a missionary. It could be that God continually drew your attention to a particular place in the world. He may have linked your life with people of that nationality who have immigrated to your country. As you read your Bible you were increasingly compelled to spread the gospel. When you prayed, God sensitized your heart for those people in the world who had no access to the gospel. Then you met someone. You began to develop feelings for this person and to consider the possibility of marriage. There is just one problem: your sweetheart has no interest in missions and has no plans to ever live in a foreign country. You're in a heart-wrenching position. You care very much for this person, yet you know the marriage would cancel what God has been saying to you since you were a child. This is a time to carefully review your spiritual markers!

Some who have experienced this dilemma have concluded: "God wouldn't have allowed me to fall in love if he did not want us to get married!" or, "I can still be a missionary but not leave my country!" or, "I guess God has changed his plans for my life." The first claim relies totally upon feelings, which can be incredibly deceptive. If there is ever a time to rely on the objective reality of spiritual markers, it is when strong emotion is involved. The second response disregards the specific nature by which God has led thus far. And finally, God is not arbitrary with people's lives. He is thorough and purposeful. He does not suddenly change his mind. If he has consistently led you for years in one direction and has prepared you for a task, he will not abandon that will at the first obstacle.

When you face a major decision, review the spiritual markers of your life. Spiritual markers identify times of transition, decision, or direction when you know God clearly guided you. When you face a new decision about God's direction, rehearse those spiritual markers. Don't take another step until you have fully reviewed God's previous activity in your life. This will give you a better perspective. As you examine the options before you, look to see which is most consistent with what God has already been doing in your life. An opportunity may clearly lead you in a direction consistent with God's leading thus far. Or it may go against everything God has said until now. If circumstances do not align with what God has said to you through the Bible, through prayer, and through other believers, hold off on your decision. Continue to pray and watch until God gives you a clear revelation of his will.

There are many ways to denote spiritual markers in your life. One method is to write the date and a brief notation beside verses in your Bible as God speaks to you through them. For example, you might be preparing to undertake a challenge that scares you to death. It might be something you have never done before. As you read the Bible, the Holy Spirit might direct your attention to Isaiah 41:10: "Do not fear, for I am with you; do not anxiously look about you, for I am your God. I will strengthen you, surely I will help you, surely I will uphold you with My righteous right hand." At that moment, the Spirit may impress this verse so powerfully upon you that you know God is speaking these words of comfort directly to you. Write the date down beside the verse so when times become difficult, you can look back in your Bible and remember the day God made this promise.

Journaling is another effective way to keep track of spiritual markers. Each day as you spend time with your Lord, write down what you sense God saying. Remember, anything Almighty God says is important! If God says something to you, it's worth writing down. At the time you might not understand why God is speaking to you about a particular matter. However, later, when you suddenly face an unexpected situation, you might be surprised as you review in your journal how God prepared you in advance for that event.

There are innumerable creative ways to commemorate times when God speaks to you. If God assured you he would provide for your financial needs, you might frame a dollar bill with the date God spoke and a Scripture he used (such as Phil. 4:13), to assure you of his care for you. God may lead people to write notes of encouragement to you at key times in your life. God may have used those notes to confirm the direction you were going in your life. Keep a special file of correspondence God has used to speak to you over the years. You might even frame special letters that God used in a powerful way to speak to you. If a particular verse has guided you and your family, buy a piece of artwork that reminds you of the event and have the Scripture reference inscribed on it. Then your children will have a visible daily reminder of God's personal caring guidance.

Lessons from Childhood
(a personal testimony from Richard)

God may give you a special word about one of your children. When I was born, God assured my parents he would one day use my life in Christian ministry. When

I was four years old, our family visited a large seminary. One of the adults took a picture of me as I stood beneath the sign at the school's entrance. My parents wrote "future student" at the bottom of the picture and saved it as a reminder of God's promise. Many years later, after I had earned two degrees from that school, I stumbled upon that picture with the inscription at the bottom. It was extremely humbling to realize my life had fulfilled a promise God had given my parents years earlier.

Spiritual markers provide a history of how God has led you, your church, or your organization. Whenever God speaks, his Word becomes a north star for your life. It doesn't change. It is sure. As you accumulate a record of God speaking to you over the years, you will have a clear picture of where God has led you. This will give you powerful assurance as God continues to lead you in the future.

Summary

God does not speak in a vacuum. What he says today will fit perfectly with what he said yesterday. One of the best ways to ensure you are hearing God correctly is to keep a record of what you clearly heard him say before. Take time to review what you know God has already told you. It will help you determine where he is leading your life today.

Questions for Reflection

1. Have you discovered things God said to your family in previous generations? If so, what were they?

2. Are you presently facing a decision? If so, how does your possible new direction fit with what God has been doing in your life thus far?

3. How do you build spiritual markers for your life? How do you rehearse them?

LEARNING TO RESPOND TO GOD'S VOICE

CHAPTER 11

Wipe Your Nose!
(a personal example from Richard)

I have the humbling privilege of speaking in many different churches and conferences. The major drawback to my travel is that my wife and children are generally unable to accompany me. To my great delight a pastor friend from Edmonton, a three-hour drive north of where I live, called to ask if my wife Lisa and I could lead his church in a marriage enrichment weekend. I was thrilled with the prospect of being able to minister alongside my wife, and I readily agreed. There was just one problem. Even though my wife is a gifted speaker, she does not enjoy public speaking. When I told her I had agreed for the two of us to lead the conference, she was shocked. "You agreed I would do what?! Why didn't you ask me first?" I could see this was heading toward a disagreement, a bad sign for a couple about to lead a marriage enrichment weekend. I hastily promised to help her in any way she needed. I would even write her script for her.

The first session was on Friday evening. As I expected, Lisa did a fantastic job. Everyone loved her! The people's warm response boosted her confidence, so I knew we would have a great second session Saturday morning. The Saturday morning program opened with another couple performing a humorous skit on marriage.

As I watched, I suddenly had an allergy attack. I have several allergies but my worst allergy is to mornings. For some reason I get a runny nose and a sneezing attack at the start of every day. I whispered to Lisa, "Do you have a Kleenex?" She frantically searched through her purse and finally discovered a thin fragment of tissue. I hurriedly dabbed at my nose as I prepared to get up and speak.

Somehow in the process, a small piece of tissue became attached to the end of my nose! As I stood before the congregation to speak, the fragment fluttered in the breeze every time I exhaled! I was busy expounding truth, and I didn't notice, but Lisa, who was standing next to me, did. She was mortified! Out of the corner of her mouth, Lisa discreetly whispered, "Wipe your nose!" I didn't understand what she said. Quite honestly, I was slightly annoyed that she would try to cue me in on what I should be doing. I thought to myself, *One night's success and she thinks she can just walk up and start telling me what to say! Obviously she has forgotten who the professional speaker is and who is the rank amateur!* I ignored her and kept talking. The Kleenex kept flapping.

Lisa was becoming more frustrated with me, so she whispered more urgently, "Wipe your nose!" I still did not understand what she said. I assumed she was worried I would leave something out of my presentation. I thought, *If she would just quit interrupting and watch carefully, she could learn much from the master!* I continued.

Meanwhile, Lisa spotted a blue dry-erase marker on the podium in front of us. I had placed a stack of handouts on the podium and on the top copy she scrawled, "WIPE YOUR NOSE!" then circled it. At this point I was getting extremely frustrated with my wife. She seemed intent on distracting me. However, knowing I was about to hand out the survey for the couples to fill in, I hurried to finish my presentation. At the same time I thought, *What a great teachable moment!* The mark of great public speakers is that they rarely, if ever, look down at their notes! So I modeled constant eye contact with my audience, and I never looked at what she had written.

I reached down and picked up the top copy of the handout (ironically it was about "communication in marriage"!). Still not looking at it, I held it up for everyone to see. I said, "Everyone, your handout will look just like this." Desperately, Lisa snatched the sheet from my hand. By this point I was getting downright perturbed! When the couples were finally working on the handouts, I turned to Lisa and hissed, "*What* is your problem?!" She pointed to the handout on which she had written her note, "Read it!" she moaned. I picked up her note and read the message. "Oh no!" I cried as I frantically, and finally, wiped my nose!

As I reflected on what I had done, I was disappointed in myself. No one in all the world loves me more than Lisa. No one is more interested in my success. Yet when she saw me in trouble and wanted to help, she could not get my attention. Is that what it is like for God? When he sees things in my life that need adjusting, does he have as much trouble getting my attention? When he alerts me to my bad attitudes and destructive habits, how receptive am I to his loving, corrective voice?

The wonderful news of the gospel is that God wants such a close relationship with us in the first place. Jesus died on a cross to secure this privilege for us. The apostle Paul declared: "So then you are no longer foreigners and strangers, but fellow citizens with the saints, and members of God's household" (Eph. 2:19). With the gift of hearing God speak to us comes the responsibility of obeying what he says.

In many ways the Christian life parallels the growth of a person from birth to adulthood. Babies learn early to recognize their parents' voices, but responding to what they hear is another matter. Parents devote years to teaching their children the importance of obedience.

The Tragedy of Disobedience
(a personal example from Henry)

The first funeral I ever conducted was for a beautiful three-year-old girl. I remember her birth. She was the first child born to a couple in our church. She was also the first grandchild in their extended family. Unfortunately, though, she was spoiled. While visiting the child's home one day, I observed that she loved to ignore her parents' instructions. When they told her to come, she would go.

When they told her to sit down, she would stand up. Her parents found her behavior cute, and they would usually laugh heartily at her antics.

One day the gate in their front yard was inadvertently left open. The parents saw their little girl escaping out of the yard and proceeding toward the road. To their horror a car was racing down the street. Their daughter was running out between two parked cars into the traffic. They both screamed at their little girl to stop and turn back. The girl paused for a second, looked back at her parents, then gleefully laughed as she turned and ran directly into the path of the oncoming car. The car struck her violently, critically injuring her. The horror-struck parents rushed their little girl to the hospital, but she died from her injuries. I was in the hospital room when the parents realized their only daughter had died. The outpouring of grief at the funeral was absolutely heart-wrenching. That was the first funeral I ever conducted, and it haunts me to this day.

This was a profound lesson for me, a young pastor, as I witnessed firsthand the enormous grief that came because a child was not disciplined to heed her parents' voices. I realized it was imperative that I teach God's people not only to recognize his voice but also immediately to obey his voice when they heard it. Deuteronomy 30:19–20 says, "I call heaven and earth to witness against you today, that I have set before you life and death, the blessing and the curse. So choose life in order that you may live, you and your descendants, by loving the LORD your God, by obeying his voice, and by holding fast to him; for this is your life."

To know the voice of God, and to obey him, is life. This truth applies not only to us but also to our families. We have both taken this word from God seriously, and we have earnestly sought to help each of our children know the voice of God when he is speaking to them. It is their life!

Develop Your Relationship

How, then, does one learn not only to recognize the Lord's voice but also to respond in a way that pleases him?

The Bible is all about God's relationship with his people. Christianity is a relationship with the person Jesus Christ. The closer the relationship, the better the communication. Observe a man and woman who have been married for fifty years and compare their communication skills with those of a newlywed couple. Both couples genuinely love each other, but the younger couple is disadvantaged in their communication because they still have much to learn about each other. A young husband can make a casual comment and be surprised to find his wife hugging him and thanking him for being so thoughtful. Shortly afterward a second casual comment can cause hurt feelings, even tears. He soon realizes there is much about his life partner he has yet to understand! The older couple, on the other hand, have walked together through life. They can communicate all sorts of information with a glance. One raised eyebrow can telegraph all the other needs to know.

As you spend time with Jesus, you will gradually come to recognize his voice more readily than you did at first. You will more easily discern what he is saying because you know his character better. You won't be fooled by other voices because you know your Lord's voice so well.

Abraham Walked with God

The Bible tells of many people who came to know and trust God more deeply over time. Abraham was not a model of faith when he began his pilgrimage with God, but he is described in the New Testament as a "friend of God" (James 2:21–23). His sturdy faith took a lifetime to develop. At each stage of his life, Abraham learned more about God. It took more than forty years before Abraham knew God well enough to be entrusted with his most difficult assignment (Gen. 40:1–3). During those forty years, Abraham learned to recognize God's voice. He came to know God's nature. Through experience he came to know God's love, his faithfulness, his power, and his wisdom. The better Abraham knew God, the more confident he became in responding to God's voice, even when it meant taking enormous steps of faith.

Moses Depended on God's Voice

Knowing and following God's voice has added implications when you are a leader. Moses had to know God's voice if he was going to lead the children of Israel successfully. A lot of people depended on him; one mistake could cost thousands of Israelites their lives. Every decision was pivotal. Moses had to know whether the voice he was hearing was from God. Making the correct distinction affected not only his life but also the lives of his entire nation.

Jesus and the Twelve

One of the hardest truths for Christians to comprehend is the reality that Almighty God wants a personal relationship with us. Yet the pattern of Scripture is that God not only desires such a relationship, but he also continually takes the initiative to draw us to himself. Psalm 23 paints the beautiful picture of what our relationship to God is to be like. If you ever doubt the tender intimacy that is possible in your relationship with your Lord, read this psalm again. Psalm 23 reveals volumes about God's relationship with his people.

The disciples came to know Jesus as their Good Shepherd. The more time they spent with him the more they knew his nature. They learned he was trustworthy and gentle (John 10:3–4, 27). They came to understand that he would lay his life down for them. They couldn't see what lay ahead for their lives, but it was enough that their Shepherd could.

As he did with Abraham, Moses, the disciples, and countless others, God will pursue a relationship with you. It's what he wants. How will you respond? Will you take time to read and study your Bible so God can teach you about his nature and his ways? Will you begin each day by focusing on the Lord and preparing your heart for whatever he might say to you throughout the day? Will you be alert to a word from God? (Matt. 13:9; 11:15).

When God speaks to you, write it down in a journal so you can refer back to it as you follow him. Be aware that

God often speaks to people in the stillness of the night. Pay attention when the Holy Spirit gently whispers to you. Be mindful that God often chooses to communicate his most profound truths in the midst of a crisis. Don't become preoccupied during turbulent moments by fixing your gaze on the circumstances. Rather, be watchful lest you miss a divine visitation during those tumultuous moments (Mark 6:47–52). There is no shortcut to intimacy with God. It takes time and many experiences with him as he teaches you and guides you in his ways (Ps. 25).

Seek to Understand God's Ways

God's people must heed his words: "For My thoughts are not your thoughts, nor are your ways My ways. . . . For as the heavens are higher than the earth, so are My ways higher than your ways and My thoughts than your thoughts" (Isa. 55:8–9). One reason God's people miss hearing him speak is their disorientation to his ways. Sometimes Christians expect God to do one thing, and when he does another, they miss him. The truth is, God is not our servant. He does not speak to us on demand. He communicates on his terms, in his timing, in his way.

God's supreme way for Jesus and his disciples was the way of the cross. Jesus understood this; the disciples did not. Satan sought to have Jesus circumvent the cross, but Jesus knew God's way, so he could immediately detect a counterfeit plan. Paul, too, understood that God's way is the way of the cross. Paul said the world regarded the cross as foolishness, but for God it was the life-giving power of salvation (1 Cor. 1:18). Therefore, Paul was not surprised when the risen Christ commanded him to take up his cross as well (1 Cor. 2:2; Gal. 6:14).

The more you understand God's ways, the more easily you will identify his words, and the better you'll know how to respond. For example, you may be in a business meeting in your church and become frustrated with some belligerent church members. You may want to express your frustration and put the obnoxious brethren in their place. However, you know God's way is to build up the body, not to divide it and tear it down (Rom. 14:19). That truth tells you all you need to know about your urge to lash out at those who frustrate you.

You become aware of a single mother who is struggling to make ends meet while raising her children. You know God has a special place in his heart for the widow and the orphan (Ps. 10:14; James 1:27). You know in your heart God wants you to help somehow, so you seek the Lord. As you pray, God leads you to a specific, practical way to assist the family.

You become involved in conversation with an unbelieving colleague at work. As she begins to voice questions about spiritual matters, you know God wants every person to have eternal life (John 3:16). You don't need to spend weeks in fervent prayer to determine whether God wants you to share your faith. As you quietly pray for direction, the Holy Spirit confirms he is initiating this opportunity, and you share the good news of the gospel with her. Understanding the ways of God allows you to anticipate what God will say, so you are prepared to receive the word that comes from the Lord.

Prepare Your Heart
One Couple, Two Responses
(a personal example from Richard)

While I was preaching a message one Sunday, I was intrigued by the diverse responses I observed in the congregation. Some were studiously taking notes. Others stared off into space. During an altar call at the close of the service, several people came to pray at the front of the church. As they wept tears of conviction in response to God's Word, others took the opportunity to exit quickly and beat the traffic out of the church parking lot!

As I stood at the back of the auditorium shaking hands with people, a middle-aged couple approached me. The husband was obviously deeply moved. With great emotion he took my hand in his, looked me in the eye, and said, "God gave you that sermon just for me!"

A puzzled look came over his wife's face. After a moment she confessed, "I can't remember what you just preached!" The sermon was less than five minutes old, and she could not recall a single thing I had said! A man and his wife sat next to each other in the same auditorium, listening to the same sermon at the same time. Yet one was moved to tears, and the other was bored to tears.

At the time I was puzzled that people could respond so differently. I assumed if I preached a "good" sermon, everyone would like it; and if I preached a "bad" sermon, people would politely ask me about the weather. However, I discovered that whenever God's Word is preached, some will be profoundly impacted while others will remain unaffected. It has little to do with the style or delivery of the preacher. It has much to do with the condition of the listener's heart.

There is no better way you can be ready to follow God's voice than to cultivate your heart. Jesus' parable of the four soils outlines the relationship between God's Word and the heart condition of those who hear it (Matt. 13:5–23). People whose hearts are hardened will reject the word outright. This is why the prophets urged people to "break up the fallow ground" of their hearts so they could receive God's Word (Jer. 4:3; Hos. 10:12). Those with shallow hearts will look for a "quick fix" from God's Word, but they will lack the depth to persevere until they receive the entire message God has for them. Such people will never experience the fulfillment of a close walk with God.

Then there are the distracted people. They are the ones who cannot seem to focus on a word from God. Their mind wanders during prayer, and they use the sermon time to mentally plan their agenda for the coming week. The danger for the preoccupied heart is its tendency to drift toward other gods (Deut. 30:17). God's Word says, "Take to your heart all the words with which I am warning you today, . . . for it is not an idle word for you; indeed it is your life" (Deut. 32:46–47).

The fact is, everyone has the capacity to hear from God and to respond to what he says (Matt. 13:16). It's all a matter of readiness and willingness. Jonathan Edwards is considered by many to have been the most brilliant person in America during the eighteenth century. He was greatly used by God during the First Great Awakening. Yet when Edwards invited George Whitefield to preach at his church, Edwards openly wept as he listened to the sermon. Whitefield was not the scholar Edwards was, but Edwards's heart was tender to a word from God. D. L. Moody was one of the most powerful preachers of his era. Until Billy Graham, no one had preached to more people than Moody. Yet when Moody attended religious conferences, he would sit near the front of the auditorium and diligently take notes of other preachers' sermons. He did not want to miss a word God might have for him through his fellow preachers. The one characteristic common to those whom God has used mightily has been a tender heart toward God.

Learn to Concentrate

Part of preparing your heart for God's Word is to eliminate distractions. This discipline is difficult for most people. Life can be incredibly busy. But with a determined effort you can make a deliberate choice to concentrate on your Lord and what he has to say to you. Jesus put it this way: "The eye is the lamp of the body; so then if your eye is clear, your whole body will be full of light. But if your eye is bad, your whole body will be full of darkness. If then the light that is in you is darkness, how great is the darkness!" (Matt. 6:22–23).

Have you ever tried to read when there is some dust or a small particle in your eye? Even though the speck is tiny, you can be totally distracted and unable to concentrate on what you are reading. Only after you've removed the offensive particle are you free to resume reading. When you have a healthy relationship with God, it is not difficult to focus on him. When there is sin in your life, however, focusing on God's Word can be difficult. The bombardment of media images that comes with modern life can make it difficult to seek God's guidance. Exposing your mind to a graphic image on television can distract you for days and even weeks afterward. It takes deliberate, concentrated effort to steer your attention away from the cacophony of voices competing with God for your attention.

The prophet Isaiah expressed the joy of an undistracted relationship with God: "The Lord God . . . awakens Me morning by morning, He awakens my ear to listen as a disciple. The Lord GOD has opened my ear; and I was not disobedient nor did I turn back" (Isa. 50:4–5). You can enjoy the same experience. It is helpful to read Psalm 119 regularly. That great psalm teaches the benefits of concentrating on God's Word, which gives light to our path, keeps us from sin, gives us sound counsel, corrects our folly, and guides us in every area of life.

There is a broader significance in focusing on God's Word. In doing so, you will hear things that will affect not only your life but many others as well.

Jesus' prayer for his disciples reveals why he was so diligent to hear and respond to everything his heavenly Father said. Jesus prayed: "Sanctify them by the truth; Your word is truth. Just as You sent Me into the world, I also have sent them into the world. I sanctify Myself for them, so they also may be sanctified by the truth" (John 17:17–19 HCSB). If Jesus missed what his Father said, there would have been dire repercussions not only for him but for his followers. They depended on Jesus knowing the Father's will. For Jesus to be daydreaming or preoccupied when his Father sought to prepare him for what was coming would have been disastrous.

In 1954, James Stewart was traveling by car to Chattanooga, Tennessee, to speak at a meeting. As he drove, he suddenly became deeply burdened for his native land of Scotland. The Holy Spirit laid such an intense concern on him that he felt compelled to pull over to the roadside and go into the woods to pray. Stewart had no idea how long he remained in the woods interceding for Scotland, but when he returned to his journey, he knew God had given him a new assignment. The confirmation of that assignment was soon to follow.

After he spoke at the meeting in Chattanooga, a man by the name of McKay approached him. "Why do you not go home and preach the gospel there?" he asked in a Scottish burr. McKay was also a native of Scotland. He, too, had recently become strongly burdened for his homeland. McKay offered to financially support Stewart's efforts if he were to go to Scotland.[1]

Soon after, Stewart received a letter from an elderly English gentleman. He lived in the very region of Scotland for which Stewart had been praying. The man wrote: "I am praying that the Lord will send you back to these parts with the gospel. I am willing to do all I can to help."[2]

Stewart did return to Scotland, and God began to mobilize others to assist him in the work. One young American missionary who came to work with Stewart eventually became his son-in-law. God did an enormous work through Stewart's life and through his family. It all began when he was sensitive to God's voice as he drove his car. Because he was alert to God's voice, Stewart could make the clear connection between what God said to him in prayer and what he heard next through other believers. The result impacted thousands of lives.

For you to miss what God is saying will affect more people than you know. Your spouse and children need you to follow the Holy Spirit's guidance as you relate to them in your home. Your friends and fellow church members will go lacking if you are not the instrument of grace to them God wants you to be. When a voice is broadcast over a public-address system, or a newscaster appears on the television screen to deliver a special news bulletin, people stop what they are doing to hear the important announcement. How much more critical to stop whatever you are doing when God speaks to you and pay attention so you don't miss anything he says. Robert Murray M'Cheyne's challenge to pastors is relevant to Christians everywhere: "Above all things, cultivate your own spirit. A word spoken by you when your conscience is clear, and your heart full of God's Spirit, is worth ten thousand words spoken in unbelief and sin."[3]

Discipline yourself to concentrate. Set aside a time each day that you can devote purely to seeking the Lord. For many people, the early part of the day is the best time to meet with God. Oswald Chambers gave this counsel to those who struggled to rise early to meet with God: "Get out of bed first and think about it later."[4] In one of his spiritual journals, Robert Murray M'Cheyne wrote: "Rose early to seek God, and found him whom my soul loveth. Who would not rise early to meet such company?"[5] Some people find it difficult to seize much time in the mornings because so much work cries out to be done. They find the quiet of the evening affords fewer distractions. Regardless of the time that works best for you, the important thing is to be purposeful in setting it aside.

Likewise it is important to find a room or a private place for prayer and Bible study. If you are a business-person, it may be hard to concentrate on the Lord while you sit at your desk in your office. Too many work-related tasks stare you in the face for you to focus on God. If you spend time with the Lord in your home, you may want to avoid a place like the kitchen where dirty dishes and other unfinished projects beckon you to complete them first.

If you find yourself continually distracted, there are other things you can do. It might be that you don't get enough rest to enable you to concentrate on anything. If you have a quiet time in the early morning, you may find it impossible to focus on the Lord for long if you stayed up late watching television the previous night. Focusing on the Lord is easier with preparation. Some people concentrate more effectively with music playing softly. Others need absolute silence. Be diligent to create an atmosphere conducive to optimum concentration. At times you will not be able to escape to a place of solitude, yet you will still need to focus on the Lord. That is when spiritual concentration is particularly important.

Occasionally, if possible, set aside a time for prolonged meditation on God's Word. Escape for the morning, the afternoon, or the entire day to a peaceful venue and spend uninterrupted time seeking the mind of God. Richard has a habit of spending one day a month at a local retreat center. There he can pull out of the rat race, if only temporarily, and devote unhurried time with the Lord. It is always a sweet time of communion with God. We highly recommend it.

To stay focused on the Lord, you have to discipline your mind, which naturally wants to dart from one thing to the next. When you find your thoughts beginning to drift away from the Lord, make a conscious effort to refocus on him. You can train your mind just as you train the rest of your body to submit to your will. You do not have to be subject to the whims of mental distraction. You can teach your mind to stay focused on the same subject for an extended period of time.

Once you train your mind to focus on the Lord, any location can become a place of worship. Even in the midst of a turbulent, chaotic day, you can focus on the Lord and hear his soothing voice. Once you learn to do this, you will be prepared to learn deeper truths about God.

Henry Alline learned to focus on the Lord even in extremely adverse circumstances. A revival preacher in Nova Scotia during the eighteenth century, Alline rode on horseback from town to town preaching the gospel. He was not always well received. Sometimes he was mocked and ridiculed. He was harassed by angry thugs. People sought to publicly discredit him. Many a night he was left to fend for himself in the cold, damp outdoors with no place of shelter. He would often be soaked to the skin by a storm or chilled to the bone by the penetrating winter winds. Yet Alline managed to keep his focus on his Lord. He noted, "God's presence begins my joy and makes my heaven."[6] Alline's journal expresses his ability to experience God's presence even under the most contrary conditions:

> I rode through the woods about 50 miles to where it was inhabited. I was then in a strange place, where I had never been before; but O the Lord remembered his poor unworthy servant, and gave me many blessed moments when riding alone/ O the worth of an invisible, kind, infinite and unchangeable friend. . . . I traveled to Barrington, and, indeed there was nothing but the joys of that that the world cannot give or take away, could make me happy, in such a walk. When much worried with the walking and not a dry thread about me, and my boots all the way full of water. O my God what shall I render for thy goodness?[7]

There are some truths God reveals only as you spend prolonged, focused time in his presence. The reason many
Christians have a shallow understanding of God is they
have never developed the ability to stay in God's presence
for a protracted period of time to focus on him in the
midst of their busy lives.

Develop Habitual Obedience

James Chalmers, the great missionary martyr to the
savage cannibals of New Guinea, once said, "Let us be men
with men, but always children before God."[8] Obedience is
the key to experiencing God. Jesus said the way we
respond to God's Word is a direct reflection of our love for
him (John 14:15). Jesus said, "If you know these things,
you are blessed if you do them" (John 13:17 HCSB). The
blessing comes not in the hearing but in the doing. One of
the most disturbing questions Jesus asks is, "Why do you
call me 'Lord, Lord,' and don't do the things I say?" (Luke
6:46 HCSB).

Many in Jesus' day did not consider it unusual that
they never heard from God. They carried on with their
work in his name and never saw the need to develop a
relationship with him. Jesus cautioned that only those who
hear his voice and respond in obedience are his true followers. He said, "Not everyone who says to Me 'Lord
Lord!' will enter the kingdom of heaven, but the one who
does the will of My Father in heaven. On that day many
will say to Me, 'Lord, Lord, didn't we prophesy in Your
name, drive out demons in Your name, and do many miracles in Your name?' Then I will announce to them, 'I never
knew you!'" (Matt. 7:21–23). Christians must never lose
sight of the huge difference between doing what God
specifically tells us to do and merely doing what makes the
most sense to us. If we settle ahead of time that we will
obey whatever God tells us, we will go into our time with
him ready to hear his voice.

Conclusion

God said, "Then you will call upon Me and come and pray to Me, and I will listen to you. You will seek Me and find Me, when you search for Me with all your heart" (Jer. 29:12–13). God's promise remains the same today. The depth of your walk with God is directly proportional to the zeal with which you seek him. If you seek after God in a halfhearted, inconsistent manner, you cannot expect to hear him speaking at the deepest levels. But if you will discipline yourself to concentrate on the Lord and if you diligently obey everything he says, then you will be prepared to experience God at an increasingly profound and personal level. God has invited you to go deeper in your relationship with him. The depth of that relationship ultimately rests with you.

Learning to Recognize God's Voice

1. Develop your relationship
2. Seek to understand God's ways
3. Prepare your heart
4. Learn to concentrate
5. Develop habitual obedience

Questions for Further Reflection

1. Are you purposefully developing a deep relationship with God? What do you think God would have you do differently in your relationship?

2. How well do you know God's ways? How has your knowledge of the ways of God helped you recognize a word from God?

3. To which type of soil would you compare your heart right now? In what areas does God want you to cultivate your heart so it is more responsive to a word from him?

4. What do you do to concentrate on God? Is it effective? What might you do to be able to focus more intently on God so you can clearly hear when he speaks?

5. Are you obeying everything God is telling you? Are there some things God has said that you have not fully processed in your life yet?

QUESTIONS OFTEN ASKED

CHAPTER 12

The Christian community is desperate to know God's will and to understand how God communicates with them. We wrote this book in response to questions we have been asked about how to know when God is speaking. People want to know how God's Word applies to their lives. Many people are not having their questions answered. Sometimes it is because their spiritual leaders are unsure when God is speaking. Some Christians claim God does not have a specific will to communicate. In this final chapter we will address some questions we are regularly asked by Christians. We have already touched on some of these issues in earlier chapters, but here we will provide a direct response to several commonly voiced concerns.

1. Question: What if my church does not respond to what I sense God is saying? Should I find a church that is willing to do what God says, or should I stay where I am? Is it right to challenge the leadership of my church, or am I obligated to submit to their authority even if I think they are wrong?

Answer: To feel your church is not hearing from God and following his will is frustrating. The problem is particularly acute when you have a family and you want your spouse and children to experience a healthy church. First Corinthians 12:18 teaches that God adds members to the body as he desires. You are not in your church by accident. If God led you there, then only he should lead you away. God may have guided you to your church because of your spiritual sensitivity. God may intend for you to be a catalyst to bring about positive changes. Perhaps God has alerted you to a problem so you can begin praying.

The apostle Paul urged believers, "Do nothing out of rivalry or conceit, but in humility consider others as more important than yourselves. Everyone should look out not only for his own interests, but also for the interests of others" (Phil. 2:3–4 HCSB). Sometimes we can grow frustrated with our church or our pastor or our church leaders because they do not seem to meet our needs the way we think they should. The model of Jesus' life is to humbly consider the needs of others. Search your heart to make sure you are not the one out of God's will rather than your church. You may simply be wanting to impose your agenda on your church. Be careful not to allow yourself to develop a critical spirit toward fellow Christians. Determine to make a positive difference by your actions and your attitudes rather than exerting a divisive influence. Ask the Holy Spirit to show you specific ways you can be a change agent in your church. Changes may not take place overnight; they usually don't. But God will work through your life so you and others will be blessed as a result.

2. Question: I did what I thought God told me to do, but everything went wrong. What happened?

Answer: God never promised that if you did his will everything would work out your way. (Read Heb. 11:36–38.) The key is not your success but your obedience. Moses delivered God's message as God told him to, and what happened? Things got worse (Exod. 5:1–23). The young shepherd boy, David, was anointed as the future king, and what happened next? The paranoid King Saul chased him around the countryside for years until David finally found refuge among his enemies. Jesus obeyed his Father's will perfectly; it led to a cross.

Joseph learned you shouldn't draw conclusions about God's will for your life until the last chapter is written. He endured years of suffering at the hands of his brothers, his Egyptian masters, and his jailers until finally he was made a powerful leader in Egypt, second only to Pharaoh himself. He was influential in saving the lives of thousands of people. Only then could he fully see God's divine plan and realize he had been in the center of God's will all the time. Joseph's famous words to his brothers speak volumes, "As for you, you meant evil against me, but God meant it for good in order to preserve . . . many people alive" (Gen. 50:20). Once you hear from God, don't let anything cause you to lose heart. Don't quit until you sense God's will has been done.

3. Question: What if there is silence when I pray? What does it mean, and what should I do?

Answer: If you don't sense God is speaking to you in response to your prayers, there are at least three things you should consider.

First, it may be that God is speaking but you have failed to recognize his voice. Would you know if God were speaking to you? If not, the problem may not be silence but deafness. Make certain you know God well enough that you can recognize his voice when he speaks. Take time to review the way God speaks and learn the nature of the one who speaks.

Second, examine your heart for sin. The psalmist declared, "If I regard wickedness in my heart, the Lord will not hear" (Ps. 66:18). Silence is a powerful method by which God may be alerting you to sin in your life. When you experience silence from God, take a spiritual inventory and ask God to reveal any sinful ways in your life (Ps. 139:23).

Finally, if you are familiar with God's ways and you are not aware of any sin in your life that could be causing God's silence, wait upon God in the midst of the silence. The Lord may simply want you to trust him and to wait until he reveals something greater to you than you have known before.

Mary and Martha sent word to Jesus that their brother, Jesus' good friend Lazarus, was gravely ill (John 11:3). Jesus' disciples assumed he would immediately set out for Bethany to heal his friend, but instead he delayed his departure. By the time Jesus and his companions arrived, Lazarus had been dead four days. Pitifully, Mary and Martha acknowledged that Jesus could have healed Lazarus from his illness if only he'd arrived sooner. The

Bible indicates that Jesus wept (John 11:35). It is doubtful that Jesus was weeping because Lazarus had died, for in just a moment he was going to resurrect him! It may be that Jesus grieved because he could see there was so much about him that even his closest friends did not yet understand. God was about to reveal a colossal truth: Jesus was not only a healer; he was the resurrection and the life. Jesus' followers had learned they could receive healing from him in times of illness. Now they discovered they could find hope even in the face of death. The initial silence from Jesus led to a greater revelation of his nature.

We struggle with waiting. It is one of the most difficult things we do! We would rather climb Mount Everest than wait for the Lord to speak in the stillness of the day. In times of silence we tend to begin speaking rather than continuing to listen. Yet if we are in too much of a hurry to speak or to rush to action, we may miss an incredible revelation God wants us to experience. Waiting on God can be one of the most profound, faith-stretching experiences of your life. Trust in God's sovereign control of your life even in moments when you cannot hear him speaking. If you reverently wait upon him, you will hear him when God knows you are ready.

4. Question: What if I know what God has said I should do, but my spouse and children are unwilling to obey. What should I do? Is there a time when I should go without them?

Answer: This question touches on a painful reality present in many Christian homes. The Bible is clear that we reap what we sow (Gal. 6:7). Sometimes our family's present response to God's voice may be largely the result of what we have sown in our family. If we have nurtured a reverence for God's Word and a willingness to obey what God says, our family will be accustomed to responding positively when God speaks. If God speaks and our family digs in its heels, it may reveal that past priorities in our home have not been God-centered. Perhaps we have neglected to guide our family by a model of ready obedience. When an angel warned Lot that Sodom was about to be destroyed in judgment, it was all Lot could do to drag his wife and daughters away from the city limits! (Gen. 19:14–16). Lot's spiritual credibility with his family was so weak that in a matter of life and death, he was barely able to convince them to save themselves. So the first thing to do is shoulder any responsibility that is yours. Seek your family's forgiveness for not being the spiritual leader you should have been.

Of course there could be extenuating circumstances. Perhaps you are a new believer and your family has not had opportunities to learn obedience to God from your leadership. When you sense God speaking to you about his will for you and your family, you must take your family with you. Don't race ahead of them or abandon them. Recognize that you may need to take time to help nurture your family's walk with God until they are spiritually mature enough to obey what God is saying. You can't bypass stages of spiritual growth. You must be willing to expend the necessary time and effort to bring your family with you as you respond to God's will. Your first priority is to take good care of the lives God has placed in your care. If you neglect your family in your quest to have a ministry, you will lose both in the process. God will never lead you to do anything that violates his Word. You can know with certainty he wants you to be a faithful parent and spouse. You know he wants you to love and cherish your family. He has entrusted them to your care. Focus on keeping your heart right before God, and ask God to work on your family.

5. Question: Is there a Plan B? I fear I may have missed God's Plan A for my life.

Answer: We regularly meet people who struggle with this issue. That's why we began the book with the example of Doug, the physician. First, it is unfathomable that God has any plan for our lives at all. But in his mercy he has graciously reached out and invited us into a love relationship with him. What happens when we reject that invitation initially but later repent and want to follow him? Can we pick up where we left off years ago? The answer is yes and no!

We often hear God referred to as the "God of second chances." Certainly the Bible testifies overwhelmingly to that truth. God is gracious and forgiving. Still, we must not try to superimpose our human perspective upon God. Doing so would be trying to make God into our image. It doesn't work that way. Some people say, "I know I sinned, but I'm forgiven. So God won't hold me accountable." But this only reveals their humanistic view of God. The point is not what we think is fair but what God considers righteous. To be forgiven is one thing; to be accountable for our choices is another.

When Jesus approached Jerusalem, he paused to weep over the city (Luke 19:41). He wept because he knew what could have been. The people had received an invitation to know the Messiah, but in their stubbornness they squandered that opportunity.

We meet so many people who tell us God called them into Christian ministry when they were young but they resisted. Ten, twenty, or even more years have passed, and now they want to serve God in ministry. But during the intervening years they married and made a number of significant financial and lifestyle decisions. These choices, made apart from God's guidance, have produced long-term consequences, some of which will cost them dearly now. As the Bible points out, we must live with the consequences of our decisions (Gal. 6:7).

Jesus told the parable of the ten virgins who were invited to a wedding feast. Five of them brought enough oil for their lamps, while five came unprepared and had to go buy more oil. Meanwhile, the bridegroom arrived and invited those who were ready to the banquet. When the women returned with additional oil, it was too late. They had missed out (Matt. 25:1–13).

The window of opportunity is sometimes brief. Life cannot wait for our response. As Doug's life proves, God may certainly choose at any time to accept someone's service and to work powerfully through his life. He is God; he has the power and the right to do that. However, a spiritual principle applies here: You may depart from God on your terms, but you return to him on his terms.

All of that being said, the Bible also chronicles more than one example of God's patience with his people. Abraham's life is a textbook case for studying God's long-suffering nature. Abraham and Sarah seemed to work hard at thwarting God's plan. When famine struck the land, Abraham chose to move to Egypt without consulting God (Gen. 12:10–20). While in Egypt, they ran into difficulty with Pharaoh that could have been fatal had God not intervened on their behalf. When the promised birth of a child was not forthcoming, Abraham and Sarah sought other options rather than wait on God. They considered Plan B, which was adoption, and Plan C, which was a surrogate mother (Gen. 15:2–3; 16). Over and over God's relentless love for the patriarchal couple saved them from tragically settling for much less than God intended. So it is with us. We tend to drift away from God and his purposes. God graciously keeps us on track. Only God knows what we miss by our disobedient choices, and only God is capable of redeeming our lives for his service.

Don't dwell on past mistakes. Be like Paul; forget what lies behind and press on to what God has for you next (Phil. 3:13). Don't compare God's activity in your life with what he is doing in others' lives. Trust that God's love is perfect; his plans are always best for you, at any point in time. Jesus evaluated his cousin's life this way: "I assure you: Among those born of women no one greater than John the Baptist has appeared" (Matt. 11:11 HCSB). Yet how long was John's public ministry? Six months. God did more through John's life in six months than others accomplished in a lifetime.

Choosing at any point to surrender to God's will is certainly better than the alternative. God's Plan Z is better than our Plan A! The key is not to focus on what might have been but to embrace God's will enthusiastically from this day forward. God always has a plan for where you are today. Trust him with your life and allow him to decide what is best for you. Graciously accept his will for your life now with the realization that for God to use your life at any time is a privilege.

6. Question: Is it OK to wrestle with God's will and to express my anger at God as long as I am being honest about how I feel?

Answer: The short answer is no! A popular teaching says we are not responsible for how we feel. If we become angry, we are simply expressing a natural feeling. And taking our feelings to God is always good. However, a person who argues with God obviously does not really know God. God is perfect love (1 John 4:7–8). If you experientially know God's love to be perfect, how could you become angry with him? If you truly know God as he is—holy, almighty, perfect and just—will you be inclined to wrestle with him? Not likely.

People who do not know God as he really is will act inappropriately toward him. One thing is certain. There are no wrestling matches in heaven! No one will approach the throne of God to express anger at how he runs the universe! When we truly see God, only genuine worship and adoration will escape our lips! When we say we are "wrestling with God's will," we are announcing our distrust of him. Whether we ultimately give in or not is not the point. Resisting God's word, even for a time, expresses our lack of faith. More than that, it reveals that we really don't know who God is.

When God called Moses to deliver the Israelites from Egypt, Moses argued with God. He spent the rest of his life paying the price (Exod. 4:14–16). Jacob wrestled with the angel of the Lord, and he walked with a limp the rest of his life (Gen. 32:24–32). Zacharias questioned the Lord, and he was struck mute until the birth of his son, John (Luke 1:18–20). It is one thing to ask God questions in faith (Luke 1:34); it is another to ask in doubt or in anger.

There is no reason to wrestle with God or try to coerce him into doing something. God will only give you that which is an expression of his perfect love for you. If he is not answering your prayers as you think he should, you may be insisting on something other than what his perfect love inclines him to give (Eph. 3:20). Far better to elevate your request to what he wants to give.

7. Question: People talk about "putting out a fleece" to determine God's will. Is that an act of faith or a sign of doubt?

Answer: Some people believe that by regularly asking God to prove himself in a particular way they are demonstrating their faith that God will respond. But the biblical account of putting out a fleece on which this practice is based was not a show of faith at all but an expression of doubt. God, in his grace, wants to do a divine work in your life, so he may make allowance for your lack of faith. That's what he did for Gideon. When God came to Gideon the unlikely warrior was hiding from his enemies, the Midianites.

God sent an angel to convince the doubtful Gideon. It wasn't enough (Judg. 6:11–12). Then the angel sent fire out from the end of his staff to consume Gideon's sacrifice (Judg. 6:21). Gideon still wasn't convinced. After the angel vanished from Gideon's sight, God spoke to Gideon directly (Judg. 6:23). That should have settled the matter, but even after all the miraculous encounters, Gideon asked God to prove himself still further with the fleece (Judg. 6:36–40). Was his request an act of faith? Certainly not. Gideon knew exactly what God wanted him to do. He did not set out the fleece to clarify God's will. God's will was undoubtedly more clear than Gideon wanted it to be. Perhaps Gideon was looking for an out from having to obey what he had been told.

God's Word says genuine faith doesn't require a miracle or a sign (Heb. 11:6). True faith takes God at his word and moves forward. Asking for God to clarify his will for you is one thing. Asking God to prove himself when you already know what he wants you to do is another. The first is motivated by a desire to obey. The second comes out of reluctance to take action as God has directed.

There is a marvelous biblical account of true faith involving Daniel's three friends, Shadrach, Meshach, and Abednego. These men knew God's will concerning worshiping idols. Consequently they refused to bow down to an idol even when it meant they would be thrown to their deaths in a fiery furnace. Observe their brave words to the king: "If it be so, our God whom we serve is able to deliver us from the furnace of blazing fire and He will deliver us out of your hand, O king. But even if He does not, let it be known to you, O king, that we are not going to serve your gods or worship the golden image that you have set up" (Dan. 3:17–18). This was faith that did not require a miracle! The greatest demonstration of faith is when you take God at his word without asking God to prove himself. If you are always testing God, examine your heart to see if you truly trust him as you should.

8. Question: Will people always know when God is speaking to them?

Answer: Jesus said his sheep would know his voice (John 10:4–5, 14, 27). The Bible's overall testimony is that when God spoke, people knew it was God, and they knew what he was saying.

Relating to God is relating to a Person. The more time you spend with someone, the more you come to know him. It can be awkward when people call on the phone and do not identify themselves. Or worse, they put you on the spot by asking, "Do you know who this is?" What they are really asking is, "Do I really matter? Do you know me well enough to recognize my voice?" Thank goodness for Caller I.D.! It isn't always easy to detect the voice of a casual acquaintance over the phone, but when our wives call, there is no question who it is.

When you are a new Christian, you may not readily recognize God's voice. Young Samuel needed help in recognizing it (1 Sam. 3:1–14). However, the biblical pattern is that in most cases people struggled not in identifying God's voice but in deciding whether they would obey what the voice was commanding! In the parable of the sower, seed fell on four types of ground—hard soil; rocky, shallow soil; weed-infested soil; and fertile soil (Matt. 13:3–17). All four types of soil received the same kind of seed. The resulting growth depended on the condition of the ground. That's how it is with us. The problem is not that we don't get a word from God. The problem lies in the way we receive that word. It all depends on the condition of our hearts. To clarify the point, Jesus quoted the prophet Isaiah,

You will keep on hearing, but will not understand; you will keep on seeing but will not perceive;
for the heart of this people has become dull, with
their ears they scarcely hear, and they have closed
their eyes, otherwise they would see with their eyes,
hear with their ears, and understand with their heart
and return, and I would heal them. But blessed are
your eyes, because they see; and your ears, because
they hear (Matt. 13:14–17).

The implication is that God's people should naturally
be able to hear God's voice and see him at work. However,
people can choose to block out God's voice. They can
allow apathy to dull their senses to God's activity. They
can let sin drown out God's voice. Only repentance can
restore the relationship so Christians can once again
clearly hear what God is saying.

9. **Question:** Must I always confirm with Scripture
what I sense God is saying to me?

Answer: When you believe God is telling you something, the Bible is your best guide to ensure you are hearing him correctly. You will not always come across a verse
that speaks directly to your situation. There is no Scripture
passage that reads: "Thou shalt marry Greta Smith on June
12." However, you will be able to verify anything you hear
God say to you by the teachings of Scripture.

Why is this important? Many doctrines and practices
are advocated today that make perfect sense to the world
but do not align with biblical teachings. It is critical for
Christians to be so familiar with the Bible they are able to
match consistently what they hear against what they know
to be true in God's Word. For example, some Bible teachers claim that wealth is a sure sign of God's blessing. Yet
many Scriptures challenge this assumption. Any word that
comes from God will always be confirmed in the Bible.
When we were pastors, we would regularly say from the
pulpit, "Don't take my word for it. Check it out in the
Scriptures." We wanted our church members to develop
the habit of measuring everything they heard against the
plumb line of God's Word.

Don't be in such a hurry to make important decisions that you neglect to test the authenticity of what you hear against God's written Word. Remember, if you are only half a degree off in making the right decision, that half degree can eventually land you far from God's will. Jesus based his decisions on God's Word. That is the safest practice for us as well.

10. Question: Some of my friends claim they have known all their lives what God wanted them to do (i.e., be a pastor, missionary, Christian doctor). Am I less spiritual because I do not have a clear word on my future?

Answer: Perhaps no area of God's speaking is of more concern to Christians than knowing God's will for their future. We have an innate desire to know what God intends for us and where our life is going. Sincere Christians dread the thought of missing God's will for their lives.

God wants you to depend on him, not on his plans. The children of Israel had to collect manna every day. They could not store up God's provision; they had to depend on him daily. Whatever God has revealed to you, that's what you should obey. If he has called you to be a missionary, you should seek the next step in preparing your life for missions. On the other hand, perhaps God's will is for you to enroll in a particular school even though you are not sure where the degree will lead you. Do it. You'll understand why God led you that way when the time comes.

11. Question: Is there anything wrong with randomly opening my Bible, pointing to the first verse I see, and taking that verse as God's word for me? Sometimes the verse I find seems to apply directly to me.

Answer: It is true, sometimes a verse will "jump out" at you, and you will know in your spirit that the verse speaks directly to your life situation. However, you must be extremely careful about this approach to receiving a word from God. For one thing, this method presumes upon God. God is sovereign. He will speak to you in his time and in his way. To force God to speak to you by picking a verse when you want to hear from God is to tell God what to tell you! He is not your servant. You are his servant. It is far better to regularly read God's Word and to allow him to speak to you through his Word as he chooses. The reason this "open and point" method appears to work is because the Bible is God's living Word. Any Word from God can impact your life. Some people don't want to discipline themselves to regularly read God's word. They would rather just pull out their Bible in a moment of crisis, flip to a page, and claim the first verse that catches their eye. Such a lackadaisical, undisciplined approach to finding God's will is an insult to his holiness. If you will regularly immerse yourself in the Bible, Old Testament and New, you will have opportunities every day for God to speak to you and to build his truth into your life.

12. Question: When you talk about "hearing from God," I picture God speaking in an audible voice. Does that ever happen?

Answer: When we talk about God speaking in this book, we are referring to any way God communicates with people. Neither of us has ever heard God speak audibly. However, God has clearly communicated his will to us many, many times. God is sovereign. He can choose to speak to us any way he chooses, and that includes speaking audibly. However, God also relates to us in ways that build our faith. If God spoke out loud every time he wanted our attention, we would not need to concentrate on him, nor would we require faith.

Just as we are forced to listen carefully when someone speaks softly, so by God speaking to us in many ways, we are forced to pay close attention to what he is communicating. People are usually fascinated by the spectacular. They seek the miraculous. We ought not to seek the spectacular when we listen to God. Rather, we should be pleased that God communicates with us in any way he chooses! Keep your heart open to all the ways God wants to communicate with you.

13. Question: What does God generally speak to people about?

Answer: When God speaks, he usually reveals truths about himself and his activity. People tend to be self-centered. We want God to merely speak to us about our problems and concerns. At times Christ is inaccurately viewed as a cosmic best friend who only exists to make us happy and successful. God turns our focus away from us and on to him. When Christ speaks to us, it is to express his lordship in our life and in the lives of those around us. Some skeptics have turned this truth around and asked ridiculous questions such as: "Do you need to pray and ask God what type of toothpaste you should purchase at the store?" Such questions reveal a fundamental lack of understanding about why God speaks. Unless your choice of toothpaste affects Christ's lordship in our your life, it is undoubtedly of no consequence to God. Our choice of spouse, or career, or place to live, on the other, hand dramatically impacts how we can serve Christ in the future. Whether we decide to order a cheeseburger or pizza for dinner will not alter eternity. Placing ourselves in crippling debt to start our own business may be important to God, however, if it prevents us from fulfilling his future assignment for us.

Ultimately our lives will be enriched by focusing on him rather than focusing on ourselves. The most important truths God communicates are truths about what he is like and what his purposes are. God has revealed all we need to know about himself, his ways, and his purposes in the Bible. We will not discover new attributes of God as we pray. The Bible tells us everything we need to know for salvation and for living the abundant Christian life. The Holy Spirit will use the Bible, prayer, circumstances, and fellow believers to apply scriptural truths to our lives. The Holy Spirit will show us what adjustments we must make for God to work out his redemptive purposes in the world around us.

14. Question: What should I do when someone declares what God wants me to do?

Answer: Many sincere Christians believe they know what God desires, not only for them, but also for others. As we've discussed, God does work through others to help you clarify his word. The following are some guidelines for responding to people who say they know God's will for you.

Treat those who claim to have heard from the Lord with due respect. You never want to develop a calloused heart that is skeptical of hearing from God through others. Showing respect indicates you believe God does speak through other people and you are open to what God might say to you through them. It does not, however, mean you automatically believe every word they say.

Test their words against the Bible's teachings just as the Bereans compared Paul's claims against the Scripture. A person who truly has a message from God will not be offended when you check the Scriptures to verify his message. Genuine messengers of God will encourage you to take their words and validate them with the Bible. Self-seeking prophets, however, will become defensive when you corroborate their message with Scripture.

Examine the track record of those who declare a word from God. The surest way to test a prophet's words is to see whether the prophecy comes to pass (Deut. 18:20–22; Jer. 28:8–9). God honored Samuel by guaranteeing everything he said (1 Sam. 3:19). Like Samuel, some people can be trusted to share a word from God only when they actually have one. Others, however, are constantly claiming new and exciting revelations from God. Yet their track record reveals that their declarations are continually off base. They may have the best of intentions. They may talk about exciting things. But they should not be taken seriously.

Another way to test someone's words is to examine his or her relationship with God's people. False prophets pass through churches looking for followers. However, they have no genuine concern for people. They are only interested in accomplishing their own purposes. The apostle John identified such people by saying, "They went out from us, but they did not belong to us; for if they had belonged to us, they would have remained with us. However, they went out so that it might be made clear that none of them belongs to us" (1 John 2:19 HCSB). Genuine messengers of God will care for God's people. They will remain steadfast regardless of the response they receive. When the children of Israel rejected Moses' word to enter the promised land, Moses did not abandon them. He knew if there was ever a time the people needed him, it was after they refused a word from God. The people in Jeremiah's day constantly dismissed his message, but God refused to release the prophet from his people. If people leave the church when others don't accept their "word from the Lord," John's words indicate their departure says it all.

When someone shares a word from God for your life, seek confirmation from the Holy Spirit. The Holy Spirit residing within you will verify truth (Rom. 8:15–18). There may be times when people pronounce "truth," but the Spirit does not give you peace about their words. Listen carefully to what the Spirit is saying. The Spirit knows the mind of God, and he knows what lies within people's hearts (1 Cor. 2:10–11). If the Spirit makes you uneasy about what someone is saying, pay attention to his promptings and follow his guidance.

Baker James Cauthen was the pastor of Polytechnic Baptist Church in Fort Worth, Texas, before becoming a prominent missions leader. A woman renowned for being a gifted Bible teacher joined his church from another church in the city. She informed her new pastor that the Lord had come to her in a vision and told her that the church was to combine all the adult Bible study classes into one class and she was to teach them. Cauthen questioned her on the details of her vision, but the woman insisted the church was to obey her heavenly vision. Cauthen finally responded, "Well, I'll not argue with you or anyone about something that came to them in a vision. But since he holds me responsible for shepherding his flock, I feel sure he will also appear to me to confirm this. As soon as he does, I'll get in touch with you."[1]

Compare what the messenger is saying with what you already know God has told you. If the two contradict each other, be alert to the discrepancy and be cautious in responding. At one point in Jesus' ministry, his right-hand disciple Peter declared that Jesus would never have to suffer or die. This would have seemed like a word in season at any time! Yet Jesus already understood God's intentions for him. The Father's assignment was for him to die on a cross. Knowing this to be true, Jesus instantly recognized that Peter's message contradicted his Father's will. Therefore, what Peter was saying could not come from God. In fact, Jesus said it came from Satan (Matt. 16:23).

When the famed Charles Spurgeon was the pastor of the enormous Metropolitan Tabernacle in London, he received numerous messages from people who purported to have a word from God for him and his church. On one occasion a stranger told Spurgeon God had instructed him to preach at Spurgeon's church the following Sunday. Spurgeon replied, "That is singular, for I am in daily communication with the Lord and he said nothing to me about it."[2]

Examine whether the speaker is sharing a personal conviction but mistaking it for a corporate assignment. At times people will receive a genuine word from God that is meant for them alone. Nevertheless, out of their excitement over what God said, they may enthusiastically encourage everyone to obey the word God gave them. Then when others do not respond with the same level of enthusiasm, they grow frustrated. The response tells you what you need to know. If it is a corporate word, others will verify that the word is from God and it applies to them.

Conclusion

There is nothing more important in life than understanding when God is speaking to you. If you are disoriented to God's voice, your life is dangerously vulnerable. The Bible indicates conclusively that God does speak to people and that he does guide them to his will. The problem of not hearing from God never lies with God. He does communicate his will. It is not a matter of us searching in vain for God's hidden will. He readily reveals it to those who show themselves obedient to do it. If you do not hear God's voice, could it be your heart is not ready to respond to what he says? Are you clinging to sin or holding out against what you already know of his will? No matter what the reason for the silence, there is a remedy: repent and return to God. Allow God to soften your heart so you are ready to hear his voice and to respond in obedience. Continue seeking and listening until you have heard him speak to you in his unmistakable voice. When he does, it will change your life.

NOTES

1. The Question: Does God Speak to People Today?

1. Doug's name has been changed for the purposes of this book.
2. Gary Friesen, *Decision Making and the Will of God: A Biblical Alternative to the Traditional View* (Portland: Multnomah Press, 1980; reprint ed., 1982), 428.
3. Ibid.
4. Ibid., 248.
5. George H. Williams, *The Radical Reformation* (Philadelphia: Westminster Press, 1962), 368–81.
6. *Winnipeg Free Press*, April 20, 1993, A1, A4.
7. Henry T. Blackaby and Claude V. King, *Experiencing God: How to Live the Full Adventure of Knowing and Doing the Will of God* (Nashville: Broadman & Holman, 1994), 7–8.
8. Andrew Bonar, *Robert Murray M'Cheyne* (London: Banner of Truth Trust, 1844; reprint ed. 1962), 78–79.
9. Andrew Murray, *The Inner Life* (Pittsburgh: Whitaker House, 1984), 55.
10. Ibid., 60.

2. For the Record: God Speaks

1. W. Y. Fullerton, *Charles Haddon Spurgeon: London's Most Popular Preacher* (Chicago: Moody Bible Institute, 1966), 197.
2. See Henry and Melvin Blackaby (Nashville: Broadman & Holman, 2002).

3. God Speaks: His Way

1. David McCasland, *Oswald Chambers: Abandoned to God* (Grand Rapids: Discovery House Publishers, 1993), 217.
2. Ibid., 51.
3. See Henry's book, Henry Blackaby and Roy T. Edgemon, *The Ways of God: How God Reveals Himself Before a Watching World* (Nashville: Broadman & Holman Publishers, 2000).
4. W. Y. Fullerton, *F. B. Meyer: A Biography*, 2d ed. (London: Marshall, Morgan and Scott Ltd., n.d.), 170.

5. *The Autobiography of George Muller* (Springdale, Pa.:Whataker House, 1984), 31–32.
6. Billy Graham, *Just As I Am: The Autobiography of Billy Graham* (New York: HarperCollins, 1997), 179.
7. J. Edwin Orr, *An Apprenticeship of Faith* (Wheaton, Ill.: International Awakening Press, 1993), 25–27.
8. Ibid., 28.
9. Ibid., 31–32.
10. Duncan Campbell, *Revival in the Hebrides* (1949), http:/www. gospelcom.net/npc/Campbell.html
11. *Hudson Taylor's Spiritual Secret*, 77.

4. The Holy Spirit: God's Presence in Our Lives

1. Basil Miller, *Praying Hyde: A Man of Prayer* (Greenville, S.C.: Ambassador Publications, 2000), 17.
2. Fullerton, *Charles H. Spurgeon*, 23.
3. Augustine, *The Confessions of Saint Augustine: Books I–X* (London: Griffith, Farran, Browne and Co., 1886), 38.
4. Miller, *Praying Hyde*, 58–59.
5. Jesse C. Fletcher, *Bill Wallace of China* (Nashville: Broadman & Holman, 1996), 13–15.
6. Graham, *Just As I Am*, 63.

5. The Bible: God's Word

1. Richard Ellsworth Day, *The Shadow of the Broad Rim: The Life Story of Charles Haddon Spurgeon, Heir of the Puritans* (Philadelphia: Judson Press, 1934), 57.
2. Courtney Anderson, *To The Golden Shore: The Life of Adoniram Judson* (Grand Rapids: Zondervan Publishing House, 1972), 30–44.
3. Augustine, *Confessions*, 154.
4. Iain H. Murray, *Jonathan Edwards: A New Biography* (Edinburgh: Banner of Truth Trust, 1987; reprint ed. 1992), 35.
5. Helen Wessel, ed. *The Autobiography of Charles Finney* (Minneapolis: Bethany House Publishers, 1977), 17–18.
6. Quoted in Roland H. Bainton, *Here I Stand: A Life of Martin Luther* (New York: New American Library, 1950), 49–50.
7. Leslie F. Church, *Knight of the Burning Heart: The Story of John Wesley* (New York: Abingdon-Cokesbury Press, n.d.), 96.
8. *The Autobiography of George Muller*, 73.
9. Ibid., 74.
10. Ibid., 73.

11. Ibid., 139–40.

6. *Prayer: What It Is and What It Isn't*

1. John R. Sampey, *Memoirs of John R. Sampey* (Nashville: Broadman Press, 1947), 62–63.
2. Ruth Stewart, *James Stewart: Missionary* (Asheville, N.C.: Gospel Projects, Inc., 1977), 34–35.
3. Hudson Taylor, *A Retrospect* (Philadelphia: China Inland Mission, n.d.), 38.
4. Howard and Geraldine Taylor, *Hudson Taylor's Spiritual Secret* (Grand Rapids: Discovery House Publishers, 1990), 38.
5. Ibid., 39.
6. J. C. Pollock, *Moody: A Biography* (Grand Rapids: Baker Books, 1963; reprint ed., 1995), 64–65.
7. Taylor, *Hudson Taylor's Spiritual Secret,* 117–18.
8. Ibid., 120–21.
9. McCasland, *Oswald Chambers*, 110.
10. Miller, *Praying Hyde*, 21.
11. Ibid., 125.

7. *Circumstances: A Time for God to Speak*

1. Taylor and Taylor, *Hudson Taylor*, 71.
2. Miller, *Praying Hyde*, 114.
3. Bonar, *Robert Murray M'Cheyne*, 27.
4. Taylor and Taylor, *Hudson Taylor*, 46.
5. Ibid., 91.
6. Ibid., 100.
7. Powhatan W. James, *George W. Truett: A Biography* (Nashville: Broadman Press, 1939; reprint ed. 1941), 88.

8. *God Speaks to People through People*

1. Fullerton, *Charles Haddon Spurgeon*, 99.
2. Stewart, *James Stewart*, 159.
3. Truett, *George W. Truett*, 48–49.
4. Pollock, *Moody: A Biography*, 78–79.
5. Fullerton, *Charles Haddon Spurgeon*, 168.
6. McCasland, *Oswald Chambers*, 162.
7. John Newton, *John Newton: Letters of a Slave Trader* (Chicago: Moody Bible Institute, 1983), 69–70.
8. Brian H. Edwards, *God's Outlaw: The Story of William Tyndale and the English Bible* (Darlington, England: Evangelical Press, 1976; reprint ed., 1999), 137.

9. Lies and Half-Truths

1. Fullerton, *Charles Haddon Spurgeon*, 92.
2. Murray, *Jonathan Edwards*, 227.
3. James Beverly and Barry Moody, eds., *The Journal of Henry Alline* (Acadia, Nova Scotia: Acadia Divinity College, 1982), 216.
4. Jonathan Goforth, *By My Spirit* (Grand Rapids: Zondervan, 1942), 28.
5. Elisabeth Elliot, *Shadow of the Almighty* (New York: Harper & Row, 1956), 196.
6. Ibid., 100.

11. Learning to Respond to God's Voice

1. Murray, *James Stewart*, 207.
2. Ibid., 208.
3. Bonar, *Robert Murray M'Cheyne*, 93.
4. McCasland, *Oswald Chambers*, 177.
5. Bonar, M'Cheyne, 23.
6. *The Journal of Henry Alline*, 151.
7. Ibid., 172, 190.
8. Richard Lovett, *James Chalmers: His Autobiography and Letters* 5th ed. (London: Religious Tract Society, 1903), 43.

12. Questions Often Asked

1. Jesse C. Fletcher, *Baker James Cauthen: A Man for all Nations* (Nashville: Broadman Press, 1977), 92–93.
2. Fullerton, *Charles Haddon Spurgeon*, 168.

SCRIPTURE INDEX

ABOUT THE AUTHORS

Henry Blackaby (B.A., M.Div., Th.M., D.D.) has extensive leadership experience. He has been a senior pastor for almost thirty years as well as a Director of Missions in Vancouver, Canada, and a special consultant to the presidents of the North American Mission Board, International Mission Board, and LifeWay Christian Resources of the Southern Baptist Convention. Henry regularly consults with CEOs concerning leadership issues. Currently Henry resides in Atlanta with his wife Marilynn. He leads Henry Blackaby Ministries, which provides ministries to leaders in Christian as well as secular organizations. Henry travels frequently with national and international speaking engagements and has written books such as *Experiencing God: Knowing and Doing the Will of God, Experiencing God Day–by–Day, The Man God Uses, Created to Be God's Friend, The Ways of God, Spiritual Leadership*, and *Experiencing God Together.*

Richard Blackaby (B.A., M.Div., Ph.D.) is the oldest son of Henry and Marilynn Blackaby. He has served as a senior pastor and currently is President of the Canadian Southern Baptist Seminary in Cochrane, Canada. Richard is a popular speaker on leadership and has coauthored books with his father including *When God Speaks, God's Invitation, CrossSeekers, Experiencing God Day-by-Day, The Experience*, and *Spiritual Leadership*. Richard lives in Cochrane, Canada, with his wife Lisa and their children Mike, Daniel, and Carrie.

HENRY BLACKABY MINISTRIES

Henry Blackaby Ministries exists to help people experience a life-changing relationship with God that dynamically affects their home, church, and business through a message of revival and spiritual awakening.

We seek to help people experience God through preaching, teaching, conference speaking, leadership training, the production and presentation of ministry materials, and various media outlets including radio and the Internet.

For further information about Henry Blackaby Ministries, please contact them at:

Henry Blackaby Ministries
P.O. Box 161228
Atlanta, GA 30321
hbm@henryblackaby.com
www.henryblackaby.com

DATE DUE

			PRINTED IN U.S.A.